Dressing Up Debutantes

Dress, Body, Culture

Series Editor **Joanne B. Eicher**, *Regents' Professor, University of Minnesota*

Advisory Board:

Ruth Barnes, *Ashmolean Museum, University of Oxford*
Helen Callaway, *CCCRW, University of Oxford*
James Hall, *University of Illinois at Chicago*
Beatrice Medicine, *California State University, Northridge*
Ted Polhemus, *Curator, "Street Style" Exhibition, Victoria & Albert Museum*
Griselda Pollock, *University of Leeds*
Valerie Steele, *The Museum at the Fashion Institute of Technology*
Lou Taylor, *University of Brighton*
John Wright, *University of Minnesota*

Books in this provocative series seek to articulate the connections between culture and dress which is defined here in its broadest possible sense as any modification or supplement to the body. Interdisciplinary in approach, the series highlights the dialogue between identity and dress, cosmetics, coiffure, and body alternations as manifested in practices as varied as plastic surgery, tattooing, and ritual scarification. The series aims, in particular, to analyze the meaning of dress in relation to popular culture and gender issues and will include works grounded in anthropology, sociology, history, art history, literature, and folklore.

ISSN: 1360-466X

Previously published titles in the Series

Helen Bradley Foster, *"New Raiments of Self": African American Clothing in the Antebellum South*
Claudine Griggs, *"S/he: Changing Sex and Changing Clothes"*
Dani Cavallaro and Alexandra Warwick, *"Fashioning the Frame: Boundaries, Dress and the Body"*

DRESS, BODY, CULTURE

Dressing Up Debutantes
Pageantry and Glitz in Texas

Michaele Thurgood Haynes

Oxford • New York

First published in 1998 by
Berg
Editorial offices:
150 Cowley Road, Oxford, OX4 1JJ, UK
70 Washington Square South, New York, NY 10012, USA

Berg is an imprint of Oxford International Publishers Ltd.

Library of Congress Cataloging-in-Publication Data
A catalog record for this book is available from the Library of Congress.

British Library Cataloguing-in-Publication Data
A catalogue record for this book is available from the British Library.

ISBN   1 85973 934 2 (Cloth)
          1 85973 939 3 (Paper)

Typeset by JS Typesetting, Wellingborough, Northants.

To all those who work with needle and thread.

Contents

Acknowledgements

First I must thank the two people most responsible for this publication: Kathryn Earle, Editorial Director of Berg, for her persistence and Joanne Eicher, series editor, whose enthusiasm has been extremely important. I feel greatly honored to be part of the series.

Secondly, I want to thank all of the people associated with Coronation who have shared their information, their memories, and their royal robes with me. The dresses and trains may be examined, but despite their glittering splendor they are only costumes without their stories. Each and every person I have talked to has contributed to this book, and a number of people have been classic primary informants, patiently answering questions – even repeatedly when I could not read my own notes! I would like to list everyone, but my promise of anonymity prevents that. I hope all of you know how much I appreciate you.

The people outside of Coronation who have talked with me about everything from Cornyation to the experience of being a Charro queen have been extremely important also. My students, who have filled out questionnaires or just talked with me about their perceptions or experiences of Fiesta and Coronation, have added immensely to my overall understanding of the relationship between these events and ordinary San Antonio citizens.

Two people must be thanked for their influence on my choice of topic – Cecilia Steinfeldt and Carol Canty. Many years ago Cecilia hired me as a temporary part-time assistant at the Witte Museum and introduced me to the Coronation robes. If I had not had that hands-on experience, I am not sure I would have had the curiosity to find out what these dazzling dresses and trains were all about. Later, I met Carol, who taught me about Fiesta and its importance to San Antonio – and took me to my first Coronation. She continues to be a prime informant regarding many nuances of Fiesta and Coronation, in addition to being an excellent reader who keeps me on track. Most importantly, as a dear friend, she has always provided sustenance for the body and the spirit.

Without the guidance and counsel of my dissertation committee at the University of Texas at Austin this book, if even possible, would be much the poorer. They made writing a dissertation almost a pleasure. The unfailing encouragement and insight of my co-chairs, José Limón and Katie Stewart, were and continue to be most important to me personally.

It is with great pleasure that I thank colleagues Lynn Denton, Richard Flores, Pam Frese, Dan Gelo, Marise McDermott, Roberta McGregor, John Martin, Shirley Mock, Linda Pershing, Linda Pritchard, Richard Reed, Linda Schott, and Anne Winkler for their continued encouragement and interest. And Bob Hill gets special thanks, or blame, for starting it all. Rebecca Huffstutler, my curatorial colleague at the Witte, has to be particularly thanked for her ability to always go beyond what is asked of her. Before we even met, I called the museum to ask a question about the collection of royal robes, and she not only gave me the answer but also told me a great anecdote about one of the gowns. Tom Shelton of the photographic collection at the Institute of Texan Cultures also goes the extra mile.

This would be a much less colorful book without the generosity of Carol and John Canty, dear friends and now patrons, and the J.E. Smothers, Sr., Memorial Foundation whose trustees, particularly Mary Ann Bruni, well understand the importance of photographs. Thanks also to Tom Guderjan, director of the Maya Research Program, for facilitating the financial arrangements. It is with great pleasure that I acknowledge their support. I must thank again those dear friends who have loved me and my family throughout the long process of writing a dissertation and then turning it into a manuscript. Over the graduate school years you invited us to dinner and parties with little hope of receiving reciprocal invitations since our dining room table was always covered with papers. And just when repayment time was in sight, out came the papers again. We are going to install a machine to automatically clear off the table so that the pleasure of being together again may begin.

I want to thank my beloved daughter Victoria, who managed to grow up into a beautiful, strong, intelligent, and wonderfully caring adult while her mother was going to school and working and trying to figure out what she was going to be when she grew up.

And finally I must thank the most precise – almost to compulsiveness – and most patient and loving copy editor an author could have. In my enthusiasm for sharing experiences with people and then writing of them, I am somewhat careless about the little things – names, numbers, pages, etc. I have not always behaved as if I properly appreciated his attention to detail, so I now publicly thank David for all of his help on this book and for much, much more over our long years together. I hope we continue our fights – over manuscripts, the house, and anything else we care enough about to produce prolonged, and loud, discussions.

Michaele Thurgood Haynes

San Antonio

An Introduction to San Antonio's Coronation

A young woman wearing an ornately trimmed velvet gown and a twelve-foot-long train, embellished with hundreds of glass stones and beads, appears at the back of a large auditorium. She is helped onto the long raised runway by two older men in full evening dress. A bright spotlight focuses on her as the orchestra begins to play Dvorak's *New World Symphony*. She has difficulty in starting her walk to the stage because of the weight of the long train but quickly finds the step and pace at which she can make her way, smiling and nodding at family and friends in the audience. In pealing tones the costumed lord high chamberlain introduces Margaret Rowen of the House of Smith, Duchess of the Triumph of Discovery in the Court of Imperial England. The duchess crosses the stage twice, providing the audience with multiple views of her royal robes. Duchess Margaret then meets her escort, dressed in full evening dress and purple baldric, at center stage. With some trepidation she executes an extremely low "formal court bow," her head almost touching the floor, then rises without assistance from her duke and acknowledges the audience's applause with a radiant smile. She climbs up steeply raked steps to her assigned position, while her escort and two younger girls help with the train, for she cannot pull the weight up the steps by herself. As she moves up the steps, the carefully worked designs on the train are almost obscured by the glitter of the refracted lights created by the glass stones. The duchess takes her seat on a small pedestal, and the young pages arrange the train so that its full splendor may be seen. The duke exits into the wings. One by one, twenty-three more duchesses, each as elaborately dressed as the first, move to their assigned places and then wait for the appearance of the princess and the crowning of the queen. They will then be entertained with a short ballet performance.

The young women are not taking part in a sixteenth-century tableau staged in honor of Queen Elizabeth I's birthday, but in a family tradition in San Antonio, Texas, in the late twentieth century. It is the annual debutante pageant presented by a men's social organization, the Order of the Alamo, and referred to by participants simply as Coronation. The twenty-six young women are living out a fantasy held dear by many little girls – to be a "fairy princess" in a beautiful dress sparkling in the spotlight of affection and attention. Most girls never get to be the princess, or even a duchess, but in San Antonio the fantasy can be played out if one not only has the discretionary income to purchase the required costumes and props but, more importantly, is also a member of the Anglo aristocracy.[1] The term "aristocrat" is specifically used with its connotations of consanguineous or affinal kinship that are not found in the terms "elite" or "upper class."[2] The queen and most of the other court members have royal genealogies with mothers, aunts, and grandmothers having held similar positions. Unlike beauty pageants, in which young women are chosen on the basis of personal characteristics, Coronation royalty hold ascribed positions.

Coronation began in 1909, when John Carrington founded the Order of the Alamo to elect a queen and to crown her, amidst her court of twenty-four duchesses, in an elaborate pageant. Almost all of the royal debutantes are daughters of, or related in some way to, Order of the Alamo members. The duchesses make their royal debuts, and two from the previous year are crowned as princess and queen. The ritual pageantry reifies for the participants their "ethclass" claim to the crown – the crown of socioeconomic dominance in the past and the present.[3] It also reproduces the boundaries of San Antonio's aristocrats for another year. The aristocratic group itself is reproduced because the royal young women are debutantes: women of marriageable age who are introduced into society and are expected to marry endogamously.

Coronation is an overwhelmingly Anglo and upper-class event in a city with a more than 60 percent Hispanic population. The full significance of Coronation comes from its larger Fiesta context and history. It is embedded in Fiesta San Antonio, a ten-day, community-wide festival with four parades and over a hundred other events. The Spanish title and the use of images of Mexican popular culture, such as sombreros and *folklórico* dancers, in promotional material imply that the festival celebrates the city's Hispanic heritage. Ironically, however, Fiesta originated in the 1891 Battle of Flowers parade staged by a group of socially elite women to honor the veterans of San Jacinto, the final battle in Texas's 1836 war against Mexico. After Texas's independence from Mexico, Anglo Americans and other immigrants, many from Germany, began to dominate San Antonio demographically, econ-omically, and politically.[4] The Anglo Americans and Germans gradually came to share values and a feeling of separateness, leading to cooperative ventures such as the staging of the Battle of Flowers parade and the later organization of the Order of the Alamo.

The presentation of debutantes as duchesses and the crowning of a queen have taken place for more than eight decades with few alterations while the city of San Antonio, the Fiesta celebration, and the world at large have undergone profound changes. Virtually unchanged is the effectiveness of Coronation in the recognition and reproduction of aristocratic identity. Most of the women who currently don the royal robes are descendants of the nineteenth-century banking and entrepreneurial families who developed Fiesta and Coronation and still hold many positions of social and economic power.

Ideally the royal court is divided into twelve in-town and twelve out-of-town duchesses. When there are not enough relatives of Order of the Alamo members to fill the in-town duchess slots, close friends of the duchesses are invited to participate. The out-of-town duchesses are also usually related to, or at least friends of, the old San Antonio families. The vast majority of all duchesses are Anglo, but during the eighty-eight-year history of Coronation seventeen duchesses have had Spanish middle or surnames. The vastly disproportionate ratio of Anglo to Spanish names is noticeable in a south-western city where Mexican Americans have appeared regularly on lists of political leaders for the last thirty years and are increasingly seen on lists of economic leaders. The extremely limited number of Hispanic duchesses is noted and decried by some, but more concern is voiced over the cost of the elaborate Coronation clothing. Older members of the Coronation families talk wistfully of the relatively lower costs of their own royal robes but still accept the much higher price of a granddaughter's regalia because they love seeing the young women in their fairy-tale dresses.

Although supposedly superficial, the royal gowns and trains are central to the continuation of Coronation itself and its affects. If classic white debutante dresses were worn instead of the specially designed, custom-made gowns and trains, highly embellished with iconography relating to the court's theme, Coronation might have ceased years ago. However, San Antonio elite families and their daughters continue to succumb to the seduction of the family tradition to clothe themselves in the magic garments of a fairy princess – at least for Fiesta week. The royal robes are superb examples of Sherry Ortner's "key symbols" for they well match her five indicators of cultural interest.[5] More specifically, they may be characterized as summarizing symbols, for they are emotionally powerful (Ortner 1979: 94). The dresses and trains are the objects of strong feelings: "I love it! It's just beautiful." "I can't believe how perfect it is."

The elaborately bejeweled gowns and trains can be compared to the costumes of the circus and Ice Capades in terms of the glitter and the flash of the fabrics and glass stones. They are comparable to costumes of grand opera or Renaissance theatre in terms of the countless yards of velvets and brocades, laces and braids, and the care with which they are made. However, rather than costumes that enable an actor to take on a role, San Antonio's Coronation robes are specialized clothing worn not by actors, but by young women to manifest the status, and adjacent role, to which they were born. The careful hand finishing on hems and interior seams, a practice not usually found in costumes, demonstrates that the royal robes are viewed as clothing rather than costumes. According to one of the people who help construct and embellish the robes, the young women themselves expect the dresses to be as comfortable as their day wear even though the design may call for specialized construction methods not conducive to wearability.

The eight hundred members of the Order of the Alamo and their families obviously have a particular interest in Coronation dresses. Other San Antonio citizens are interested in them for a variety of reasons – from employment as seamstresses to aesthetic appreciation. But few people outside of San Antonio are aware of these extraordinary markers of attainment. I grew up in Austin, ninety miles from San Antonio, but never heard of or saw the royal robes of Coronation until I moved to San Antonio after college and saw photographs of the court members published in a newspaper. Since I was interested in costumes, I did notice the photographs, but even in color a flat image conveys little of the complex adornment with rhinestones and beads that is the trademark of the royal garments. I paid little attention to them until I worked on some of the older gowns as part of my duties as a textile assistant at the Witte Museum in 1975. I only handled a small number of the dresses and trains in the extensive collection at that time but was greatly intrigued by the details that can only be seen at close range. My childhood vocational ambitions had centered on life either as a dancer or circus performer. Having pursued neither, this was the closest I was going to come to bejeweled, glitzy costumes. Politically I was perturbed at the cost of the contemporary royal wardrobes, but I loved the ones from the 1920s and 1930s on which I was working.

I soon left the museum but did pay more attention to the duchesses and their dresses when I saw them in the annual parades. However, I did not know anyone associated with Coronation and did not think about it outside of a continued belief that the money spent on the dresses would be better spent on charitable causes. Much later, when I began graduate school in anthropology, I had years of experience in making ballet costumes, sewing for boutiques, and buying and selling vintage clothes. I wanted to add the conceptual to the hands-on work I had been doing with fabrics and clothing for so long, and began reading the literature on personal appearance.[6] I researched and wrote about the changes in the tribally identifiable clothing of the Lenni Lenape. I examined the concept of fashion as part of the "code of true womanhood" and the hold it had for women in the nineteenth century even on the frontier. But I did not consider the Coronation dresses an appropriate topic for study until I began to learn the history of Coronation and its place in San Antonio's Fiesta from a new friend with a long association with Fiesta. I attended Coronation for the first time in 1987. I was amazed at the visual impact of twenty-six young women arranged on a stage all wearing garments designed to "catch the light," the expression used by participants to describe the desired result of using reflective materials in elaborate patterns. Seeing a stage full of sparkling dresses and trains, bathed in professionally designed lights against an elaborate set and accompanied by the full San Antonio Symphony orchestra, gives quite a different view than the photographs in the paper or even seeing the young women riding in the parade. I finally realized that the royal robes are central to the enactment of a ritual, a ritual that is part sheer spectacle, part family tradition – and wholly concerned with class boundaries.

Research and Analytical Concerns

I began my research at a time of renewed academic interest in material culture. Artifactual evidence is a rich source of information because of its historicity and enactment of values (Glassie 1983: 376–80), but it was largely ignored by most anthropologists from the 1920s to the 1970s. Artifacts were collected along with other kinds of information by early anthropologists, but material culture then became the domain of archaeologists and museum curators. Folklorists have been in the vanguard of material culture studies since the 1960s and have directed their attention to such diverse items as vernacular architecture, furniture, home altars, wooden carvings, and special foods. José Limón and Jane Young's review article (1986) notes a variety of perspectives in contemporary work, including viewing objects as texts that mirror culture, as integral keys to cultural processes, and as markers of group identity.

The renewed recognition of the importance of material culture by cultural anthropologists was exemplified in the title of the 1993 spring meeting of the American Ethnological Society – "Arts and Goods: Possession, Commoditization, Representation." Marcel Mauss's (1967) work on the ramifications of gift exchange had foreshadowed more recent theoretical approaches to understanding the importance of objects. Goods as commodities were treated as visible markers of cultural categories (Douglas and Isherwood 1979) and as anything whose "exchangeability for some other thing is its socially relevant feature" (Appadurai 1986: 13). Igor Kopytoff's (1986) biographical approach to objects demonstrated their variable status as commodity. Daniel Miller

(1987) also went far in remedying anthropological neglect of objects. He investigated the relationship between society and material culture and critiqued the Marxist emphasis on production and relative neglect of consumption. Miller also criticized the overemphasis on linguistics in symbolic anthropology at the expense of artifacts, stating that there is a "tendency to perceive objects as being reflective in a relatively passive sense" (1987: 96).

Jane Schneider's review article, "The Anthropology of Cloth" (1987), as well as Annette Weiner's (1988) significant work in the Trobriand Islands, demonstrate the range of recent work on cloth as it relates to social relations. Even seemingly unimportant goods, such as banana leaf skirts, are an inherent aspect of socioeconomic systems and additionally have embedded existential values "that are both the animating armature and the fuel of all social activity" (Weiner 1988: 164–5). Weiner, in collaboration with Schneider, edited the significant cross-disciplinary volume *Cloth and Human Experience* (1989). However, these works examined non-Western or historical Western cloth and clothing only.

Many authors do recognize the semiotic importance of personal appearance, including that of contemporary Western cultures (Barnes and Eicher 1992; Barthes 1983; Bogatyrev 1971; Davis 1992; Eicher 1995; Goffman 1973; Holman 1980; Joseph 1986; McCracken 1987; Sahlins 1976), but little work has been done on specialized elite clothing as an element of hegemonic class construction. An exception is Angela Rundquist (1995), who examined the forms of dress required for presentation at the Swedish court from 1850 to 1962. Although Swedish court dress was quite modest in design and expense, it was "a class sign with magic power" (1995: 361). In contrast to the Swedish court dress, San Antonio's version is anything but modest in design and expense. The royal robes, the most significant material culture associated with San Antonio's Coronation, must be fully examined in order to understand the extent to which they act as Weiner's "animating armature." The materiality of the dresses and trains enables them to "make visible and stable the categories of culture" (Douglas and Isherwood 1979: 59), in this case of a specific ethclass, San Antonio's aristocracy. Wearing the robes in the Coronation signifies a specific socioeconomic category based on historical ties to the city.

Two years are spent in researching the designs of the robes, which then take months of intensive labor to construct. Fine fabrics are used, and all embellishment is applied by hand. Families of the chosen young women each spend an average of $18,000 for the duchesses' royal gowns and trains, while the cost of dressing the princess or queen can be as high as $35,000.[7] The elaborately bejeweled royal robes appear to be prime examples of Thorstein Veblen's (1934) term "conspicuous consumption"; however, such an analysis of the material culture aspect of Coronation would be simplistic. As are all symbols, the gowns are multivocal and have multiple meanings for wearer, creator, and viewer – meanings explored in chapter 4.

Coronation has been performed annually (with the exception of the war years of 1918–19 and 1942–45) since 1909 through the Depression of the 1930s, the social upheaval of the 1960s, and the 1980s Texas recession. The cumulative effect of wearing and viewing all of those royal robes is central to an analysis of the event. Clifford Geertz (1973) provides a framework within which to analyze the affect of the ritual of being a fairy-tale princess for a week. Ritual's ability to create, not just reflect, reality has been well documented (Moore and Myerhoff 1977: 4; Ortner 1978: 9). Geertz characterizes this double aspect of ritual as being not just a model "of" but a model "for" reality. Rituals give meaning to social and psychological realities: "both by shaping themselves and by shaping it to themselves" (Geertz 1973: 93). Coronation, the presentation of San Antonio's aristocrats as court members, is a model of their historic socioeconomic dominance and is a model for the continuation of that hierarchical positioning. The themes of Coronation, with their emphasis on beauty and attainment, provide both an idealization of the participants' lives and also a goal for reality. In the earliest years the themes referred to nature, Court of the Flowers (1909), or imagination, Court of Fairies (1916). But by the late 1920s themes began to be derived from geography, Court of the Mediterranean (1928), or history, Court of Louis XIV (1929). Almost all courts are now historically based: Court of the Imperial House of Hapsburg (1987), Court of the Napoleonic Empire (1993), and Court of the Age of Discovery (1997). The texts, heavily laced with historical thematic information, and the royal robes, covered with arcane iconography, exemplify Pierre Bourdieu's markers of social distinction that are "predisposed, consciously and deliberately or not, to fulfill a social function of legitimating social differences" (1984: 7). The annual enactment of Coronation, based on those markers, reinforces group identity for the aristocracy – members of the Order of the Alamo and their families.

Catherine Bell (1992), through a practice-based framework of ritualization, analyzes the efficacy of ritual activity. She focuses on the creation of reality through "redemptive hegemony," the way ritualized activity makes the participants cognizant of the social order and their potential personal empowerment (1992: 84). The court presents a model of hierarchically ranked status from the youngest pages up through the ranks to the queen and to the President of the Order of the Alamo, who bestows the crown. If one is born into the proper family, one usually can achieve the highest ranking of queen or president of the Order simply by choosing to go through the progressive steps toward that attainment. The community ritual has an internal hierarchical ranking that is assailable, just as many of life's hierarchies are assailable by the members of the socioeconomically advantaged. The structure of participation naturalizes social positioning. Coronation also has a pragmatic effect on one's status as it identifies and maintains the elite. Personal networks are nurtured throughout the six-month-long social season preceding Coronation and can be turned to economic or social advantage in any number of formal and informal ways. Bourdieu refers to this phenomenon as "social capital," defining it as "the set of actual or potential resources related to the possession of an enduring network of relations of inter-cognition and inter-recognition, which are more or less institutionalized" (Bourdieu as translated in Lomnitz and Perez-Lizaur 1987: 104). Such social capital can be invested when one needs a job, a recommendation, a loan, or a referral. These benefits extend not only to the royal young women but also to their families and close friends. They are invited to Coronation and the many associated social events where contacts are made and relationships developed, thereby accruing social capital with interest.

Ritual is intimately related to issues of gender identity, particularly in rites of passage (Frese 1991; Herdt 1982; Watson 1993), as well as being an important means of considering class issues. San Antonio's Coronation can be viewed as a rite of passage and is outlined as such in chapter 3. An analysis must also look at the ways in which the ritual, as played out by the members of the elite families, reinforces traditional gender identity. Women take prominent roles as court members, mistresses of the robes, and court artists. Women also act as active lobbyists on behalf of kin and friends for membership in the Order or in the royal court. Significantly, marrying or fathering a queen or princess is one of only two means to an automatic invitation to become a member of the Order.[8] A study of debutantes demonstrates the continued importance of young women as representatives of the family, the basic unit of the elite social class. Through participation in Coronation and its attendant social season, the royal women are keys to social reproduction: the families mark their continued membership among the elite, the social class reaffirms its group identity, and the next generation is assured through endogamous marriage.

The endogamous marriages make the reproduction/production framework highly germane to a study of Coronation gender roles. However, analyses using production and reproduction have often been contradictory and unclear because of the variation in the definitions of the term "reproduction," leading to confusion between the biological reproduction of the working class and social class production (Mukhopadhyay and Higgins 1988: 479–86; Yanagisako and Collier 1987: 20–4).[9] Coronation both produces the elite social class and biologically reproduces the next generation because of the endogamous marriages resulting from the Coronation season. Although a separation is made for analytical purposes, the ritual of Coronation precludes a separation of social and biological reproduction for in it the two forms are collapsed. In classic terms the young women are the reproducers – virgin–daughter–future mother; the male members of the Order are the producers.

While somewhat concerned with gender relations, Randall Collins (1992) concentrates on the importance of women in creating class difference. Many upper class women have the privilege of spending less time in household labor because of the ability to hire help. Their surplus time is then spent in status production: "[W]e have here a siphoning off of female energies into the realm of status and apparently under the strong initiative of women themselves" (1992: 216). His work applies to the women in Coronation as they design and create the royal robes, the markers of status.

Although the dichotomous model of gender roles to explain universal asymmetry has fallen out of favor, particularly in cross-cultural applications, the model of separate domains is still a useful tool, particularly when looking at American material (Frese 1991: 101; Lamphere 1993; Moore 1988: 21). The historicity of Coronation makes binary domains highly appropriate when analyzing an event that was begun in the late Edwardian period by a trans-planted southerner who romanticized the past in general and chivalrous gentlemen in particular. The participants as a whole make a concentrated effort to maintain the "tradition of Coronation," and it is not surprising that gender roles do fall into separated domains of public and private, political and domestic. However, the differing domains are seen by most participants as complementary, rather than being used to create asymmetrical relation-ships. This emic view corresponds to Ortner's point that the highest social levels in hierarchically arranged societies do not divide the genders but unite them in deriving their primary status (Ortner 1981: 397). Men and women both gain social stature from the Order of the Alamo and participation in the Coronation ceremony.

Methodology

Being a graduate student in the late 1980s and early 1990s, I was keenly aware of the quandary self-reflexive anthropologists found themselves in when choosing an area for advanced study. The traditional "other," subjects of American and European colonialism or ethnic minorities in the United States, could no longer be so freely appropriated as objects of study. I had long been drawn to Laura Nader's (1964) call to "study up," when she questions anthropologists' proclivity for asking why some people are so poor rather than finding out why some are so affluent.[10] But, to study the elite, one first has to identify them – not always an easy task given the hesitancy many feel in identifying themselves as privileged. Fortunately, Coronation's boundaries easily identify the elite.

George Marcus's (1992) work on group reproduction of dynastic families in Galveston, Texas, provides an interesting contrast to San Antonio. Marcus explored the families' creations of ancestral personal narratives, biographical texts that are ways to transmit concepts of the family's character, its unique distinctiveness, to the younger generation (1992: 182). Unlike San Antonio's Coronation families, Marcus's elite families have to create such texts as embodiments of family tradition because there are no rituals or collective representations left in which the families may participate and "assert and glorify in public their superior distinctiveness" (1992: 182). Marcus also reports that some dynastic families, in attempting to create familial distinction, turn to anthropological terms to create an "emblematic association of the family with some other cultural model (e.g., clan or tribe)" (1992: 181). San Antonio's aristocratic families not only share the Coronation family ritual, but also use an "emblematic association" when they refer to it as a "tribal ritual." However, such terms also seem to be an effort to neutralize the elitism, to create a connection to the exotic Other whose activities must be seen as culturally relative and classless.

The current academic interest in domination and hegemony also coincided with my interest in the class issues inherent in the Coronation robes and ritual. However, the virtually unlimited access mandated by the methodology of participant-observation is not usually made available by the elite, and many of the Coronation participants are no exception. The Order of the Alamo is concerned about criticism of both the costs of the gowns and minimal Hispanic participation, and it carefully controls any kind of media access to members or events. Coronation itself has always been a public event, but all associated meetings, rehearsals, and parties are quite private.

However, I was in a somewhat fortuitous position to do an ethnographic study of this group, although I am a total outsider in terms of socioeconomics and ties to San Antonio. To begin with, I believe that my forty-something age kept me from being seen as a typical graduate student who would automatically be considered a potential adversary. Also I have lived in San Antonio for over twenty years and have friends in social circles peripheral to Coronation. I happen to dress in a style somewhat similar to the relaxed denim and cotton look adopted by many middle-aged elite women in San Antonio for everyday and therefore am perceived as potentially acceptable for social contact. Most importantly, I am Anglo. However, even with those positive factors, my access was somewhat limited.

I could have interviewed former court members through the friends-of-friends method, but contact with the current court and the board of directors of the Order of the Alamo had to be made formally. I began by contacting the current president of the Order by letter. He was cooperative and helpful but did lay down specific rules regarding the events I could attend and asked for a list of the people I would be interviewing from both past and present courts. While I chafed a bit under the restrictions, I eventually realized that the president would be held personally responsible by the board of directors for any unwelcome results of my research. I began to understand the difficulties of studying up. I was allowed to attend several rehearsals and in subsequent years have always been welcomed into the backstage area to view and photograph the royal robes prior to Coronation, but I have had to repeatedly reassure members of the Order that I would not write anything that would appear in the popular press.

I had extended interviews (from two to three hours in length) with about fifty people. The oldest Order member I interviewed was eighty-four, and the oldest duchess was ninety-two. My youngest informants were in their twenties. I have had both formal and informal follow-up interviews with a number of my informants. I am certainly aware that most people were careful about their responses to my questions, particularly regarding the costs of the robes and the limited participation by non-Anglos. I was given permission by most informants to tape interviews in addition to note taking, but I promised anonymity to all (I have changed details in the following descriptions to conceal identities). Many people have been cooperative, friendly, and a bit surprised, and sometimes even pleased, that an academic is interested in their traditional spring event. The women, particularly older ones, were happy to talk about their royal memories, and they got out scrapbooks and even dresses for me to see. I interviewed more women than men because most men who had not been officers of the Order of the Alamo did not have that much to say. Many of them referred to Coronation as something that they attended because their wives wanted them to. Also, my focus on the dresses required more interviews with the women who are involved in designing, making, and wearing them.

I am fortunate to now have half a dozen good friends who are closely involved in Coronation and are willing to discuss both their experiences and concerns with me. Also, due to my current museum curatorial position, I continue to interact on several levels with people connected with Coronation. As the history curator, I have literally handled every dress and train while doing an inventory of the museum's current collection of 163 royal robes. I have selected the royal robes for three different exhibits on Fiesta. I have resewn many loose rhinestones and picked up far more from the floor. These hands-on experiences have made me even more certain that the royal robes – these often beautiful, sometimes poorly designed, or just plain glitzy, dresses and trains covered with rhinestones and beads – are central not only to the continuation of Coronation but also to the reproduction of social class and gender roles.

The heavy, carefully fitted royal robes, with their accompanying under-structures, literally reconfigure the wearer's body. They are not just superficial clothing. Wearing a gown and train heavily laden with symbols of beauty and achievement transfers the message onto the body of the wearer. Clothing is the most discernible indicator of personal characteristics and is also the most malleable. It may be changed, and the princess may appear on the streets as part of the proletariat by exchanging her crown for ordinary headgear. The malleability extends to the body and mind of the wearer for the physicality of clothing may shape both physical and mental perceptions. As the young Coronation women are physically transformed by the clothing, so are they psychologically. Susan Kaiser, in her text on the social psychology of clothing, points to the work of Susan Sontag and Jean Schlater, who state that "clothes are not only contiguous to the body in a physical sense, but they also may be close to the self in a psychological sense" (Kaiser 1990: 147). Through proximity to the body, clothes incorporate several constructs, including that of positive or negative acceptance of self based on other's judgements of one's personal appearance. It is impossible to wear the royal robes, weighing up to a total of seventy-five pounds or more, without considering the implications of being attired in clothing considered beautiful and highly desirable by one's family and social group. Parents who have both the social connections and economic ability to clothe a daughter in the Coronation robes can make the young woman into the fantasized fairy princess of her childhood dreams.

Before examining the fairy-tale clothes in detail, an overview of the history of San Antonio and that of Fiesta is presented in the next chapter to contextualize Coronation and its royal robes. When asked why he thinks that Coronation continues, Carrington's son replied, "Well, I'd hate to try to analyze it because it doesn't make much sense except as part of Fiesta." Chapter 3 lays out the mechanics of participation in Coronation. The qualifications for membership in the Order of the Alamo and for participation as a member of the court are discussed, pointing to the continued importance of residence in one of three older neighborhoods. The effect of Coronation participation in gender roles and relationships is also discussed. The royal robes and the contexts in which they are viewed are the focus of chapter 4. The lives of the royal robes from design to deposition are presented, following Kopytoff's (1986) biography of an object. Details in the text, setting, and royal robes are used to demonstrate the specific ways in which Coronation reifies elite identity. The last chapter steps back from the microanalysis of the royal robes to look again at the larger context of Fiesta San Antonio. The relatively few public criticisms of the embellished robes, from satires and parodies to newspaper columns, are reviewed. Consideration of the importance of the fixity, of the predictability, of the boundedness, of Coronation in a postmodern world completes the study.

Notes

1. The term "Anglo" designates members of the core culture of San Antonio and is primarily a twentieth-century term (Feagin 1978: 58). "Anglo American" refers to immigrants to Texas from 1820 to 1900. "Mexican American" refers to Texans whose ancestors emigrated from Mexico or are themselves immigrants. "Hispanic" is used when an inclusive term is necessary and includes Mexican Americans, immigrants from Spanish-speaking countries, and Mexican and Spanish nationals.

2. Ilse Hayden in her work on British royalty defines "aristocracy" as "the top pinnacle of a hierarchical society" and refers to Simmel's requirement that "relations of blood and marriage must be ramified and traceable throughout the whole group" (1987: 8–11). Much of the core group in San Antonio's Coronation is made up of the dozen or so families who are all distantly related due to the marriage between John Smith, an Anglo immigrant to San Antonio, and Maria Curbello, daughter of one of the Canary Island founding families, in the early nineteenth century (and some later distant cousin marriages).

3. Milton Gordon (1964) uses the term "ethclass" to designate the intersection of class and ethnic group: the group that allows a member to both share a sense of peoplehood and behavioral similarities; a shared "consciousness of kind" (1964: 53). I feel the term is specifically accurate in reference to the elite in San Antonio.

4. In 1856 San Antonio's population was 10,500: 4,000 were Mexican, 3,000 German, and 3,500 were Anglo Americans (Montejano 1987: 29).

5. Ortner's indicators of a key symbol are 1. "Natives tell us that X is culturally important." All discussions of Coronation at least begin with talk of the royal robes. 2. "Natives seem positively or negatively aroused about X." Participants love the robes, even when seen with a slightly jaundiced eye. The general population has a low awareness level, but those on the periphery of the aristocratic class usually have strong feelings, pro or con. 3. "X comes up in many different contexts." The robes are present in North Star Mall as well as on the stage at Coronation. 4. "There is greater elaboration surrounding X." The techniques involved in making the robes and the resulting discourse are ever evolving. 5. "There are greater cultural restrictions surrounding X." The Order has strict rules regarding the length of trains and where the robes are worn. Informal restrictions, based upon tradition, also govern the materials and how they are used (Ortner 1979: 94).

6. Goffman (1973), Horn (1968), Kuper (1973), Roach and Eicher (1965, 1973), and Stone (1965) provided the foundation for my further reading.

7. These figures do not include the additional basic costs of a party for the honoree, a wardrobe for the numerous social events, and rooms in a downtown hotel for the duration of Fiesta week.

8. Sons of former presidents of the Order of the Alamo are automatically offered membership at the appropriate age.

9. Current usage usually follows the tripartite division developed by Olivia Harris and Kate Young (1981): biological reproduction, reproduction of the labor force (housework), and social reproduction (the maintenance of institutions and practices that lead to the continuance of production relations), although slippage may occur between the latter two terms (Yanagisako and Collier 1987: 23).

10. Since the development of an elite perspective to explain agency in the late nineteenth and early twentieth centuries (Mosca 1939; Pareto 1935), sociologists have been virtually the only social scientists to research the upper class as a powerful social organization (Domhoff 1967, 1971, 1974; Mills 1959; Warner 1941). The historical work of Frederic Jaher (1973, 1982) is an important exception. Although many anthropologists have increasingly recognized the importance of understanding the cultures of the United States, most have focused on ethnic or blue-collar groups (Achor 1978; di Leonardo 1984; Foley 1990; Myerhoff 1978; Rose 1987; Stack 1974; Sutherland 1986; Varenne 1977).

2

The History of San Antonio and Fiesta

The Order of the Alamo's Coronation was established to create monarchs to reign over Spring Carnival, the original version of the city-wide celebration now known as Fiesta San Antonio. In 1891 the Battle of Flowers parade was staged to honor the veterans of San Jacinto, the 1836 concluding battle in Texas's revolt against Mexico (Figure 1). The parade remains the focal point of Fiesta San Antonio, now ten days long with over a hundred events including three parades, a band festival, military reviews, and a carnival. Although Fiesta is held in memory of the war's successful concluding battle, which took place outside of Houston, the overall tenor is affected by the fact that the Alamo, the site of Texas's most important defeat, in which all the men inside the mission compound were killed by Mexican forces, is located in San Antonio.[1] The Alamo is the site of the oldest ritualized Fiesta activities. The symbolic flower battle, the highlight of the early Battle of Flowers parades, took place in front of the Alamo, when the procession split in half and began to toss flowers at one another. The parade has taken different routes over the years but always passes in front of the Alamo, where many of the participants stop to lay flowers or wreaths on the front lawn (Figure 2). The Pilgrimage to the Alamo, a solemn procession of representatives of local organizations and institutions, has been part of Fiesta since 1918. A guided tour of the Alamo by costumed living history association members is presented annually during Fiesta by the Sons of the Republic of Texas to "honor the heroes of the Alamo . . . on the very site where Travis and his men made their heroic stand for Texas independence."

Food and drink are indulged in to excess at some Fiesta events, but the overall emphasis on patriotism and history, and the constant presence of the Alamo, prevents the development of the carnivalesque atmosphere associated with seasonally based observations such as Mardi Gras in New Orleans.[2] Comparing the behavior of parade participants and spectators in San Antonio and New Orleans illustrates the quintessential difference between the two events. In New Orleans riders on the floats in Mardi Gras parades throw

Figure 1. Fresh or artificial flowers were used to decorate buggies and carriages for early Battle of Flowers parades. Courtesy: Witte Museum.

Figure 2. The Alamo remains the focal point for many Fiesta events including the Battle of Flowers parade. Courtesy: Institute of Texan Cultures, Zintgraff Collection.

beads and coins to observers. Some of the men on the floats challenge young women in the crowd to reveal part of their upper anatomy in exchange for the beads, calling "Show us your ____!" In San Antonio young men in the crowd that always forms in front of the Menger Hotel, adjacent to the Alamo, yell at the duchesses on the floats, "Show us your shoes," and the girls raise their heavy skirts to flash their Reeboks or other comfortable shoes. The irony of tennis shoes being worn under elaborate dresses is enjoyed, but does not lead to requests for further revelations.

The Alamo is also intimately associated with Fiesta monarchs. King Antonio is crowned in front of the Alamo and the voting for the Queen of the Order of the Alamo takes place inside the chapel – Texas's most sacred shrine. These facts most clearly reveal the intrinsic tie between Coronation and Fiesta San Antonio, the commemoration of Texas's successful revolt against Mexico. In order to understand the implicit hegemony in the royal ritual and its themes of beauty and grandeur, both Coronation and Fiesta must be examined as examples of pageantry, popular theatrical productions commemorating a historical event using amateur casts. Pageantry was a way to present a popular view of local history and identity (Glassberg 1990: 1). Fiesta as a whole is an example of the pageantry movement for it has always included events drawing attention to the history of San Antonio and Texas: the defeat of Mexico, settlement by Anglo pioneers, the rise of cattle ranching, and the establishment of five military bases. Pageants present an idealized view of history by ignoring class and ethnic divisions and tensions in a community, yet by "giving recognition to various group and individual histories, [pageants suggest] categories for our understanding the scale of our social relations and the relative position of groups in our society" (Glassberg 1990: 1). Coronation's thematic emphasis on the elite and their attainment creates a framework within which participants may place themselves in relation to the rest of San Antonio. Coronation was begun at the height of the pageantry movement, and the origin of its thematic emphasis on history can be traced to the influence of that movement. However, unlike most examples of pageantry, Coronation did not die out in the 1940s but became institutionalized as an annual ritual, varying little from year to year in format and function.

The historical pageantry of Fiesta is an attempt to justify the political and cultural conquest of Mexican Texas, while the pageantry found in Coronation itself is a mythologized ethnic and class history that justifies the hierarchical positioning of its Anglo participants; albeit, the intentionality may be subconscious in both cases. This symbolic justification is accomplished in Fiesta through the associated patriotic and historic events, the Pilgrimage to the Alamo and the Pioneer Ball, and in Coronation through the theme selection and the elevated imagery carried out in the set, text, music, and most visibly in the gowns and trains. The text focuses on glory and beauty and power, regardless of whether the theme is of nature, literature, or history. All of the themes become transformed into a public presentation of class consciousness. These qualities are embodied in the royal robes worn by the young women, who represent the oldest, monied Anglo families.

An overview of San Antonio history is necessary to provide the context in which Anglo debutantes are crowned as the city's aristocrats, in a city founded by Spain and now dominated demographically by Mexican Americans. The history of Fiesta San Antonio and its royal figures reflects the socioeconomic and political changes in San Antonio.[3]

History of San Antonio

Hierarchical positioning has been a part of San Antonio's history since 1731, when the Spanish settlers from the Canary Islands arrived. This chapter traces the formation of an elite ideology from the first Spanish arrivals in the eighteenth century to the development of the Tejano (those of Mexican and Spanish blood who lived in Texas) upper class and its rapid replacement by Anglo American immigrants during the period of the Republic (1836–45). San Antonio's Spanish speaking citizens became anathema to many of its Anglo American immigrants from the southeastern United States even before the end of the Republic, despite the many contributions of Tejanos to the revolt, for they were seen as part of Texas's monolithic enemy, Mexico. Early in the nineteenth century, Anglo Americans and Tejanos, for a time, had shared goals and desires in their settling of Texas. These were lost as increasing segregation took place as a result of a basic Anglo belief in Manifest Destiny. The rest of the nineteenth century was a time of increasing prosperity for the more recent German arrivals and of diminishing social and economic power for the Tejanos who remained in San Antonio. As Anglo Americans and European immigrants increasingly united through mutual business interests, Tejanos became isolated from the sources of socioeconomic power. A history of Fiesta San Antonio, beginning at the end of the nineteenth century, reveals the separation between Tejanos and Anglos that had taken place and the subsequent shifts in relationships throughout the twentieth.

Spanish Period: 1691–1820

The bands of indigenous hunter-gatherers who traveled throughout what was known in Europe as New Spain offered an excuse to the rulers of Spain to establish their presence in the area to protect it from the encroachments of France. Spain's earliest attempts to establish missions in the northernmost parts of New Spain both to protect the nation's interests and to convert the indigenous inhabitants were sporadic and largely unsuccessful. Despite two official namings of the river, San Antonio de Padua, in 1691 and again in 1709, it was not until April 1718 that the Mission San Antonio de Valero was founded at the site of present-day San Antonio. Personnel included thirty-five soldiers, six chaplains, and thirty-one other people, including wives, vaqueros, mule drivers, and a blacksmith, as well as assorted livestock (Davis 1978: 4). In addition to the mission, the Villa de Bexar came into being to serve the presence of the soldiers and their families.

In 1721 a new expedition of two companies of men and livestock arrived and proceeded with preparations to finally build the proposed adobe presidio on what is now Military Plaza. From the inception of the first mission, fires, floods, epidemics, lack of money, and the presence of unfriendly indigenous tribes, such as the Apache, all plagued the development of the missions, the presidio and the town itself. Many more colonists were needed to hold the vast stretches of the frontier but economic measures prevented the planned development. The one official effort at settlement was the transportation of fifty-six Canary Islanders to San Antonio de Bexar in 1731. The local contingent of fifty-three soldiers and officers with families and four civilian families assisted the new arrivals, little suspecting the approaching disruptions they would soon face (Ramsdell 1959: 23).

The newcomers arrived with a belief in their inherent superiority that was reinforced when they were given the title of Hidalgos, the lowest order of nobility. They were given land on the river side of the fort, land the soldiers felt was theirs. Because their deeds had not been registered, the soldiers had no recourse but to give up their lands. The Hidalgos were also given full control of the town's *cabildo* or city council with ten receiving lifetime appointments as *regidores* or councilmen (Poyo 1991a: 42).

The Canary Islanders caused ill feelings among the other settlers and soldiers by their acquisition of land and political power. Their complaints and requests for special rights and benefits, including use of mission Indian labor in their fields and a monopoly on selling produce to the military, caused further alienation. The viceroy's auditor lost his patience and suggested that "they desire to be left alone in undisputed possession" (Ramsdell 1959: 25). The first hierarchical socioeconomic positioning from politics to location of homes had begun. José María Rodríguez in his memoirs described the "right" and "wrong" sides of the San Antonio River. "The west side of the river was supposed to be the residence of the first families here, and the descendants of the Indians and Spanish soldiers settled on the east side"

(Rodriguez 1913: 37). De facto segregated settlement patterns based on class and ethnicity continued throughout San Antonio's history and are clearly seen in the clustering of home addresses of Coronation participants in three older neighborhoods.

Conflicts over economic and political advantages abounded between the groups; however, the two communities increasingly found themselves allied against the officials of the Church and Crown, who pushed changes such as attempts to expand mission property boundaries, a move that would benefit neither group of settlers. The Canary Islanders originally controlled the cabildo, but the mutual interests of farmers and ranchers as opposed to those of the Crown led to a general integration and opening up of local political positions to members of both groups.

Intermarriage between the settlers from New Spain and those from the Canary Islands and between new and old settlers was also an important means of creating a more united citizenry, although elite family lines were still acknowledged. At first the Islanders had looked down upon soldiers and settlers of mixed blood but, as the social networks merged, "suspect bloodlines became less of a problem socially" (Poyo 1991a: 47). Marriage between Indians and non-Indian inhabitants, often those of mixed ancestry, also occurred with some frequency, just as it had in the interior of New Spain (Hinojosa and Fox 1991: 118). Immigration finally began to increase in the 1770s, and those newcomers, whether Indian or from New Spain or Europe, with artisans' skills were able to acquire wealth and land and to become part of the social hierarchy (Poyo 1991b: 102). However, economic stratification remained firmly in place, as a 1783 inventory of Fernando de Veramendi's store indicates, with its bolts of coarse fustian cloth and unbleached blanket cloth from Puebla in contrast to fine French fabrics and gold and silver thread (Almaraz 1993).

In the eighteenth century most of San Antonio's problems came from disagreements with the Church and Crown over land use and governmental control, although there was internal strife among colonists as well. The Catholic Church's control of the best lands created bitter feelings among many of the settlers.

Revolts: 1821–36

In the early nineteenth century the problems of San Antonio and its environs were far more dramatic, as it became the site of battles first of the Mexican War of Independence against Spain (1810–21) and then of the Texas revolt against Mexico (1835–36). San Antonio's population decreased steadily throughout the Mexican War of Independence. In 1819 a flood, following a drought and pestilence, made the city even less desirable until 1821 when the war was concluded and San Antonio began to recover. In 1824 the new federal constitution of Mexico joined Texas and Coahuila (the Mexican state across the Rio Grande from most of Texas) into a single political entity, with Saltillo as the capital and Texas as a Department of the Republic of Mexico. San Antonio's recovery was to be short-lived for it was soon to be the center of the unrest and dissatisfactions that culminated in the Texas Revolution.

An atmosphere for eventual revolt was created by both the influx of American immigrants and Mexico's internal political problems, which left few resources for the frontier. At the beginning of the *empresario* movement Texas had a total population of 4,000, but within fifteen years there were 20,000 to 25,000 inhabitants (Thompson 1929: 14).[4] The newly independent Mexican government was initially quite generous in its inducements to the new immigrants; however, an unsuccessful attempt in 1826 to declare Texas independent of Mexico led to efforts to check the high numbers of immigrants from the United States.

Popular representations of Texas history depict the Texas Revolution as simply one of the newly arrived Anglo Americans versus Mexicans, making no distinction between Tejanos who were loyal to Mexico and those who were greatly dissatisfied with the Mexican government's movement away from federalism. There is little recognition of Anglo Americans who fought on the side of Mexico, such as Col. John Bradburn, or of Tejanos who fought for Texas Independence, such as Juan Seguin and José Antonio Navarro. The majority of Tejanos remained loyal to Mexico, but a number of the elite did side with the revolutionaries. The involvement of Tejanos in the Texas Revolution was primarily a result of the accommodations made by the elite to the new demographics.[5] Elite Tejanos, such as Seguin and Navarro, often developed economic and personal ties to the new Anglo settlers. Well-connected Tejanos received large land grants just as did Anglos in the early 1830s and, just as in the previous century, intermarriage was an important way of interconnecting the new and old elite (Gonzales 1989: 25; Montejano 1987: 36). Newcomers with no local background could establish a family network, as did James Bowie when he married Ursula Veramendi, the daughter of a prominent San Antonio shopkeeper.[6] Personal ties were also deepened through the Masonic movement, in which Navarro, Seguin, and Lorenzo de Zavala were members, as were Stephen F. Austin, Sam Houston, and Mirabeau Lamar (Gonzales 1989: 21). In 1830 John William Smith, later mayor of San Antonio, married Maria Jesusa Curbelo and had five children, whose descendants form ten of the foremost Coronation families.[7] All reported intermarriage between Spanish and Anglo was unidirectional: Spanish females married Anglo males, thus losing the Hispanic name.

Mexico's economic and political inability to properly support and maintain its northern frontier led to feelings of alienation and disillusion. The perceived abandonment of the north also led to accommodationist stances and eventually to decisions by a minority of elite Tejanos to support the Revolution, primarily economically. A belief that participation in Anglo economic and political institutions would benefit the community as a whole and the Mexican segment specifically also explains some of the Anglo-Tejano cooperation among the elite prior to and during the Revolution and subsequent Republic. In addition to the more altruistic reasons for cooperation, a desire "to maintain social status, which in turn is based on political and economic power, was a prominent, perhaps even predominant, factor in explaining inter-ethnic cooperation in the American Southwest" (Gonzales 1989: 24–5). Manuel Gonzales goes on to note that the Tejano elite were not trying to attain higher status but were trying to maintain what had belonged to their families for two generations. Seguin and Navarro were both second-generation Tejanos whose fathers had been alcaldes in San Antonio, both were friends of Stephen F. Austin (as was Seguin's father Erasmo), both received large grants from the Mexican government and became successful plantation owners. After initial hesitations both joined the Anglo Americans in the move for independence. Navarro was one of three Tejano signers of the Texas Constitution of 1836, and Seguin fought at the battles of the Alamo and San Jacinto, winning a rank of lieutenant colonel. After the war, Navarro served as a representative from Bexar County while Seguin was a senator.

The average Texan does not know that men with Spanish surnames fought in the battles or served in Congress; fewer still know that the earliest formal call for reform came not from the new Anglo immigrants but from Tejanos. Elite Tejanos from San Antonio published *Representación* on 19 December 1832, stating their dissatisfactions and concerns.[8] This was not a call for revolution but a statement of needed reforms. However, little change resulted. Instead more difficulties arose, including a tariff, pitting some of the Tejanos with the Anglo American settlers against the Mexican government led by Santa Anna.

Tensions gradually eased as the tariff was lifted and Anglo settlers themselves voted against independence from Mexico during a convention held in 1833 "to decide the future of Texas" (Guerra 1985: [14]).[9] Austin himself led the effort against revolt and William H. Wharton and Rafael Manchola were selected to present a petition in Mexico City, to illustrate the shared feelings of both Mexican and Anglo Texans. Austin went to Mexico to discuss separating Texas from Coahuila (while remaining in the Mexican Union) but was arrested on his return home. However, by 1835 many problems had returned and Austin felt there was no alternative and gave the call to arms.

Some Tejanos joined the newly formed Texan army while others, such as Don Erasmo Seguin, aided effort through sending horses, mules, and supplies (Lozano 1985: 22).

The war lasted less than a year, but San Antonio was the site of one of the earliest victories of the Texans, led by Ben Milam, and then the most important defeat, which took place at the abandoned mission San Antonio de Valero and became known as the Battle of the Alamo. Although the defenders of the old fort inflicted heavy losses on Santa Anna's troops, the Alamo fell on 6 March 1836. There were no survivors and no prisoners, and the battle has been raised to legendary status. On April 21 Santa Anna and his troops were defeated on the field of San Jacinto, near present-day Houston. Santa Anna was taken prisoner and signed the Treaty of Velasco, ending the Texas Revolution.

The Republic of Texas: 1836–45

After the war the American elite, the lawyers and merchants, were superimposed atop the old hierarchy. Lawyers acted as intermediaries between what remained of the Mexican landed elite and the Anglo merchants who had capital and wanted to invest it in land, often with Mexican merchants as minor partners. Social events, such as the visit of President Mirabeau Lamar to San Antonio, took place at the home of the Seguins with guests whose names reflected both Mexican and Anglo American backgrounds. Mary Maverick moved with her husband from Alabama to San Antonio in 1838. In her memoirs she described the social scene, noting, "We exchanged calls with the Navarros, Sotos, Garzas, Garcias, Zambranos, Seguins, Veramendis and Yturris" (Maverick 1921: 54). Intermarriages did continue to occur and Jovita González noted that daughters "were married at an early age, and not for love, but for family connections and considerations" (1930: 27). David Montejano notes that "ethnic divisions were secondary to those of class" in the post-annexation politics of the area (1987: 36).

Tejanos who had been active in the Texas Revolution became political leaders in the new Texas Republic, but the memory of their part in the Revolution quickly faded, as did their names from the lists of Texas statesmen. In the years immediately following the war, San Antonio's city council was ethnically mixed. However, as early as 1844, just eight years after the conclusion of the war, Anglos dominated local politics. "San Antonio was now an Anglo town – even though the population count was not" (Davis 1978: 19). Political representation by citizens of Mexican heritage dropped throughout the nineteenth century from a high of forty-one Spanish-surnamed candidates for city aldermanic council in 1837 to one or two by 1866 and even fewer thereafter.

Some Tejanos did acquire land through entrepreneurial activities, primarily those along the border area (de León 1991: 45). A handful managed to hang on to their lands, but most Tejanos lost political power, land, property, and, to a lesser extent, their lives during the Republic. Montejano states that the character of the Texas revolt changed after its successful completion and that former alliances immediately began to break down. There was now a prevailing "spirit of revenge and abandon" among many of the ex-soldiers and they grabbed Mexican-held lands, stock, and lives without regard to the Mexicans' former places in the battle lines. Most of the initial rampaging violence took place in southern Texas, with La Bahía (Goliad) being razed in 1837. However, life was not secure even in San Antonio. Threats against lives and confiscation of property drove many prominent families out by the 1840s, including Juan Sequin and his family. Tejano-held land, the principal source of wealth, was taken by force, fraud, or even bought legitimately when the owners were so frightened by the prospects of Anglo American dominance that they felt unable to remain in Texas (Montejano 1987: 26–8). William Bollaert recorded his observations on the three classes of Hispanics during his visit in 1843, noting that the old Spaniards, or Gauchupins, were gone and that their descendants were "very few indeed. . . . The days of the Governador, alcalde, and Regidor are gone – gone for ever" (1956: 218).

Annexation and After: 1846–75

Vengeful acts were once again perpetrated against the relatively small remaining Mexican-Spanish population in the 1850s after the Mexican War.[10] There was wholesale eviction in some Texas towns by posses, but, when the San Antonio sheriff tried to raise a posse for similar purposes, the high number of Germans who refused to take part made the effort unsuccessful (Davis 1978: 25). Although San Antonio Tejanos were not expelled, most had very little in terms of resources.

In the 1840s the economy of San Antonio was based on the land, but a decade later it had changed to one based on the presence of the military and the city's location as the hub of a trade network reaching from Mexico to California. Nearly 60 percent of the Mexican work force was engaged as teamsters taking goods both within the city and to areas outside, but even that source of income evaporated for many when masked bands attacked and killed several of the Mexican teamsters who worked the San Antonio–Goliad route (Montejano 1987: 29). United States troops were quartered in San Antonio during the Mexican War and then became permanent residents when the headquarters of the Eighth Military District was established. European goods came into San Antonio through Indianola while Mexican pack trains brought in cotton goods, tobacco, chocolate, and silver. San Antonio was primarily an importer and exported only pecans, cattle, and a little wool.

By mid-century ethnic as well as class differences had become more visible as the physical and social appearance of San Antonio changed. Fueled by political idealism, German immigrants had begun arriving in the Texas Hill Country in the 1840s seeking social and economic opportunities. By the 1850s many German immigrants had moved into San Antonio. The first German club was organized in 1853, an opera house quickly followed and Sangerfest Hall was built in 1854. A German brewery, a German–English school, the Menger Hotel, and Guenther's Grist Mill all were established in that decade. A visitor, Frederick Olmsted, pointed out that many of the Mexican-style homes of adobe or plaster that edged Alamo Plaza were being remodeled, and that German stone houses and Irish flats were more in evidence (Lich 1981: 16–25). The Beethoven Mannerchor, a German singing society, was founded in 1867 and in 1895 built Beethoven Hall, considered the finest concert hall of the southwest in its prime. It was the site of the first Coronation staged by the Order of the Alamo.

The German immigrants did not use intermarriage as a means of consolidating themselves with the local elite, as had the earlier Anglos. They also further separated themselves from the rest of the city's economic elite by refusing to support the Civil War.[11] Many of the most prosperous German immigrants built large homes in an area known as King William after its main street, reputedly named by an early resident in honor of the Prussian ruler Wilhelm I. The grandparents and parents of many of the earliest Coronation royalty lived in its Italianate Victorian, Greek revival, and neoclassical homes.

Despite the intermarriages (with the German exceptions) and the other mechanisms of accommodation between Tejanos and Euro-American immigrants, particularly between the two elite groups, there was still an underlying feeling of acquisition or Manifest Destiny rather than accommodation. An 1854 magazine declared that San Antonio was being "developed under the brighter auspices of Anglo-American energy and enterprise. . . . The Mexican will soon disappear altogether" (Ramsdell 1959: 40). The comment would not be true numerically, but the Civil War set up the conditions under which Anglos would emerge as a dominant force in the San Antonio economy and politics in contrast to what formally had been a fairly bicultural elite. The social interactions that had taken place among the elite gradually were eroded.

[T]here is at the present time but little, if any social intercourse. Once or twice, perhaps in the course of a year, a public ball will summon the fair representatives of both nations to terms of amity. But then ceases all social intercourse. The breach seems to be widening, and for the soul of us we cannot tell why. Some of our most reputable and wealthy citizens have intermarried with ladies of Mexican origin; the result has been prosperous and intelligent offspring; and yet this social coldness and frigidity seems to strengthen daily. (San Antonio *Ledger*, 1 September 1853, quoted in Everett 1975: 25)

Trade boomed during the Civil War years for the enterprising men who moved cotton to the Mexican border where it could be shipped to European markets, avoiding the Federal blockade. Commission companies and merchants all profited from the war, partially from supplying the Confederacy with meat and canned goods and from their successful diverse investments. Thus, the war strengthened San Antonio's mercantile enterprises and also led to some industrial development (Booth and Johnson 1983: 6). Profits were used to start banks in the postwar period by men whose names are still recognized as being among the socioeconomic elite – Oppenheimer, Groos, Frost, Brackenridge, and Maverick. These names also continue to be those of Coronation's royalty, from duchesses to queens.

Politics and Power: 1875 to the Present

The arrival of the railroad in 1877 furthered the economic divisions between all classes of Mexicans and Anglos. The railroad marked the demise of the old animal-drawn freight trains, many of which had been Mexican-owned. In the 1870s Mexicans owning commercial lots on the plazas sold out "either because they had fallen into debt or because they thought it best" and moved to the west side of the river (Montejano 1987: 92), foreshadowing the emergence of the "westside" as the Mexican business and residential area. Gradually Anglos acquired the best business sites on the plazas as Mexicans were being numerically as well as physically displaced. In 1876, of the total city population of 17,314, 5,630 were Germans and Alsatians, 5,475 Americans, English and Irish, and 3,750 were Mexicans (Ramsdell 1959: 154). "By 1900 the Mexican upper class would become nonexistent except in a few border enclaves," such as Brownsville, Roma, San Ygnacio, and Laredo (Montejano 1987: 50).

As Mexicans gradually diminished in number among the city's elite, Germans, French, and Anglo entrepreneurs began to enter into partnerships. "Spurred on by San Antonio's opportunities, the various factions within the elite – Germans, Anglos, and French, Republicans and Democrats – began to cooperate for their mutual benefit" (Booth and Johnson 1983: 7). Donald Everett points to the 1881 establishment of the San Antonio Club, a private club made up of professionals and businessmen interested in promoting San

Antonio's growth through investment and outside contacts, as the most important marker of the growing unification of non-Hispanic citizens. The membership list of 1887 includes German, British, and French names (Donald Everett, pers. comm.). Significantly, the one Spanish name is that of Yturria, a name dating from the early nineteenth century in San Antonio, and one of the very few Spanish surnames in the current membership list of the Order of the Alamo.

The cooperation brought the European Texans both greater economic benefit and more political power. The German community had already experienced a burgeoning political power when their loyalty to the Republican Party was rewarded after the war through appointments by the Republican government to most public offices (Booth and Johnson 1983: 7). The previous internal dissension over city control ended in a new coalition of ethnic values and ambitions and Reconstruction politics that shaped "a very different community ethic characterized by a remarkable absence of public spirit and by intense conservatism" (Johnson 1990: 36). The elite were not intrinsically interested in such power but were interested in electing leaders who would implement policies that would allow San Antonio to grow and prosper.

Between 1885 and 1889 Bryan Callaghan II, the first "machine politician," created a multiethnic, multiclass organization "based on patronage for the faithful and solid policies for the elite" (Booth and Johnson 1983: 9). His family background exemplified the history of the elite of San Antonio. His father, a merchant, alderman, and mayor, was married to Concepción Ramón, a descendent of one of the original settlers. Bryan helped consolidate the European elite by marrying Adele Guilbeau, the daughter of a wealthy French merchant. By the early twentieth century "the Mexican voice in city politics was symbolically represented by Anglo officials with familial ties to the Mexican upper class." Bryan's mother's Spanish heritage put him in good stead with the lower-class Mexican Americans, "who regarded him, as they had his father, as their patron" (Montejano 1987: 40).

Callaghan was mayor on and off from 1890 until his death in 1912 but not without difficulties. After his death there was a change to a commission form of city government that lasted until 1941. Machine-controlled voting prevailed, and most of the city's business leadership "tacitly accepted the pattern of machine control, which had historically provided the public spending and improvements necessary for urban development and expansion" (Sanders 1990: 156).[12]

The machine-controlled commission form of city government that had been in place from the late nineteenth century until the 1940s allowed for the distribution of patronage jobs among its Mexican American and African American loyal followers, with a small amount of neighborhood improvement but no real representation. With small fluctuations between the older and newer, the socioeconomic elite maintained control of city politics. It was self-perpetuating and many of the pre-Civil War names and families remain prominent to this day in economics and politics (Booth and Johnson 1983: 25). Continued fiscal and political problems finally led to the formation in 1954 of the Good Government League, which promised to establish a city manager plan and deliver good government. The northside Anglo voters supported infrastructure bonds but the spending did not necessarily benefit the east and west neighborhoods. The Good Government League prevailed until 1975, followed by a change to a district-based city council and the possibility that a variety of interest groups could gain political power.

Historians John Booth and David Johnson assert that the socioeconomic (and therefore political) inequalities of Mexican and African Americans were purposely constructed and maintained by the economic elite. The changes that occurred in the 1980s were imposed by outside forces, such as civil rights legislation, changes in voting laws, and restructuring of local government (Booth and Johnson 1983: 26–7). The district city council system varies somewhat in terms of ethnic balance but since 1977 generally has four or five Mexican Americans and one African American on a ten-member council in contrast with the token minority representation in the 1950s and 1960s. In 1981 a Mexican American, Henry Cisneros, was elected mayor of San Antonio, receiving as much as 45 percent of the votes in predominantly Anglo precincts (Brischetto et al. 1983: 91). Mexican Americans continue to play an important role in local politics while gaining economic importance.

History of Fiesta San Antonio

The multiethnic, multiclass characteristic of San Antonio's modern political scene is the antithesis of the beginnings of Fiesta San Antonio. The celebration began almost as a private party played out in the public streets. Now there are hundreds of parties associated with Fiesta, and a large percentage of San Antonio citizens, from all parts of the city, take part in Fiesta in some way. Hundreds of thousands of people attend the various events. People of all walks of life take their vacations during Fiesta in order to thoroughly enjoy the week. Adult children who have moved as far away as Michigan come home for Fiesta. Some of the events are private and many more are public, but the elitist origins of Fiesta are still visible in the oldest organizations: the Battle of the Flowers Association, the Order of the Alamo, and the Cavaliers.

San Antonio has a long history of fetes, processions, or parades held in honor of saint's days, patriotic dates, and civic events. The Spanish friars used Christian celebrations to entice the indigenous Indians into participation in church activities. By the late seventeenth century saint's days festivities had become so common that a document signed in 1781 by Don Domingo Cabello, the military inspector for San Antonio de Bexar, banned parades on horseback held in honor of the feasts of St. Peter, St. James, and St. Ann, because they inevitably end up as horse racing "creating dangerous situations" (Dora Guerra, pers. comm.). In the 1820s prominent citizens assumed responsibility for "expenses and preparations of religious celebration" as was the Spanish custom, with individual dances for the different classes (de la Teja and Wheat 1991: 15–16). In the latter part of the nineteenth century, parades with elaborate floats were sponsored by the German organizations in honor of German holidays. By 1897 Diez y Seis (Mexican Independence Day) festivities lasted for three days with a parade, a program of oratory and music, a salute of twenty-one cannons, and a ball attended by "patriotic Mexicans and scores of their American friends" (Hinojosa 1997). The development of Fiesta San Antonio follows a long history of celebrations in San Antonio.

Origins and Early Development of Fiesta

As in any large celebration, Fiesta has multiple voices, and the hundreds of thousands who attend respond to different calls, attending favorite events and paying little attention to the rest. The westside family that goes to all of the parades, the carnival, and the St. Mary's Oyster Bake experiences a different Fiesta than that of Order of the Alamo members and their families who attend only the crownings and parties associated with the oldest and most exclusive Fiesta royalty.

The origin of Fiesta San Antonio is the Battle of Flowers parade, first held in April 1891. The formation of the Battle of Flowers parade and its founding organization by the town's leading women is an example of what Sara Evans (1989) refers to as "women's conceptions of citizenship." Evans notes that an important principle in the development of American ideals was that of an active citizenry and a deep belief in popular sovereignty. However, since an active citizenry inherently meant one involved in public politics, women were barred from such republican ideals. Throughout American history women have struggled to reshape the boundaries of the public arena and to situate themselves in the public and civic life (Evans 1989: 2–3). By the 1840s women, as well as men, actively formed voluntary associations that carved "out a public space located between the private sphere of the home and public life of formal institutions of government" (Evans 1989: 67). The Battle of Flowers organization was, and is, a highly valued volunteer activity where women are able to use an enormous array of organizational skills and to feel that they are contributing to the community. The parade is proudly touted as "the biggest parade in the world put on by women" (McGimsey 1984: 1).

The specifics of the origin of the first parade are somewhat obscure, but it is generally accepted that a visitor from Chicago, W.J. Ballard, suggested that the city hold a bicentennial celebration in honor of the first naming of San Antonio de Padua as well as honoring the fifty-fifth anniversary of the San Jacinto battle. San Jacinto Day had been celebrated with speeches and music in the past, but no parades had been held. Ellen Maury Slayden, wife of James L. Slayden, who became a congressional representative in 1896, was the chief organizer of the event. She asked her friend Mrs. J.S. Alexander to help and immediately the latter's husband, a bank president, joined the organizing committee. The three decided the parade would incorporate a mock flower battle, similar to those held in France, Spain, and Mexico.[13] The committee was enlarged to include some men who belonged to the San Antonio Club and their wives. Few of the original names are those of the most elite families, but they did take part in the parade itself, according to newspaper accounts.

After plans for a parade on April 21, San Jacinto Day, were well underway, President Benjamin Harrison announced that he would be visiting the city on April 20. Since this was the first presidential visit ever paid to the state, it was decided to hold the parade to coincide with the presidential visit. A call was made in the daily paper for "every citizen having a vehicle and flowers" to participate. To the dismay of the organizers, a torrential rain forced the postponement of the parade, but it was still held four days later, after Harrison had left the city.

Veterans of San Jacinto were the honored guests in the parade and remained so for the next several years. Decorated bicycles, several floats, a military band and marching units, as well as the flower-covered carriages, were part of the procession, which divided in half at Alamo Plaza. Going in opposite directions, each half pelted the other half, as well as the onlookers, with fresh flowers, "which were returned at the hurlers with vigor" (McGimsey 1984: 4). The flower battle lasted one hour, and the entire event was considered so successful that plans were immediately made for it to be an annual event. The local newspapers covered the event extensively, listing each participant and describing his or her conveyance and decorations in flowery Edwardian language, with numerous references to "tasteful," "artistic," and "dainty."

In the succeeding years the parade got larger and more elaborate, as did the sponsoring committee. Additional events, such as band concerts and charity balls, quickly began to take place throughout the week of April 21.

The celebration expanded in 1899 with the addition of a Grand Military and Patriotic Carnival. By 1900 numerous parades began to be added, from industrial and military to those based on baby carriages or automobiles, and even burlesque parades that made fun of all the others had been added to the week's activities. The local military took an active role in the celebration, from loaning wagons and horses to the parade to presenting jousting tournaments at Fort Sam Houston for the enjoyment of the visitors. In addition to the parades, street carnivals with aerialists, dancers, and sideshows were held in the public plazas by 1905, giving rise to the entire event being called Spring Carnival.

Emphasis on History

Despite the ever increasing additional activities, the Battle of Flowers parade (without the actual exchange of floral ammunition) emerged as the focal point, just as it is today. Then and now, it is always held on Friday of the week of April 21 and includes military and school bands and marching units, floats, mounted horses, antique cars, and assorted dignitaries. The most public appearance of the Queen of the Order of the Alamo and her court is in the Battle of Flowers parade. Many older members of the Battle of Flowers organization still think that the court section is the most important part of the parade.

Women were annually elected as presidents of the informally organized Battle of Flowers committee until 1902 when a man was elected president with a women appointed as chairman of the ladies committees. A woman was president in 1904 and 1905 but was replaced by Frank Bushick, who then quickly formed the first Spring Carnival Association with himself as its first president. In addition to Bushick, representatives of the organizations that sponsored events were members of the association. The official Battle of Flowers history booklet discreetly explains the 1906 split by saying that "business men began taking an even greater responsibility for features of the week-long celebration, which made it even more desirable that the Battle of Flowers ladies confine themselves to the social and patriotic parts of the festivities" (McGimsey 1984: 7). However, the split reflects the larger issue of what was considered the proper role of each gender within voluntary associations. The disagreement underlying the Battle of Flowers split was over the relative number of commercial and carnival-type entertainments versus patriotic events. As early as 1896 concern was expressed by the Battle of Flowers women that the entire event had become too commercialized and had lost its original patriotic intent (Everett 1979: 66). Commercial promotions and carnivals constituted the male venue, while women took on the loftier ideals of patriotism. Although the men formed the new organization, the influence of the feminine interest in preserving the patriotic emphasis can be seen in the name change in 1913 from Spring Carnival to Fiesta San Jacinto to emphasize the history and patriotism. The Battle of Flowers organization itself adopted a constitution for the first time, was granted a charter by the State, and stated its purpose as educational and patriotic (McGimsey 1984: 8).[14]

In 1918 no parade was held because of World War I. However, the Battle of Flowers women organized a solemn procession of thousands of citizens to the Alamo. That event has continued as the Pilgrimage to the Alamo and is now sponsored by the Daughters of the Republic of Texas (another women's voluntary association). It is a most solemn occasion with music by a military band, a speech by the Fiesta military coordinator, and the names of the fallen heroes read in sonorous tones as wreaths or bouquets are laid on the lawn in front of the Alamo. The 1918 procession foreshadowed the historical pageantry that was established primarily in the 1920s and remains characteristic of Fiesta, despite the ever increasing number of new events based primarily on an exchange of money for food, drink, and music. In a specific move to turn the thoughts of the citizens to the original purpose of the parade, the Battle of Flowers organization sponsored a historical pageant in 1922 and for several years thereafter. Additionally, prizes were offered by the Battle of Flowers women for the best one-act play based on local color or a historic poem. These were dropped in 1926 when the Oratorical Contest began. Cash prizes are still awarded to the college students who write and deliver the best speeches on some phase of Texas history.

In addition to these historical and patriotic events, the State Association of Pioneers was founded in 1919 and held annual meetings during Fiesta. They sponsored Pioneer Day with a parade of ox-pulled wagons and other representations of the past. Although it has been years since the meeting and parade were held, a Patriotic and Historical Ball, to which all of the military Fiesta representatives are invited, is still held the second night of Fiesta. Texas's cattle ranching history was emphasized in the 1940s when a stock show and rodeo were added to Fiesta week (now held in February as a separate event). Texas history is also emphasized in the San Antonio Conservation Society's Night in Old San Antonio (NIOSA), its major fund-raising event. It was added to the Fiesta lineup in 1948 and is held in La Villita, a downtown area with restored and reconstructed buildings representing the Spanish period of San Antonio. The early NIOSAs featured food and music of different periods and ethnic heritages, including sections devoted to "Indian, Spanish, Mexican, Texan, Pioneer, Old South, Western, and Gay Nineties." The specific groups have changed somewhat but the various ethnic heritages still provide the framework for the highly successful event. Interestingly, despite the range of booths, an emphasis on Mexico is evident for not only are the longest lines always in front of the stands selling handmade tortillas, but also many of the Conservation women wear Mexican folk clothing, at least for the opening night. Some are essentially folkloric dance costumes, while others are authentic indigenous costumes complete with jewelry.

Military Presence

San Antonio's four military bases provide an almost pervasive presence, from bands in the parades to military reviews, with flyovers at the military bases adding another patriotic overtone to Fiesta. The military loaned horses to pull the floats in the earliest parades, replacing them later with jeeps. All of the bases send official representatives to Fiesta events and host their own special events. Lackland Air Force Base's special parade, with a review staged for Fiesta civilian and military dignitaries and royalty, is typical. A high-ranking officer of Fort Sam Houston, the army post established in 1878, acts as the official Fiesta coordinator. San Antonio is said to be the only place in the world in which military personnel in uniform may wear the commemorative medals presented as souvenirs during Fiesta. Interestingly, the military events seem to provide a neutral ground where new friendships may take place among the various royalty and event sponsors, from the San Antonio Conservation Society to the African American Zulu Association, sponsors of Taste of New Orleans.

Changes and Developments

In addition to the historical and patriotic events many other activities were added throughout the years. Some lasted only a short time while others have become a permanent part of Fiesta. During the 1920s and 1930s a children's fete sponsored by all of the dance schools, a flower show, and a number of military events were added as well as others that lasted for a year or two and then disappeared. In the 1940s two more parades were added to the official processions. A King's river parade was added in 1941 by the Cavaliers, the sponsoring organization of King Antonio. In 1948 Fiesta Flambeau, an illuminated night parade, was instituted, and in 1950 it began to feature Miss Fiesta and her maids of honor. In the 1950s numerous events were added to Fiesta as a whole, some focusing on the German community with a tour of King William, the historic residential area, while others focused on the more modern attractions of water skiing on Woodlawn Lake and appearances by popular screen personalities. The carnival remains an important event, but Fiesta never reclaimed its earlier street entertainment flavor when all of the public plazas and side streets were filled with circus acts and carnival entertainment.[15]

By the end of the 1950s discontent was brewing within the ranks of the Fiesta San Jacinto Association. The association itself sponsored the Fiesta Flambeau parade and Miss Fiesta, and some of the older sponsoring organization members – Battle of Flowers, Cavaliers, and Order of the Alamo – felt that the association gave undue favoritism to its events to the detriment of theirs. They threatened to pull out of the Fiesta Association, and the Chamber of Commerce was called in to mediate. In 1959 the Fiesta Commission was organized, with bylaws specifying that it could never sponsor an event itself, thereby avoiding charges of favoritism. It is made up of representatives from its eighty-plus participating organizations, whose annual dues, in addition to fees paid by commercial participants, support the celebration.

Although there had long been some Mexican American participation, several Mexican American organizations were reluctant to participate in Fiesta because of the "implications inherent in naming it after the battle of San Jacinto." One of the first decisions made by the new commission in 1959 was to change the name of the celebration to Fiesta San Antonio (Canty 1991: 22). The charter expressly states that part of the commission's purpose is "to encourage the study of history and culture of Texas and Latin America; to cultivate and enhance the importance of San Antonio as the meeting place or confluence of the great Anglo and Latin American cultures; and to encourage Pan American friendliness, understanding and solidarity" (Maguire 1990: 109). The name change and more inclusive statement of purpose reflected the political tenor of the 1950s in San Antonio. Additionally, improved occupational opportunities for Mexican Americans provided the economic stability needed for the luxury of supporting community-based organizations (Montejano 1987: 280–99).

The name change was the first public acknowledgement of a feeling of alienation or disenfranchisement by segments of the Mexican American community of San Antonio regarding the city's largest civic event. Mexican American participation as observers at the parades, as student musicians in the band contest, and as consumers at NIOSA had largely been taken for granted. There had been Mexican Americans on various floats and as parts of riding groups, such as sheriff's posses and *charro* groups, and Mexican American politicians joined their Anglo peers in riding in as many parades as possible. The street carnival was seen as largely a Mexican American attraction. However, events sponsored by or directed towards the Mexican American population were few in number. The Mexican American Chamber of Commerce, an example of the middle-class civic and patriotic organization of the 1930s, sponsored La Noche de Fiesta, an evening of professional entertainers from Mexico. The event was begun in 1938, later dropped for some years, and then reinstated in 1961 under the name Noche Mexicana.

In an effort to follow its stated purpose of furthering Pan-American friendship, in 1961 the Commission invited three young women representing Tampico, Mazatlán, and the border cities to take part as special guests. These international exchanges no longer occur. In 1968 Noche Mexicana's incorporation into Fiesta was marked by King Antonio's official visit and his presentation with a medal. Noche Mexicana in the 1970s became a street event with music, food, and drink rather than the more formal earlier revue but was later dropped. A *charreada* or Mexican rodeo became a permanent part of Fiesta activities in 1972 and King Antonio began officially visiting it the next year.

In 1960 the Mexican American Chamber of Commerce was the only Hispanic member of the Fiesta Commission but participation by both African American and Mexican American associations and individuals has increased steadily. The number of events has also increased, giving greater representation to all segments of San Antonio. The Fiesta Commission remains in place today and oversees the ten-day-long affair with its 150 separate events. Paradoxically, although Fiesta San Antonio was founded by and, until recently, controlled by Anglos, it has long used Mexican imagery, from the name itself to the iconic use of sombreros, *cascarones*, and *folklórico* dancers on related advertising. Tex-Mex food can be found at virtually every event, even at those sponsored by German heritage organizations.

Fiesta Royalty

The redistribution of political power beginning in the 1950s was demonstrated in the revised structure and content of Fiesta, but nowhere is it more clearly delineated than in the matter of Fiesta royalty. In accordance with America's insatiable desire to place temporary crowns upon the heads of its citizens, a king and queen were chosen in 1896 as part of the Battle of Flowers parade activities. In the country that rejected titles and royalty, there are queens and kings of everything from kindergarten classes to senior citizens centers. However, Americans do recognize the ironic incongruity between monarchs and democracy so our royalty is usually elected, sometimes by popular vote (as in high-school contests) or by judges (as in Miss America contests). San Antonio Fiesta has multiple duly elected monarchs: King Antonio and Rey Feo, military queens, charro queens, queens of soul, and Miss Fiesta. These monarchs are voted on or appointed. The Queen of the Order of the Alamo, the oldest Fiesta royal figure, is the closest to the tradition of a monarch for the title is largely restricted to a branch of one of a dozen oldest socioeconomically prominent families. The story of Fiesta royalty is a reflection of San Antonio's class and ethnic differences and difficulties.

The earliest royalty of Fiesta was haphazardly selected. The Battle of Flowers committee in 1896 selected Ida Archer and Alex Walton to reign over a charity cotton ball, but San Antonio citizens reacted quite uncharitably for Archer was a citizen of Austin. This mistake was never repeated, and the subsequent queens and kings have all been San Antonians. Selection continued to be somewhat random: in some years there was no queen, in others no king. Although the king and queen both rode in the parade, they apparently were seen as individual roles, not as a king and his consort. Not until 1900 and the choice of Queen Lola Kokernot was there a royal court and royal robes. Formerly the young women wore evening gowns but did not have a train as did Kokernot (Figure 3).

Queen of the Order of the Alamo

In 1909 John Carrington organized the Order of the Alamo, a private men's social club whose sole purpose was to elect a queen crowned in an elaborate coronation. They also sponsor a private reception following the Coronation, a garden party, and a Queen's Ball. Although the Order assumed responsibility for the queen, the close relationship between the Battle of Flowers parade and royalty remained (Figure 4).

Carrington was born in Halifax County, Virginia, spent his youth in Louisville, Kentucky, and attended the University of Chicago. As a young man Carrington was told that he was threatened with tuberculosis. The family moved to the central Texas hill country and settled in the small German town of Comfort because the climate was reputedly beneficial for respiratory problems. Carrington became interested in Texas history, but Virginia and its southern traditions remained paramount in his self-identity. Described by one of his sons as a would-be writer and a romantic, Carrington was imbued with a sense of the importance of the past, of Southern chivalry, of being a gentleman. He made books for each of his four children based on photographs and words of advice that reflect these interests. The very first inscription in his youngest son's book explains that he was named in honor of someone whom Carrington considered as "the truest gentlemen that ever lived. There are gentlemen and gentlemen, and some who wear the name have not the spirit. Seek then to get the spirit my son, for it is indeed something worth achieving . . . it is an immortal something that never dies."

After marrying a young woman from Comfort, Carrington moved to San Antonio and become involved in real estate and other business enterprises. He was active in the Chamber of Commerce and apparently worked with

Figure 3. This 1900 Carnival Ball and early Coronations took place in Beethoven Hall, the site of today's satirical Cornyation. Courtesy: Ann Russell and the Institute of Texan Cultures.

Figure 4. Queen Josephine Woodhull rides on a horse-drawn float in 1915, accompanied by mounted aides. Courtesy: Witte Museum.

the Spring Carnival association in promoting the Battle of Flowers parade and related activities. Early in 1909 Carrington, with the help of Franz Groos and J.H. Frost, gathered a small group of his friends to form the nucleus of the Order of the Alamo. "Some one hundred selected men of recognized social position" made up the membership in the early years (Order of the Alamo [1925]). He was obviously influenced by his family's English ancestry for the Order of the Alamo and the Coronation are modeled on the English court and its aristocracy.[16] The name of the organization and titles of the participants – queen, princess, duchess, mistress of the robes, prime minister, prince, duke, and lord high chamberlain – are all taken directly from British royalty and ceremony. The court has always included twenty-four duchesses split between those from San Antonio and visitors from other towns, primarily in Texas. In the early years each of the out-of-town duchesses also had a lady-in-waiting escorted by her esquire. The members of the Order were required to wear knee breeches, the style of the English court, until 1921 when a change was made to formal dress with a purple ribbon across the chest similar to the royal baldric.

Although the English court is the prototype for San Antonio's royal rites, certain practices have been exaggerated. The trains and headpieces that have always been worn are based on the British requirements, issued by the Lord Chamberlain's Office, regarding the dress of ladies at court (Arch and Marschner 1987: 57). In the 1840s a three-and-a-half foot train was required for the English court, but the length increased to eight feet or longer by the end of the century. From 1922 until the abolishment of court presentations in 1958, the train was restricted in length to eighteen inches from the heel of the wearer (Arch and Marschner 1987: 105–24). However, San Antonio trains have always been longer, reaching a maximum length of fifteen feet, for they provide the surface upon which the theme of the court can be most easily represented in iconographic embellishment.

The greatest exaggeration of English court practice is in the Order's version of the mandatory curtsy to the British monarch based on the eighteenth- and nineteenth-century pause in walking and lowering of the body and head in the direction of the person whose presence is being acknowledged, historically an inherent part of good breeding. The position of the feet and the hands, and the depth of the curtsy, varied from one century to another; but the correct positioning of the feet was based on classical ballet. Therefore, curtsies were taught by dance masters (Wildeblood and Brimston 1965: 267). During the English court presentation women paused, placed their feet properly, then did a deep plié whose depth depended on the style of dress and the ability of the young woman. A woman presented at court in the 1930s remarked, "Apparently the Queen used to get seasick with all those people bobbing up and down in front of her the whole time so she never looked at you but always slightly over your head" (Pringle 1977: 116).[17]

A one-knee-on-the-floor, straight-back curtsy or a moderately low bend from the waist are the most common American "debutante bows"; but San Antonio Coronation debutantes have always made the "formal court bow," elsewhere known as the "Texas dip," virtually a physical feat. The Texas version is similar to the English in the first stage, but Coronation debs take it literally to the floor. The young woman points her right foot in front and then moves it in a semicircle to the back. She lowers her erect torso, collapsing her legs until she is sitting on them. She then bends forward from the waist until her head is as close to the floor as possible. She rises, preferably without taking the hand of her escort for balance. When asked for an explanation of its origin, the answer always is, "It's the way it has always been done." The oldest former duchesses well remembered their bows but said that it was done with the foot extended to the front. That information suggests strongly that the "formal court bow" is actually an imitation of the dying swan's final pose in the second act of *Swan Lake*. Anna Pavlova's performance of "The Dying Swan" was immensely popular in the years around the founding of the Order of the Alamo. Since a ballet mistress has always been associated with Coronation, it is quite likely that the "formal court bow" was her innovation, but the origin was quickly lost due to the incongruity of young women and the death of a bird. Whatever the source, the highly exaggerated curtsy and the elongated trains remain hallmarks of Coronation.

The first five Coronations under Carrington's tutelage were held in Beethoven Hall, built in 1895 by the German community of San Antonio. In 1914 the event was moved to the Majestic Theatre and then, in 1926, to the Municipal Auditorium where it is still performed. Originally the queen made her appearance already wearing her crown. In 1914, however, an investiture was incorporated into the presentation – thus fulfilling the title of Coronation. The queen was crowned by the archbishop (the President of the Order in "regulation robes") supported by two acolytes as she took a formal oath. Three sets of royal crowns and scepters have been used in the eighty-four-year history, but the oath remains the original one. The queen is then asked if she "promises to govern your people according to the laws of happiness and joy . . . [to] bring mirth, melody and sweet music to this your kingdom? That you will always preserve gladness and banish sorrow? And that, throughout your realm, you will make each passing day brighter because of your reign" (Order of the Alamo 1991). The wording clearly reflects the typical romanticization found in the pageantry movement.

All of the courts have had specific names or themes although at the beginning there was relatively little thematic decoration on the trains or dresses. The themes conjured up images of romance and make-believe, particularly in the early years. Many of the early courts were based on nature: Court of Flowers (1909), Court of Roses (1910), Court of Spring (1913), and Court of the Birds (1920). However, in 1922 the Court of Aladdin initiated the use of a historical or pseudo-historical theme. In it the duchesses represented different civilizations and the queen ruled "the Heliolithic Empire existing about 3000 B.C. in what we now call Mexico and Texas" (Order of the Alamo [1925]). This was the beginning of an increasing use of historical or mythohistorical themes. The charter states that the organization was "formed for the purpose of educating its members and the public generally in the history of the Independence of Texas and perpetuating the memory of the Battle of San Jacinto by having an annual ceremony in Bexar County, Texas" (Order of the Alamo 1990). Although few of the themes actually refer to Texas history, a great deal of time is spent on researching each theme, and the text is seen as a means of educating the audience and the court about a specific subject. Some of the themes still refer to fantasy or literature, but historical ones have become increasingly prevalent. The implications of the increasingly historicized themes are discussed in chapter 4.

Carrington himself selected and worked out the themes as well as taking one of the leading positions in the organization until 1915. Thereafter he is listed simply as one of the seven directors. In 1920 there is no mention at all of Carrington in the program, but in 1922 he took the role of the Genie in the Court of Aladdin. His son later recalled that "once it got established, he would go off and start something else. That is when he decided that they needed a king."

Cavaliers and King Antonio

There had been earlier kings selected by the Carnival or Fiesta San Jacinto association or the Chamber of Commerce, but there was no consistency, just as in the selection of a queen. In the earliest years the king was usually a businessman chosen by the Chamber of Commerce who could afford to donate $1,500 towards the costs of the festivities. He took such whimsical names as King Selamat (tamales spelled backward), King Omala (Alamo backwards), or the more serious King Cotton, Zeus, or Rex. He did not take on the more somber title of King Antonio until 1916, and there was no systematic election until the formation of the Cavaliers in 1926.

Unlike his conception of the Order of the Alamo, Carrington had several objectives in organizing the Cavaliers, in addition to the crowning of the king. He wanted the men's private social organization to sponsor the Pilgrimage to the Alamo (although it never did), to facilitate social relations between the military and civilian populations, but primarily he wanted to "preserve the Texas tradition of horsemanship in this age of automobiles" (Graham 1976: 11). By the 1940s, many of the men had to ride borrowed horses and they were not regular riders; therefore, many stories, perhaps hypothetical, exist regarding the misadventures of horse and rider. One story involves a frightened horse entering the pre-air-conditioning open doors of a Woolworth's and running the length of the store, exiting at the other end with the rider still hanging on. The emphasis on horsemanship caused many difficulties in the following years, but even today a small contingent of Cavaliers rides in the parade.[18] Carrington himself apparently did not ride but according to his son he "loved the horseman idea. I don't think I ever saw him on a horse, actually. He was great on [the idea of] horsemanship." At one point most members did ride, and the Cavaliers built a club house and stables, but they burned down and were never replaced. Although several of Carrington's objectives were not fulfilled, the Cavaliers do interact closely with the military in addition to being responsible for the selection of the king and his activities. The military loaned horses for many years to the Cavaliers to ride in the parade and also loaned men and equipment to help in organizing the river parade, begun by the organization in 1941.

The Cavaliers elected no king the first year, but a Tournament of Roses was presented, complete with jousts and fair ladies. Carrington had conjured up a southern tradition for it was common before the Civil War to present tournaments with knights in shining armor at the resort springs area in Virginia, not far from Carrington's Halifax County (Graham 1976: 12). Not all of the young riders were experts at these activities and a member commented that Carrington "must have been the greatest promoter in the world to get those guys on horses and go at each other with wooden swords." An older member laughingly suggested that "they all got bootleg whisky to get hootched up enough to do it."

The next year the membership refused to wear the theatrical (and uncomfortable) tights and armor outside of the tournament arena and adopted a red military style jacket and blue riding breeches, boots, and cap, feeling that these were more in keeping with a gentlemen's association. Carrington was sorry to see the armor go and never wore the new uniform, saying that it was not appropriate for his "compact figure" (Graham 1976: 22). Slacks are now worn by most members instead of the riding breeches. The uniforms are rather plain and stories abound about members being mistaken for doormen or other kinds of attendants and are told with relish (Graham 1976: 143). The uniforms also perform their classic function of making members of a group more or less identical. One member who never enjoyed the financial success that many of the other members have achieved said that he particularly enjoyed wearing the uniform for it erased any feelings that he had of being an outsider.

The costume of King Antonio has also undergone several transformations, from a lace-trimmed coat to the present Cavalier jacket with gold braid, cape, and plumed hat. Following a tradition established by earlier kings, Antonio IX and his retinue rode a special train into the station on Monday evening to be greeted by the mayor, military representatives, a band, and the rest of the mounted Cavaliers. He then proceeded to the Alamo for welcoming ceremonies, after which he visited the Pioneer Ball and then attended the King's Ball. The next day he presided at the Tournament of Roses and throughout the week visited schools, made an appearance at the Pilgrimage to the Alamo, and rode in the Battle of Flowers parade. With the exception of the tournament, eliminated in 1930, all subsequent kings have followed the same general pattern. King Antonio now appears at more events, but the importance of the Alamo and Texas history is still seen in the order in which he makes his appearances.

Of the nineteen charter Cavalier members, seven were also members of the Order of the Alamo. There has always been a significant overlap in membership, but the two organizations had for many years "a curious sort of sibling rivalry" (Graham 1976: 153). The Cavaliers are seen as being more of a "men's club" while the Order is more of a social club. "The Cavalier type is a different breed of cat. They do the river parade and it is a lot of work. A lot of hard work." The Order is perceived as being more elite, more formal, more difficult to get into; while the Cavaliers, though still considered quite restricted in membership, are seen as slightly more broad based because of the greater number of newly successful businessmen who are members. The Order's queen and her court were included in the activities the first few years, but gradually the two monarchs formed different realms, reflecting separate gender domains. The king took on a more public role with royal visits, while the queen's activities were restricted to private parties. In the 1930s royal visits to schools as well as hospitals and orphanages by King Antonio became an increasingly important part of Fiesta week; however, the queen and princess were not included in visits until 1957.

As is the case in most civic celebrations with both a king and queen, the king is middle-aged, usually a successful businessman or professional, while the queen is always younger (often by a generation or two) and is unmarried, that is to say, symbolically virginal. There is no suggestion that King Antonio and the Queen of the Order of the Alamo are consorts although the close relationship has been sharply emphasized several times when the king and queen have been father and daughter (Graham 1976: 155).

King Antonio no longer arrives by train but does ride in an open carriage drawn by a matched set of four palominos to the Alamo. Although the Alamo ceremony has been both a public and private ceremony at different times, it currently combines both aspects. At the Alamo the king and the rest of the Cavaliers file solemnly into the chapel, where the roll of deceased members is read. Once outside, the current members raise crossed swords under which the new members pass. The new king then walks under the swords to the throne where the outgoing king sits. The king is publicly crowned when he is presented with the red plumed hat, saber, medallion, and a key to the city by the former king. He then turns to the crowd, which is largely made up of Cavaliers and their wives, members of the military, tourists, and some local viewers, and says "Let the merriment begin."

The current ceremony has added a historic aspect through the presentation of Texas's six flags, accompanied by music and a descriptive historical text, in an effort to emphasize the multicultural history of the state. This change may be in response to the critical questions about the exclusivity of the Cavaliers and the appropriateness of an Anglo king in a city that bases its tourist appeal on its multicultural population. Historically King Antonio has been a much more public figure than the queen and therefore is a more visible target for criticism.

Other Queens

Although the Cavaliers and the Order of the Alamo have both been charged with elitism and racism, the Order has been less frequently criticized. The more private nature of Coronation, discussed in chapter 4, has partially protected it from criticisms. More importantly, additional female royal figures have long been part of Fiesta and appear to diffuse criticism of the Order of the Alamo's queen. The military bases were represented by military queens from the 1940s until the 1980s. Most importantly, there has been a popularly elected royal figure since 1950, when Reynolds Andricks instituted the Miss Fiesta contest. Andricks's vision of Fiesta events and their royal personnel was quite different from that of Carrington, but he affected the character of Fiesta almost as much as did the older man. Andricks was not the romantic gentlemen that Carrington was, but a populist who wanted to expand interest and participation in Fiesta, including extending the royal ranks. One former Miss Fiesta suggests that Andricks was angry because he could not get into the Order of the Alamo and that was the reason that he started the Miss Fiesta contest. He was also a showman who wanted to be highly involved and control things, unlike Carrington, who retired or moved on to other projects once the current one had solidified. Andricks, a civil engineer, was elected to the board of the Fiesta San Jacinto Association in 1948. His primary interest was in adding an illuminated night parade to the lineup of Fiesta festivities. The first obstacle to starting a new parade was to get entries who were not already committed to the river parade or the Battle of Flowers parade. He invited bands from surrounding towns and suggested to the military that each of the five bases sponsor a float as a showcase for the elected military queens.

In 1950 he began the Miss Fiesta contest, open to all students at the colleges and universities in San Antonio; the winner would be featured in the night parade with her court. The contest is run in the usual fashion, with judgements based on talent, poise, and beauty. Additionally, all contestants have to research and present a ninety-second vignette of a woman in Texas history. Rather than being part of a historic family as is the Queen of the Order of the Alamo, Miss Fiesta learns and represents a historic figure. In addition to expanding the royal ranks to the populace, the Miss Fiesta position gave Andricks a bargaining chip with which to draw parade entries from other festivals. He sent Miss Fiesta to all of the Texas festival parades, such as the Luling Watermelon Thump Parade, and as far away as the Minneapolis Winter Carnival as well as the Rose Parade. In exchange he got many floats and royal personages for his parade (Maguire 1990: 71–4).

Although Miss Fiesta was not created to specifically represent the Mexican American population but as a way to break through the class lines, the result has been more balance in the ethnicity of queens, particularly in the last fifteen years, since proportionately more Mexican Americans now attend the local schools. Even in the 1950s, however, some Mexican American young women did win. One of the earliest reported that, when she rode in the parade and passed in front of her father's gas station, she felt she definitely represented the westside community.

The military bases stopped electing queens in 1987 and now each sends a male and female representative who wear uniforms rather than ball gowns and crowns. However, a number of other royal figures have been added to the Fiesta royalty. The Fiesta Teen Queen, daughter or granddaughter of a member of the Woman's Club of San Antonio, a middle- and upper-class primarily Anglo organization, has been a part of Fiesta since 1967. Most of the Teen Queens have not had Hispanic last names, but in recent years some have. In 1969 Queen of Soul, Inc. was organized specifically to select a young woman to represent the African American community during Fiesta. A panel of judges votes for the Queen of Soul on the basis of beauty, charm, poise, and intellect.

In the last decade three specifically Mexican American queens have been added: Miss Charro, representing the Confederation of Charros, Queen of the San Antonio Charro Association, and the Reina de la Feria las Flores, sponsored by the civic organization League of United Latin American Citizens (LULAC). Again, in contrast to the ascribed qualifications of the Order of the Alamo queen, the charro queens must be proficient in folkloric dancing and horseback riding while the LULAC queen wins her crown by raising money for scholarships.[19] The Fiesta Commission has decreed that no Fiesta royal figure may reign over another, but the Order implies that its queen does have special domain. Even though all Fiesta royalty is invited to their garden party, only the Order's queen is supposed to wear her crown.

Rey Feo

Since 1947 the Mexican American community has had a king, Rey Feo (the Ugly King), but he was not considered part of Fiesta royalty. He was sponsored by LULAC Council Number 2, as part of La Feria de las Flores, a parish-based fund raiser held annually in August. The council selects several nominees, both Anglos and Mexican Americans, who are well known in the community and who have been involved in civic affairs. Because the position of Rey Feo is sponsored by LULAC, even Anglos who win the crown are seen as representing the Mexican American population. Preferably nominees have experience in fund-raising since Rey Feo's crown is earned through the raising of money for a scholarship fund for disadvantaged students in San Antonio. In the early years the crown was won for a penny a vote, but stakes are much higher today. The 1997 Rey Feo, Henry Muñoz III, raised more than $250,000 in scholarship funds. The young women who compete for the crown of Reina de la Feria also raise scholarship money but on a much smaller scale than do the older men.

Despite the name, the Ugly King, the role of Rey Feo apparently has never been one of satire and inversion as was the Mock King of the medieval Feast of Fools. The carnivalesque Feast was celebrated in France and England at the end of December and was marked by social role reversal and satirical representation of authority (Santino 1995: 97). The only satirical element associated with Rey Feo is the presentation of a young goat or *cabrito* to the newly crowned king. This practice gave rise to the Order of the Cabrito, an honorary medal presented to friends and associates at the king's discretion.

As early as 1971 accusations of racism were made against the always Anglo King Antonio, and the Fiesta Commission ruled that officially neither the Queen of the Order of the Alamo nor King Antonio was a monarch of the Fiesta but that custom had made them appear to be so. The Cavaliers changed the name of the river parade from the King's River Parade to Fiesta River Parade in order to avoid legal questions, but it is still considered the king's parade. In 1972 Dr. José Cárdenas, superintendent of the overwhelmingly Hispanic Edgewood School District, announced that the king's school visits would no longer be made at his district's schools. He based the decision on the king's remarks in which he told the children "to work hard at school for you can be anything you want to be," contending that this was a lie since they obviously could not be King Antonio if they were Mexican American (Graham 1976: 177).[20]

It took the creation of single member districts and the demise of the Good Government League and, ironically, the concentrated efforts of an Anglo Rey Feo to make another male throne part of Fiesta's nobility. Mexican American members of the new city council of 1977 questioned the role of King Antonio and the Cavaliers. Councilman Henry Cisneros, who would become mayor in 1980, diplomatically stated, "I think the Cavaliers would be well-served if they would loosen up and widen access of the community to that particular event and that honor," while Councilman Bernardo Eureste characteristically stated bluntly, "In the Mexican-American community, King Antonio is like a joke" (Anon. 1977). In what appears to have been an attempt to deflect the criticisms, King Antonio (Porter Loring) in 1975 created a Royal Order of the Red Plume and had medals made at his own expense to bestow upon sixteen individuals. The recipients included two well-known Mexican Americans.

In 1979 Logan Stewart, a local newspaperman and radio personality, became Rey Feo and in early spring of 1980 began campaigning for Rey Feo to become part of Fiesta as a representative of the Mexican American community. He used his radio program to raise public awareness of the incongruity of an Anglo king reigning over Fiesta. Stewart began contacting Fiesta officials and requested a Rey Feo parade. The president of the Fiesta Commission urged Stewart and LULAC to apply for a permit and then set up meetings with both the Battle of Flowers organization and the Cavaliers to smooth the way (Maguire 1990: 58). The permit was given and the parade was underway – except that all of the local bands and floats were already committed to the older parades. The president of LULAC put together a mixture of out-of-town high-school bands, decorated flatbed trucks carrying various groups who did not fit into the other parades, musical groups, and National Guard tanks and troop carriers. It was the prototypical small-town parade. Held on Saturday afternoon the weekend before the big parades, it did not draw large crowds but they were loyal and enthusiastic. It struggled along for six years but never attained the same status as the older pro-cessions.[21] After Andricks died and the Fiesta Flambeau parade had gone through several sponsorships, it was given to LULAC as the Rey Feo parade. In two years splits within the LULAC council caused the night parade to be turned over to a new organization made up of some members of LULAC, the Junior Chamber of Commerce, and St. Mary's University alumni.

Rey Feo has been increasingly included in Fiesta events. He wears a white paramilitary suit with gold braid and buttons, quite complementary to the red and blue of King Antonio. At recent opening ceremonies an out-of-town observer was overheard asking her companion, "Which is the ugly king?" The response was, "The one in white must be the good king, so the other one must be the ugly or bad one." Both kings ride in all of the parades; both attend the Coronation and invite one another to each other's coronations and balls. In 1992 there was even talk of having the two kings make school and hospital visits together. Differences certainly still do exist. Rey Feo's crowning does not take place during Fiesta as does King Antonio's and is not within the hallowed halls of the Alamo. Rey Feo's ball during Fiesta is sponsored by LULAC and is open to anyone who buys a $20 ticket while King Antonio's is strictly by invitation. But any negative comments are about an individual Rey Feo's personality or character, not about the position of Rey Feo. Some of the Cavaliers and Order members initially were not completely pleased at the addition of Rey Feo. Almost all now realize that the inclusion of Rey Feo in Fiesta has allowed the Cavaliers to continue with their minimum of Spanish-surnamed members and their Anglo kings with only a modicum of spoken or written criticism.

Conclusion

The hundred-year history of Fiesta can be examined as a microcosm of the history of socioeconomic and political power in San Antonio. The initial events were begun by the elite – first- and second-generation Anglo and German immigrants who had become successful through a combination of tactics and abilities. The original Battle of Flowers parade, honoring the victory over Mexico, quickly grew into a multiunit event. Although the 150 or so events now encompass things of interest for almost everybody in the major local ethnic groups, many of those were not added until the last ten or fifteen years. There was always public entertainment in the form of the street carnivals, but the prestigious events and figures – the parades, NIOSA, King Antonio, and the Queen of the Order of the Alamo – all were sponsored by wholly or largely Anglo elite organizations. Mexican American participation was through school bands or clubs, as members of the military, as part of middle-class Mexican American organizations or folkloric groups, and as observers at the parades.[22] The addition of Miss Fiesta, Queen of Soul, Rey Feo, and the LULAC and charro queens has created a more balanced royal image of Fiesta; however, with the exception of some members of the charro associations, there is little visible participation by the Mexican American elite in Fiesta.[23]

Notes

1. Holly Brear presents an excellent analysis of the myth of the Alamo and its importance in Fiesta events in *Inherit the Alamo* (1995).

2. See Jack Santino's *All Around the Year* (1995) for an interesting discussion of the seasonal basis, the solstices and equinoxes, for most major holidays and celebrations in American life. Mardi Gras is a Christian observance superimposed over pre-Christian new year or midwinter festivals. Seasonal rituals are often marked by licentious behavior, inverted social or gender roles, and overindulgence in food and drink.

3. My historic overview is primarily based on the classic work of Charles Ramsdell (1959), the more recent work of John Davis (1978), and the revisionist research of Arnoldo de León (1983, 1991), Manuel Gonzales (1989), and Gerald Poyo and Gilberto Hinojosa (1991). My understanding of the emergence of Anglo dominance in the previously Hispanic town and the ensuing ethnic relations in South Texas is based on the important work of David Montejano (1987). Donald Everett's (1975) compilation of newspaper columns and stories reveals the human side of the changing political and social relationships.

4. The empresario movement was characterized by men who acquired large grants of land from the government and then brought in families to establish colonies. The most well-known Texas empresario was Stephen F. Austin.

5. The story of Tejano involvement in the Texas Revolution was largely unrecognized for many years. Ruben Lozano's 1936 *Viva Tejas* was the first published account of the participation of such men as Juan Seguin in the fight. Lozano's work is still the core of the "Tejano as Texas patriot in the fight against tyranny" school of history. Manuel Gonzales (1989) as well as other revisionists look at the same figures but interpret their actions as those of accommodationists.

6. However, intermarriages rarely occurred after more Anglo women were available and after Tejanos lost their wealth (Gonzales 1989: 25). With few exceptions elite or middle-class intermarriages have predominantly been between Anglo males and Spanish-surnamed females, leading to the loss of the Spanish name. An unsystematic survey of current marriages as listed in the local paper indicates that this is still true. The descendants are usually free to make a choice about acknowledgement of their Mexican heritage.

7. Many members of these families do state proudly that they are descendants of Canary Islanders.

8. The Mexican Constitution of 1824 promised certain rights to citizens and to the states, but Antonio López de Santa Anna repudiated the constitution and

established a centralized government. Demands by the settlers included the need for protection from Indians, roads to expand trade, a means to control manipulated land prices, primary schools, and a bilingual judiciary (Lozano 1985). The Tejano authors also decried the Law of April 6, 1830, which forbade further immigration, because they felt that settlers from the United States were the quickest and most economical way to destroy the Indians, populate the frontier, and to produce saleable crops (Guerra 1985: [11–13]).

9. Austin himself led the effort against revolt and William H. Wharton and Rafael Manchola were selected to present a petition in Mexico City pointing out the importance of the "Mexican Texan and Anglo Texan combination" (Lozano 1985: 17). Austin went to Mexico to discuss separating Texas from Coahuila (while remaining in the Mexican Union) but was arrested on his return home.

10. The Cortina Wars of South Texas, an armed Tejano response to the land confiscation and violence, added to the fear and hatred that Tejanos felt toward many Anglos, for example the new landowners and the Texas Rangers (Gonzales 1989: 6; Montejano 1987: 33).

11. In the Hill Country a group of German abolitionists from Kerr, Kendall, and Gillespie counties reorganized their Union League into a battalion. They prepared to move into Mexico to avoid conflict but were ambushed by a massive Confederate force (Lich 1981: 200).

12. See Johnson et al. (1983) and Miller and Sanders (1990) for detailed analyses of the machine as it varied through time, with elite, middle class, and lower class being pitted against one another in various combinations at various times.

13. The conflicting stories regarding the prototype of the flower battle seem to not just be a matter of simple uncertainty due to the intervening years. There is also an apparent wish by some to see the origins in France, while others want to stress the similarity to Mexico.

14. Then, as now, membership is limited to 400 active female members, who automatically move into an inactive category after twenty-five years. Like their predecessors, members are middle- and upper-class Anglo women. A prospective member must be proposed by a member and be endorsed by two others. The primary requirement is a proven record of work in a community, church, or charitable organization. For a number of years some members have felt that the organization should actively recruit Mexican American women; however, in 1997 there are still no Spanish surnames in the membership list.

15. The carnival shows in the 1920s featured dancing girls, trained animals, Siamese twins, autodromes, and wild west shows. In the 1950s an aerial act still appeared on one of the plazas. Since the 1950s the carnival has been considered primarily an event for the westsiders.

16. Carrington family history focuses on two British brothers, who immigrated first to Barbados and then to Virginia. The story includes references to markers of success, such as land and monies donated to build a library.

17. An ad in the 1935 catalogue from London's Sloan's department store states that "we remember to cut the skirt of a court gown so that one may curtsey in it

without trembling or tottering! An important point!" The store also demonstrated the curtsy in the gown department "every afternoon from 2 to 5 o'clock during the week of May 13th" (Pringle 1977: 116).

18. In 1975 Porter Loring as King Antonio gave a Royal Order of the Red Plume award to Dr. Raul Goana, President of the San Antonio Charro Association, recognizing their contributions to Fiesta through the presentation of the charreada. Later Loring commented, "It is interesting to note that their program parallels our initial purpose in the development of interest and skills in horsemanship. They just made a better job of it" (Graham 1976: 185).

19. Miss San Antonio, a beauty contest winner, has been an official part of Fiesta for eighteen years, but is not as visible as the other royalty, primarily because she does not have her own Fiesta event as do the other queens.

20. In 1968 a parent in the Edgewood School District, Demetrio Rodríguez, filed a class action suit against the State of Texas based on the inequities in school funding. The effects of the case are still felt in a continuing debate on school funding in Texas.

21. It was suggested to LULAC by a leader in the Battle of Flowers Association that the Rey Feo parade be constructed as a specifically Mexican American parade using all of the folkloric and music groups (perhaps inviting groups from Mexico) and organizations, both civil and religious, in order to create a unique parade. However, the suggestion was not followed, and the new parade never seemed to really crystalize since so many of the potential participants were already committed to the older parades (Carol Canty, pers. comm.).

22. Watching the parades is a family activity, particularly for Mexican Americans. People go to the parade route hours in advance to stake out a good viewing area and to set up chairs and ice chests. Many who have a vehicle to spare park it along Broadway under the expressway overpass in an open space and leave it for as long as three weeks. Although some Anglos also do this, most of the cars or trucks are owned by Mexican Americans. Chairs and pallets are set up for the children, and the men tend the barbecue pits that are part of the necessary equipment. Sometimes a family will sell fajitas or sodas or even space to sit on the truck, but usually it is simply a family activity. They watch the Friday afternoon Battle of Flowers parade, and then a few men stay to watch the truck and other paraphernalia while everyone else goes home until Saturday afternoon when they return for the Fiesta Flambeau night parade.

23. Rey Feo, whether Anglo or Mexican American, usually comes from the ranks of successful businessmen and is rarely part of the elite.

3

The Construction and Maintenance of Class and Gender Roles

When Duchess Margaret started down the long runway, she was actually completing a journey begun when her grandmother made her court bow long before Margaret was born. How did Margaret, and her female relatives before her, get to be royalty, and why did she even want to make that exaggerated bow in 1993? This chapter attempts to answer that question through a description and analysis of the annual reenactment of Coronation as a form of debut and how it significantly achieves the continued reproduction of San Antonio's elite ethclass and traditional gender roles.

San Antonio's Coronation embodies issues both of class and of gender, for it is a form of a debut or presentation of a woman to society, and, by implication, a readiness for marriage. Marriage in the United States primarily occurs endogamously in relation to social class, since most couples meet and share experiences through school, work place, church, neighborhood, or mutual friends (Ember and Ember 1990: 295). While there is an aspect of uniting wealth and influence through marriage between members of the upper class, the more bounded nature of elite lives also leads to an apparent emphasis on endogamy. Boundaries are created by mechanisms of restricted access, rules of membership in social clubs, or by the required expenses of specific neighborhoods or schools. San Antonio's aristocratic class is reproduced through the annual Coronation since it not only provides specific boundaries of identification – membership in the Order of the Alamo or in the royal court – but also through the intermarriages resulting from the long social season and the eventual birth of the next generation.

Many marriages still result from relationships developed during the elite debutante season in San Antonio. Even in the late 1990s there is an underlying assumption that a daughter who has graduated from college and still does not have a significant relationship can meet that "someone" during her coming-out year. Although the royal robes and wedding dresses are quite different in appearance, there are parallels; both kinds of garments evoke strong emotions and wedding dresses are the only contemporary garments with trains, remnants of past fashionable excesses. Trains in general denote status since the excess fabric is dragged through the dirt, requiring frequent cleaning, but trains on wedding dresses and the royal robes have additional implications. They imply future fertility since long trains are guided by young girls who follow in the wake of the bride or debutante.[1]

In addition to reproducing social class through social boundaries and endogamous marriage, the Coronation debut also reproduces traditional Western gender roles. Debuts in general are a remnant of familial patriarchy, with fathers presenting their daughters as potential marriage partners to other males.[2] Veblen (1934: 83) asserts that in a capitalist system the duty of a wife is to become "the ceremonial consumer of goods which he produces," but debutante daughters also symbolically display a father's ability to clothe his loved ones in finery. The construction of San Antonio's Coronation further models gender behavior because of the dichotomous division of labor. Men select the young women to be presented, pay for the dresses, and oversee the production itself. Women are presented, receive royal robes designed and constructed by women, and are responsible for the happiness and well-being of all the involved families. Men are the providers in charge of public and political domains, while women receive the beneficence of men and are in charge of those things that fall into the domestic or private domains.

Debuts and Debutantes

History

A debutante or "deb" is a young woman whose parents have agreed that she is old enough to accept social invitations to dinners and dances without her parents (Post 1937: 329). Implicit in the term is the acknowledgement that the young woman is now of marriageable age. The first English use of the French term "debut," meaning to enter into society, was recorded in 1751. The gender-specific use, a girl coming out or being presented to society, was first recorded in 1801 in reference to young women presented at court to the monarch, a practice started by King George III's consort, Queen Charlotte, during his 1760–1820 reign.[3]

In the United States the practice of introducing a daughter to society and the use of "debut" in reference to the social act was used before the Civil War among the elite. Relatively small parties were given for a daughter to which friends of her parents and unattached men, usually somewhat older than she, were invited. By the 1890s debutante parties given by the wealthy had become elaborate balls, making up social seasons varying in length from less than a month to half a year. A smaller dance or an afternoon tea was an alternative for parents without the means, or the desire, for the more ostentatious displays, which could cost as much as $200,000. One party featured an artificial lake with a huge artificial swan that exploded on cue, sending thousands of pink roses into the air. An infamous Philadelphia party involved 10,000 exotic live butterflies suspended in huge nets above the ballroom. As the debutante took her bow, the butterflies were to be released to "fly prettily around the party." Unfortunately, the heat in the pre-air-conditioning ballroom rose dramatically and when the net was opened "out tumbled 10,000 butterfly corpses" (Birmingham 1990: 234).

In addition to presentations at private balls, social clubs, such as the St. Cecilia's society in Charleston and the German Club in San Antonio, were founded in the nineteenth and early twentieth centuries. They provided an exclusive atmosphere in which groups of young women, the daughters and granddaughters of the aristocratic members, could be presented.[4] While the debutante at a private ball or dance marks her special status with a long white dress, a bouquet of flowers, a reception line with her parents (or just mother depending on the specific form and period of the debut), and introductions to her guests, the group debs have a more formalized presentation. The performance usually includes introductions made by a master of ceremonies giving the debutante's name, parent's names, sponsor, and escort; a bow or curtsy made to her escort or the rest of the guests; and a group grand promenade or a symbolic first dance, usually a waltz. She is presented by her father, with whom she has the first dance, and then she is turned over to the escort and the stag line – all, theoretically, potential husbands.

In the early twentieth century the public became aware of the lavishness of some debutante balls and the indulgent lives of the participants through increased media coverage. As a result of the criticisms, two debutantes in 1901 organized the season's debs as a volunteer force to work "for the benefit of the poor and the betterment of the city. The Junior League was born" (Birmingham 1990: 236). In many cities the Junior League still holds a debutante ball for the daughters of the members. New York cafe society debutantes in the 1930s and 1940s became celebrities, and one appeared each year on the cover of *Life* magazine as "Deb of the Year." Reaction to stories of the costs (and debauchery) of the parties was partially responsible for the creation of the subscription dance. The idea of a charitable organization giving a ball where daughters could be introduced – for a fee (and sometimes volunteer hours) – emerged by 1950 (Mills 1959: 81). In addition to couching the debutante concept within the protection of charitable donations, debutante balls, such as the New York Infirmary Cotillion and San Antonio's Symphony Belles Ball, created a conduit for middle-class participation. Parents who did not hold memberships in the exclusive clubs could now "buy" a debut for their daughters in any one of the hundreds of balls – if they met the requirement of knowing someone who would sponsor the debutante.[5] The cotillions or balls vary in prestige and exclusiveness, and the prices reflect the differences.

Additionally, several different ethnic groups in the United States have created or adapted debut events to fit their own unique needs. In San Antonio, African American debutantes are presented by the Van Courtlandt Social Club, a men's social organization. The young women are college students and are usually honored by their parents with individual teas or receptions. Mexican American and Anglo high-school students are presented as "princesses" at the Black and White Ball, started in 1933 to foster goodwill and friendship between the United States and Mexico. A queen is selected, who then represents San Antonio at Black and White balls held in sister cities throughout Mexico. She also rides in the Battle of Flowers parade. There is a Mexican American charitable debut through the Cordi-Marian Sisters Cotillion whose proceeds benefit the sisters' missionary work. Many Mexican American girls in San Antonio have *quinceañeras* to celebrate their fifteenth birthdays and their symbolic introduction to society.[6]

In the northeast most debutantes now make their official debut through one of the charitable or cultural organizations and then have a private dance or tea given by their parents either individually or with three or four fellow debs. However, elite debs in the south and in Texas still debut through the old private clubs. Most aristocratic San Antonio debs do both the German Club debut and Coronation – sometimes simultaneously, sometimes sequentially, thus stretching the season over two years. Some will also appear in Dallas or Houston at charity debutante balls. It is considered prestigious by some families to be presented at the international balls in New York and Vienna; others see this as merely ostentatious.

Debuts as Rites of Passage

The archetypal debut can be seen in the female rites of initiation found throughout the world and across time, rites marking the social maturity of young women and their readiness to accept marriage and adult status. American debutantes are eighteen to twenty-two years of age, depending on local practices. Although current eighteen-year-old debutantes do not see their social season as being put "on the marriage market," in the past a "coming out" was definitely that. San Antonio's Order of the Alamo and German

Club debuts continue to be arenas for matchmaking because the debutantes are seniors in college or recent graduates and are seen as being of marriageable age. Whether through the German Club, a traditional white dress presentation, or the Order of the Alamo's Coronation, many of the young women do end up getting married in the following year to someone who is part of the social group, particularly if the deb did not have definite career or graduate school plans.

Even when a debut is not an acknowledgement of availability for marriage, it still functions as a rite marking adulthood. In the past a debutante's long evening dress, upswept hair, and place in the reception line were visible markers of age. Today the style and the color of the dress make it still recognizable as a "deb dress," and the reception line remains a marker of adulthood, whether at weddings or debuts. From the 1930s into the 1980s a deb party was often the first time that an underage daughter publicly drank hard liquor in front of her parents. Most importantly, the debut process makes the girls feel that they have become young women. San Antonio informants specifically stated that they felt they were finally recognized as adults by others afterwards. One former queen reported that she was now seen as a person, "no longer just a cute little granddaughter." Another stated, "It put me on a different basis from a child. It puts you into the position of being equal with your parents and their peers."

San Antonio's Coronation can be seen as a classic rite of passage in anthropologist Arnold van Gennep's tripartite terms (separation, transition, incorporation) because of the age of the debutantes and the length of the season (van Gennep 1960). The royal young women are essentially separated from the rest of the world for the six-month season. They are extremely busy with multiple fittings for the royal robes and the numerous social events culminating in the last weeks with three or four parties being scheduled back to back – luncheons, teas, cocktail parties, and dinner dances. Life is tightly focused on a closed circle of people. During Fiesta week, most debs move into hotel rooms, furthering the separation. The girls who are away at college and only come home for the actual week of Fiesta are both spatially and psychologically separated from the rest of their lives, for most do not try to talk to their college friends about Coronation. "They just don't understand. They think it is all silly getting so dressed up." The sense of separation or difference is characterized by the declaration that Fiesta week should have a fairy-tale quality to it. Mothers instruct their sons who are going to be dukes that "Your job is to make your duchess feel that she really is royalty."

In van Gennep's classic rites of passages, initiates must learn the sacred lore of the tribe. Several informants specifically mentioned learning more about San Antonio and its history as part of their social discourse during the debutante season. "It opened my eyes to San Antonio. It opened a whole lot of my mind." Many also learned more about their family histories. "I learned of the tradition of my family in Coronation and San Antonio." The guest lists at the innumerable social events are often multigenerational. Informants spoke of learning to talk with not only their parents' peers but also those of their grandparents. They learned to feel comfortable asking the older friends for advice on careers or economic decisions. "You're having real discussions with these people. You ask them questions about things you really want to know about. You ask for advice or explanations."

Rites of passage often involve some kind of ordeal or deprivation in order to prove that the young person is ready for adult status. The tight fit and heavy weight of the royal robes and the resulting restriction on movement makes the long walk to the stage and extremely low bow an ordeal for many duchesses. When asked about the bow, an eighty-five-year-old informant remembered being nervous and how relieved she was when it was successfully accomplished. So many public and private appearances and social events occur during Fiesta week that all the court members are deprived of normal sleeping and eating patterns. However, the deprivation and endurance are accentuated for the queen and princess, who accompany King Antonio on his round of visits to the schools and hospitals. A typical schedule includes 140 stops in five days. They have to get up at 5:00 a.m. to be ready for the 6:00 a.m. arrival of the official royal car and motorcycle escorts. A former queen talked about how wonderful the week was, but also how exhausting. "You are on from 5:00 in the morning till 2:00 in the evening [morning]. I would say that entire week I got about fourteen hours of sleep and I just could not . . . by the end of it I had my head in my eggs [at breakfast]." There are reports of people getting B-12 shots, believed to provide extra energy, just so they can make it through the week.

Reincorporation with the society as a whole occurs when Fiesta week is over. The young women speak of the necessity of "facing the real world." The presence of Victor Turner's (1967) quality of liminality in the transition stage is revealed by the references to the return to reality in the final or reincorporation stage. "You wake up on Monday, and you are on your own. No one is there to tell you what you are supposed to do that day. It is back to reality. The schedule is gone, and you have to think of your own plans." The court robes will never be worn officially again. The fairy tale is over. However, the reality faced by many of the duchesses is not that of an average twenty-two-year-old. Many of the young royal women go on a vacation to a favored spot in Mexico or the Caribbean to recuperate from their social activities, although some, like their age-mates from less prominent families, must return to jobs or to school.

Regional Variations

Debutante rituals vary in form and content ethnically, socioeconomically, and regionally. Debuts in Boston, for instance, are considered to be more restrained, as befits the character of New England. The South, as a whole, has more debuts, and (with the exception of the extremely exclusive St. Cecilia's presentation in Charleston, a model of understated decorum) they are often marked by extravagant costumes and crowns. There are pilgrimages, cotton balls, and magnolia or cottonwood festivals all over the South that incorporate debutante presentations. The Mardi Gras balls of New Orleans are probably the most well known, but Texas has more than its share of debuts as pageantry. The required ages in the Texas debutante events vary, and they take place at different times of the year. Therefore, there are some Texas debs coming out at two or more of these events, particularly if they have relatives in the proper social circles in the other towns.

Galveston, Texas, holds a Mardi Gras with the krewes and formal balls of its New Orleans namesake, largely because it also began in the nineteenth century. Debutantes are presented at the oldest krewes' balls, but the royal robes do not have trains bearing icons of the theme, as do those in San Antonio. Waco has a Cotton Ball and pageant where high-school senior debs, wearing nineteenth-century-style evening gowns of satin and lace, are presented as part of a long pageant depicting the city's history. Laredo, a town on Texas's border with Mexico, hosts the George Washington Birthday Celebration with two sets of debutante presentations: the Martha Washington Pageant, in which the participants wear elaborately bejeweled eighteenth-century-style evening costumes, and the Pocahontas Pageant, showcasing young men and women representing different Native American tribes wearing indigenous costumes – made of Ultrasuede, sequins, and beads. Both Waco and Laredo began their celebrations at the end of the nineteenth century when pageantry was at its height.

The Rose Festival in Tyler, begun in 1930 to promote the rose industry, is highlighted by the coronation of the queen. New costumes are designed yearly by a professional theatrical designer. The queen always wears a crown with her jeweled gown and train, but the other costumes are quite theatrical. Corpus Christi's Buccaneer Days, begun in 1956 as a civic event to encourage tourism, has a court based directly on San Antonio's Coronation. The first Buccaneer court even borrowed the royal robes from San Antonio, but subsequently they have made their own, with a new theme each year. Neither the Rose Festival coronation nor the Buccaneer Days court presentation has the formality of San Antonio's Coronation, primarily because they were both started long after the heyday of pageantry.

Order of the Alamo's Coronation

Membership in the Order

Coronation's pageantry, with its historicized thematic presentations, is a major factor in its ability to mark aristocratic boundaries. Additionally, the limited membership of the Order of the Alamo and the degree of difficulty in obtaining membership assure the exclusivity needed to mark elite status (Marcus 1983: 11). The only written requirements for Order membership are that the nominee must be twenty-one years of age and a resident of Bexar County for a minimum of two years prior to nomination by a current member, but there are many more implicit restrictions. Currently the vast majority of members are Anglos, most of whom belong to the local aristocracy and are interrelated through ties of birth and marriage. The membership of 815 takes in no more than twenty-four new members yearly, and preference is usually given to legacies, sons and grandsons of members, so there are relatively few spots available for "new blood." Several men reported that they always voted for sons of members. "If I know the father and like him, I usually vote for the kid. Because I figure if the father is nice, he has usually raised the kid that way." However, newcomers do become members, and the proportion of new versus old seems to vary through time, both on the basis of available potential members and on the philosophy of the current board of directors, the final authority over membership.

Without kinship or affinal connections, the best way to become a member is to grow up in the same neighborhoods and attend school with the men who end up on the board. San Antonio's Old Guard elite and the incorporated communities of Alamo Heights, Olmos Park, and Terrell Hills are inextricably intertwined. Most Order members live in one of the communities, and it is unusual for a member of the Coronation in-town court to live anywhere outside of these contiguous older neighborhoods located a few miles northeast of the downtown area. Alamo Heights was settled in the 1890s, while Terrell Hills and Olmos Park were begun in the 1920s. They were all promoted as being a retreat from the heat and noise of the downtown area. The three incorporated communities are actually heterogeneous in terms of house values and ethnicity, particularly Alamo Heights and Terrell Hills, but the most visible inhabitants are Anglo and live comfortably in houses ranging from cottages to five-bedroom estates. Listings from one real estate company for Alamo Heights in 1992 ranged from $60,000 to $350,000, while those in Olmos Park hovered around $250,000 but could soar into seven figures. Although some of the houses are very expensive, San Antonio does have more expensive, new suburban areas. However, the aristocratic families have primarily stayed within the older neighborhoods.

Virtually all American cities have elite neighborhoods where sharing a common space "reinforces the sense of social togetherness so necessary to the perpetuation of social dominance" (Jakle et al. 1985: 51). The shared physical space both defines the inhabitants and creates a base from which shared attitudes and values can emerge. Bourdieu refers to this two-sided characteristic as habitus: it is a way of classifying but also is generative of "meaningful practices and meaning-giving perceptions" (Bourdieu 1984: 170). The inhabitants of the three San Antonio neighborhoods are called "'09ers" in reference to the last two digits of the zip code (although Olmos Park's zip is 78212). The term refers to the physical space, but more specifically to those inhabitants who are Anglo, professional, and usually from old San Antonio families that share a certain lifestyle, often including participation in Coronation. The styles of the houses vary considerably, but there is a certain style found through much of the three neighborhoods. The age of the houses creates the basis for the look, but landscaping and decorative techniques also add to the overall distinctive look. Recently, custom-made wreaths decorated with the colors and motifs of the royal robes worn by the royal daughter of the household, began to be displayed on front doors throughout April. The wreaths appear as just another example of the ubiquitous door decoration to outsiders driving through the neighborhoods, but they are instantly recognizable by insiders as the markers of royal distinction.

The single most important draw for current buyers is the Alamo Heights Independent School District shared by the three incorporated communities. It is the highest rated district according to achievement scores and percentage of college-bound graduates from its one high school.[7] People new to San Antonio move into one of the areas primarily for the school system, but second in appeal are the yards filled with large oak and pecan trees and the small-town feeling, exemplified in the commercial establishments, including a drugstore with a lunch counter where cherry Cokes are still served. And a few people straightforwardly want to live in one of the three neighborhoods because it is the best way to further the chances of becoming part of the old social set, at least for their children.

The children of the newcomers get to know children of the older families as neighbors, as fellow members of sports teams, or as campers at one of the Texas Hill Country camps, an important part of elite childhood experiences. An unconfirmed story claims that the Coronation bow used to be taught at some of the central Texas camps. Future duchesses and dukes primarily attend colleges in Texas or the southeast and pledge one of three top sororities or fraternities, often renewing friendships from summer camp.[8] When long-term friendships occur between newer and old families, the newcomers may be rewarded by invitations for the younger generation to be in the royal court or to become a member of the Order.

There are four categories of membership – single, married (thirty-five and under), married (thirty-six and older), and non-resident – with numerical allotments that may vary slightly depending on the current distribution of current members. In 1992 there was a total of 122 nominees for the twenty-two openings. There are always more spots for single men, since they are needed to act as dukes for the duchesses. Membership is highly desired for several reasons. It is a social door to "meet young people of similar interests." The Order is seen as one of the best ways a young man can renew old friendships and make new ones, both male and female, when he has been away at school or just returned to San Antonio after working elsewhere. A grandmother was sad that her grandson had not gotten in the previous year because he felt "left out," since most people he knew were in it. When he was accepted, it "helped his ego a lot." One father felt that membership would help smooth the somewhat rough exterior of a son who had spent a lot of time on the family ranch and was a little "too country."

Married men (and their wives) want in to enjoy the three parties included with the $210 dues and the social prestige accorded the Order, considered by the membership to be the highest ranked of the private clubs. Although it is strictly a social group and is not consciously viewed as a means to business connections (as is Rotary or Optimists), many members do benefit professionally. Through committee work in particular, men get to know one another's strengths and weaknesses, who can be counted on to get a job done – useful knowledge in deciding with whom to do business of all kinds. Whether a member is in banking or sales, membership and active participation and the resulting personal relationships can significantly, if indirectly, affect a man's career. The same phenomenon occurs in the Cavaliers, the social club started by Carrington to elect King Antonio.

Prior to 1980 new members were elected directly by the board, so personal friendships with the leaders were even more important. "It was a matter of who you knew on the board. There were many evenings we would stay up until 3:00 or 4:00 in the morning because somebody had a brother-in-law he wanted in. The jerk and a friend on the board would agree to blackball everyone else until the brother-in-law got in." Now the ballot, composed of all eligible nominees, is submitted to the general membership with directions for number of votes to be cast in each category. It includes the name, age, proposing member, and all past relatives in the Order and in Coronation. The proposing members (and occasionally other relatives or friends) politicize membership by sending out letters or cards extolling the virtues of their nominees. Some are straightforward letters simply stating his name and family connections; others include anecdotes or remarks, such as "He has an eye for the pretty girls and can sniff out a good party just like we did." Some look like political ads, printed on brightly colored cards with the nominee's name in bold type and asking for the reader's vote. These are often signed by several people to show the depth of the support.

When all of the votes are tabulated, the membership committee (the three or more most recent past presidents of the Order) submits to the board of directors a list of the top vote getters in each of the four membership categories. "Now if the jerk's brother-in-law doesn't get the membership's vote, we don't have to fool with him." Although the board still makes the final decisions by secret ballot, the new method is favored "because it takes the pressure off the board." However, any nominee receiving two board votes against him is rejected.[9] It is difficult to determine with any certainty why one person gets in and another does not. One informant says simply, "They have to pass the dog-sniff test." The results of the 1992 vote for new members demonstrates the reality of that tongue-in-cheek remark. Of the twenty-two new members taken in for 1992, two nominees from classic old families were not admitted, while seven men with a single or no familial connection did make it.[10] A Mexican American nominee did not make it, but neither did a grandson-in-law of the founder of the Order. Several board members specifically stated that new people, those without family connections, could join the Order. Some believe that new people are needed to "keep it alive. When it has been in the family, it is not an honor, but something that is passed down." It is felt by some that the "new blood" works harder, is more willing to be on the committees. "They appreciate their membership more."[11] The high percentage of minimally connected new members in 1992 seemed to indicate that the board acted on those beliefs in the final selection. In 1996 and 1997 the same trend continued and new members included several Mexican Americans, one of whom received the automatic invitation offered to a husband of a queen or princess.

Once you are admitted as a member, you are in for life, as long as you pay your annual dues. The only cause for suspension of membership in the bylaws is failure to pay the fine for inviting an ineligible guest or escorting more than one woman (not otherwise eligible) to the ball or reception. Several times informants laughingly said that there are convicted felons among the members as well as several waiting indictment for various white-collar crimes. Older men think about resigning but are talked out of it by their wives because they would no longer be able to attend the reception following the Coronation, the most private, and coveted, of the three parties. Attendance at the parties and membership in the Order and the royal court all mark elite status due to the restrictions involved.

Board of Directors

Although Coronation presents an overall model of social dominance, the internal hierarchical or ladder structure of the board is significant because it allows the participants to be cognizant of the order of social relations and their ability to achieve personal empowerment through "activity in the perceived system" (Bell 1992: 84). The members of the board of directors of the Order of the Alamo head the committees responsible for producing the Coronation. The twelve-member board is voted on by the entire membership from a list of nominees. Many members have no desire to be on the board of directors, but others know from the beginning that they want to be completely involved. One former board member stated that there are no rewards or additional membership benefits for putting in the long hours and effort (although there are a number of social events that only board members attend); but "It is an honor to even be nominated. It means that they think you can handle the job. [By such service] you prove something to yourself and to others."

The board is hierarchically arranged with the Fiesta committee chairman at the bottom (referred to as the "liquor boy" because laying in supplies is his primary job), then moving up through the Coronation reception, year-book, visiting court, publicity, secretary, garden party, and Queen's Ball committee chairs. "When you first get on the board, you have all the plans in the world to stay on it for ten years, but after three or four years, you go 'Oh, my God, what have I gotten myself into? Do I really need to do this?'" Many people drop off after holding the Queen's Ball position. Beginning the last four rungs of the ladder – treasurer, in-town court, Coronation chairman and president – is considered a firm commitment to "go all the way to the top." "Once you are on the ladder, that means that you are going to be doing Coronation." Although it usually takes ten or twelve years to make it through the board, sudden shifts have occurred and a man may suddenly find himself three years away from Coronation rather than the expected seven. As with much of Coronation, such spontaneity seems to have been more common in the past. Now, the ladder climbing seems to proceed in a method-ical way, just as many other areas have become more formalized and codified.

There is also an institutionalized hierarchy in the Coronation itself, which applies to women as they move up from being a ramp page, to stage page, to duchess, and to princess or queen. It does serve to naturalize female ascendancy and hierarchy, but it does not provide the individualized empowerment as does work on the board of directors ladder. The women are chosen by someone else on the basis of their family connections, not on their personal achievements or abilities. The women cannot "work" their way up. An examination of the specific positions involved in Coronation demonstrates the ways participation reinforces traditional gender roles.

Gender Roles and Coronation Positions

Males hold the majority of official roles related to the production of Coronation, including the Coronation chairman, who has the ultimate responsibility and control. Women act as mistress of the robes, court artist, ballet mistress, and dressmakers. Despite the preponderance of male roles, the importance of female participation is well recognized since the sole purpose of the Order is to create an elaborated debut venue for women. Coronation could not exist without young women or royal robes, and the men would have to find another way to mark their class identity. One former chairman asserted that the men "should do nothing but work in the background like dogs to be sure that a bunch of attractive girls have a good time. And if they start thinking that they are important or something special, that's not right."

Significantly, the sole guarantee to a male of an invitation for membership is to marry a former queen or princess or to be the father of one; however, it is quite rare that a father is not already a member. Why is the queen a conduit to male membership? Following Émile Durkheim's insight that a group must create a means of perpetuating itself past its immediate members, Bourdieu states that such mechanisms include symbolization and representation "which confer ubiquity and eternity. The representative (e.g., the king) is eternal" (Bourdieu 1984: 72). The queen (and, secondarily, the princess) is the official representative of the Order and acts as the means of reproduction of the group identity. The queen is always the woman with the oldest royal lineage, and her annual crowning reaffirms the continued recognition of the group's boundaries. Since the selection of the queen, like the social class itself, is based on family lineages, the genealogy of the highest representatives (the queen and princess) must be pure. Therefore, in the unusual case that the father is not a member, membership must be immediately extended in order to bring him into the fold. Since the daughters of queens and princesses have a good chance of becoming the highest representatives themselves, the husbands of queens and princesses must be made members so that the future children will have pure lineages. Marrying or fathering a queen or princess therefore is the only assured way to acquire Order membership. The emic explanation of the practice is usually given as, "If he is good enough to father her or marry her, he is good enough for us."

While females cannot actually nominate someone, they do write letters and make phone calls on behalf of their relatives. Such work of creating a network of connections would be seen by Carol Gilligan (1982) as part of women's work as helpmate and nurturer, but interpreted by Micaela di Leonardo (1987) as the work of kinship, an important perspective in analyzing women's labor. She emphasizes that women extend their kin work across households, that it is not restricted to the immediate domestic domain. Letters of support may be sent to literally hundreds of current members who are friends or relatives of the letter writer. Di Leonardo stresses that kin work must be recognized as a source of power and future obligations, not as simply the altruistic labor of love. Support for Order nominees or for a place in the royal court does imply reciprocal support. In effect a woman may offer to support a friend's nephew if he will vote for her daughter when it comes time for her to run for queen.

The participation of males and of females must be treated together, for the division of labor is based on separate but complementary domains, and the royal court members are set up in paired roles. In the production of Coronation, the men primarily take care of the public performance while the women concentrate on the behind-the-scenes work. The duties fall into binary domains of public and private, political and domestic. The dyadic pair who oversee the production are the Coronation chairman and mistress of the robes, while the royal pairs are the president and queen and dukes and duchesses. The other men on the board of directors are responsible for various aspects of Coronation and do not have female counterparts, although many wives do serve on the committees headed by the board members. The court artist, ballet mistress, and dressmaker are female production roles without male counterparts. They are anomalies also because they are professional or semiprofessional positions, unlike the board members and mistress of the robes, which are all filled by volunteers. Another contrast is that the women holding these paid positions may or may not be part of the Coronation ethclass.

Coronation Chairman and Mistress of the Robes

In general theatrical terms, the male chairman directs the public performance while the mistress is in charge of the behind-the-scenes area of costuming and relationships. The division reflects the traditional gender domains of the public male and the private female. The chairman takes care of all negotiations with the outsiders – the symphony members and the stage hands – while the mistress is responsible for the designs of the robes, invitations to the pages, and relationships among the insiders – the participants and their parents and the dressmakers. However, domains are not strictly separated but may overlap, depending on the individuals involved. Many of the chairman's decisions are made in conference with his mistress of the robes and other board members. The Coronation chairman issues the invitations to be a member of the court after consultation with other members of the board, but often the mistress of robes is informally included in the decisions. The chairman alone chooses the mistress of the robes and the lord high chamberlain, the only speaking part in Coronation. The chamberlain is chosen for his speaking ability but also for his friendship with the chairman and he rarely comes from outside the Order membership. As befits her more domestic domain, the mistress chooses only the children who will be pages or part of the prologue. Usually the chairman and mistress decide on the theme together, although sometimes one or the other has such strong feelings about it that the other one simply withdraws from that decision. Musical selections are made together, as is the staging, although the chairman may take the lead in the latter area. The mistress and the chairman may write the script, or it may be turned over to someone with specialized knowledge in a field related to the theme or who is adept at script writing. The amount of involvement by the chairman in the royal robes varies, depending on the individual. Most just want to see the dress designs and then leave the rest up to the mistress while others even attend the dress fittings.

Exclusive duties of the Coronation chairman include the contract negotiations with the lighting and sound technicians, the stage manager, and the musicians of the San Antonio Symphony, all of whom are union members, and arrangements with the Municipal Auditorium, the site of the event. Significantly, the chairman makes all arrangements for the queen's honor guard, always a military or paramilitary group. The chairman and other Order members do much of the physical labor, such as setting up the risers, although the scenic designs are left to professionals.[12]

The mistress of the robes has been an official figure in Coronation since the beginning in 1909; however, her duties and length of service have increased enormously. In the early years, she simply acted as a coordinator or supervisor; now she is responsible for designing the whole court, assigning dresses and colors to each young woman, supervising the actual construction of the dresses, and, most importantly, keeping all of the young women and their parents happy. Despite the extraordinary amount of time and effort involved in being mistress, the position is highly coveted. Some see it as an opportunity to work with beautiful dresses and to be a part of something they themselves loved doing as duchesses, or, in a few cases, to make up for not being a duchess (usually due to an early marriage). The chairman begins to think about his choice of mistress of the robes three or four years ahead of time. She is always the wife of an Order member, and in the past was often somewhat older than the Coronation chairman, although recently they have been closer in age. Most of the chosen women have college degrees in the liberal arts, but infrequently have utilized them in obtaining employment. Mistresses usually have years of experience in upper-class volunteerism, serving on committees in the many charitable, social, and cultural organizations, work that Susan Ostrander in her study of upper-class women points out "serves largely to uphold the power and privilege of her own class in the social order of things" (Ostrander 1984: 3). An important characteristic of a possible mistress is an interest in fashion, art history, or a related area. "I looked for someone who dresses well so I knew she could make the girls look good. Could match colors and all."

The ability to "match colors" is important because the mistress of the robes is responsible for the production of status through her cultural knowledge as exemplified in the area of artistic taste. The male chairman is in charge of the financial and material arrangements while the female mistress specializes in converting these resources into status through her knowledge of those "self-consciously aesthetic levels of culture production" (Collins 1992: 224–7). The mistress spends up to two years in researching the theme to be able to produce all of the costumes. The research itself gives great pleasure to many of the mistresses, perhaps drawing on their educational background that had not been specifically used elsewhere. "[I]t is the challenge of working with people, of learning. Everyone wants to learn something new." "It got my brain working." Typical of the extensive research is the mistress who took eighteen months off from her normal employment, spent an estimated $300 on copying, and put 6,000 miles on her car. She went to libraries, special collections, and museums and conferred with a specialist in Spanish art to gain detailed information for the theme and design ideas. One mistress went to the Museum of Anthropology in Mexico City to check the colors for her La Corte de la Tierra Mágica, while another went to India to obtain authentic fabrics for her Court of India dresses.

Some mistresses of the robes additionally view the job as an opportunity to educate, to pass on cultural information. One mistress used a newsletter to educate the duchesses, including historical facts, and suggested books of fiction and nonfiction about the court's theme for "mood reading." In addition to the drawings of the royal robes, she presented the young women with a map of the country each represented and a detailed description of the sources of the design and the motifs for her dress. Although the stated purpose of the Order is to educate its members and the public in the history of Texas, the purpose is apparently loosely interpreted as the use of any researched theme. The mistress of the robes therefore is the educator, supporting the observation that women are largely involved with teaching, in itself cultural production (Collins 1992: 224). Rather complete knowledge of the theme is necessary because the mistress must develop two separate subthemes, one each for the in- and out-of-town courts; fantasy titles, such as Duchess of the Filigreed Palace or Duchess of Exuberant Celtic Ornament, for each of the twenty-six members; and material for the text read by the lord high chamberlain explaining the theme and the relationship of each dress to it. The research is so extensive that mistresses can usually relate the exact origin of every motif used on a gown or train to a historical source, whether it be from a classic painting or a little-known piece of statuary. One woman smiled, "Afterwards, you are a walking fountain of information which no one wants to hear."

Although the artistic aspect of the position of mistress of the robes is very important, of equal consideration now is how well she gets along with the chairman and how well she works with people. The Coronation chairmen in the last twenty years have often become more involved in the area of the royal robes and may spend at least a year in frequent meetings and consultations with the mistress since so much more time is spent in the research and design. "She is a mistress in every way except sexually," one former chairman laughingly said to point out the extent of the time and energy that is shared. The feelings of the mistress of the robe's husband are also considered since "you take someone's wife away for a year." Not all of the pairs work this closely together, but many do. In addition to working closely with the chairman, the mistress directly handles all of the potential problems of twenty-six young women and their parents, who are spending large amounts of money on a dress and on an emotionally charged occasion. One former chairman, a dentist, said that the woman he picked was a patient as well as a friend and so he knew that she was "really cool under pressure. You learn a lot about a person in a dental chair." A former mistress stated, "The most important characteristic a mistress must have is the ability to work with lots of people." She works with the chairman, the court artist, the royal young women and parents, dressmakers, and up to fifty children and their parents. A recent mistress estimated that she had to "get 198 people on the same wavelength with me." The public relations aspect was summarized by one woman: "Even if the dress designs are awful, the dressmakers can help you, but if you can't get along with people . . ."

The Coronation chairman also works with a large number of people but more often in his capacity to make decisions, not as a mediator. The role of the mistress of robes falls into the classic view of women as being keeper and nurturer of relationships (Chodorow 1974; Gilligan 1982). The mistress works within the private or domestic sphere: she and her court artist work in their homes, in contrast to the chairman, who usually keeps all of his Order records at his office. Then she goes to the homes of dressmakers to supervise fittings and work out compromises when there are conflicts. In addition to maintaining smooth relationships between the dressmaker and family, sometimes even between parents and daughter, the mistress becomes the source of information and comfort to the duchesses on personal levels. "And the men in this organization don't understand that. You are their mother at times, confidante, their social secretary. They want to know what is proper for such and such a thing." One mistress described the job as being a "Brownie troop leader for young adults."

Who has the more important position? Whose Coronation is it? Both chairmen and mistresses use the phrase "my Coronation" at different times in conversation. When specifically questioned, one mistress said that "it depends on what part you are talking about and to whom." The mistress is always credited with the royal robes and is either praised or blamed for the results. Chairmen seem to use "my" when talking about the production as a whole and before actually becoming chairman when they begin to talk of themes and different kinds of music that will make their Coronation a unique production. "When you know you are going to be Coronation chairman in three or four years, you are full of ways to change things, but the closer you get to it, the more you realize that there are reasons for the traditional way things are done." The themes are actually the only element that change yearly, but even they are eventually repeated so there are few unique themes. However, many chairmen do project feelings of their ownership. "Doing the Coronation is the very best. It is very time-consuming and you do have to spend a lot of time on detail. But it is great because you get to know everybody – the in-town court, the visiting court – every aspect of it – and it is your show." Another man stated simply, "You get to be boss."

The mistresses use the personal possessive pronoun in relation to the court ("The Court of Ageless Beauty was my court") and to the royal women, emphasizing the interpersonal aspect. "I was lucky. All of my girls were beautiful and had darling figures." There is a definite feeling of accomplishment for it is seen as a tremendous responsibility.

> Just the sheer monetary responsibility makes it a huge job. One of the biggest I've done. I did not approach it as just something fun to fill my time. I have lots of things I can fill my time with. It's the most exciting thing I've ever done. You get to be creative and do your own thing. I've done a lot of other things, President of Junior League, the Symphony Board, but nothing else is as exciting and fulfilling.

The comparisons to other volunteer positions may highlight the limited number of supervisory career positions that have been held by women who have been mistresses of the robes, at least until recent years.

The roles of chairman and mistress are apparently seen as complementary. "He has his part and I have mine. So he may say 'my Coronation' when he is talking about the honor guard, but I talk about 'my dresses.'" There is an annual luncheon during Fiesta week for past Coronation chairmen and mistresses of the robes and they all look forward to attending it and recalling "their year." If there is a difference, it is because the chairman has achieved his position based on his reputation and effort. The mistress, like all of the females in Coronation, is given her role based on ascriptive characteristics. A woman who wants to be mistress of the robes can let it be known that she is interested, but can only wait to be chosen.

Court Artist, Ballet Mistress, and Dressmakers

The chairman and mistress hold the two most important positions in the production of Coronation in terms of authority and scope. The court artist, ballet mistress, and dressmakers have more specialized roles but are equally necessary. The chairman as well as the other committee chairmen and the mistress of the robes are all clearly part of the elite social group, and their participation in Coronation is voluntary and nonprofessional. The roles of court artist, ballet mistress, and dressmakers, all female, are less clear-cut.

The amount of actual designing done by the mistress of the robes depends on her individual abilities. Until the 1950s much of the actual designing was done by court members' friends involved in fashion or costuming in some way and the dressmakers themselves. In the mid-1950s costume designers, also wives of Order members, were listed in the programs in addition to the mistresses of the robes. By 1959 a court artist was hired to make precise scale drawings of the trains to be enlarged by the dressmakers and used as patterns. Several men acted as court artists, sometimes doing most of the actual design work. Farrell Tyson was court artist twice and wanted to become the permanent designer. When the Order declined his offer, Tyson started a similar coronation event through his church to honor young Christian women. The Lutheran Coronation still takes place yearly with a new theme and high-school-age duchesses wearing elaborate dresses and highly embellished trains. They are not as costly, however, as the Order's royal robes.

The mistress of the robes chooses her court artist, and with a few exceptions the artist is a former duchess or wife of an Order member or at least a friend of the mistress. All court artists have been female since 1965. Some of the artists actively pursue their art work while others are less involved but are seen as having artistic abilities. Sometimes the artist is the actual designer, while some mistresses and artists design as a team. Although the artist's name is listed in the program, it is in smaller type, and she often does not get the attention that the mistress of the robes gets. One mistress, in talking of their mutual work, stated, "As far as I'm concerned, she didn't get nearly the credit she deserves. It was every bit as much hers as mine, literally." Unlike the mistress, however, the court artist is salaried, and a few have held the job repeatedly, up to four times.

Another semiprofessional position is that of the ballet mistress. The formal court bow is considered so important and difficult that, just as in England, someone trained in dance instructs the young women and men in their courtly behavior. The ballet mistress conducts eight weeks of bow rehearsals for the duchesses and two rehearsals for the entire court – pages, entourages, and all. Until recently a dance performed by young children was always part of the Coronation entertainment and was choreographed by the ballet mistress. Over the years several different ballet teachers have held the position, but one held it for over thirty years. When asked why she would take on so much extra work, a recent ballet mistress explained that she felt it would give her school good publicity, and more importantly it would be an opportunity for her students to dance on a large stage with the symphony, something that she could never offer otherwise.

The completely professional positions associated with Coronation, filled by women, are those of the dressmakers. The dressmakers are central to the entire event, for they offer the only continuity in the actual fabrication of the royal robes. Those who hold the positions of control, the Coronation chairman and the mistress of the robes, are elected or appointed annually and are always newcomers to the jobs. The dressmakers have years of experience. The two most well-known dressmakers of the past each made the gowns and trains for over thirty years, and two of the current seven have each worked for over twenty years. Competition among the royal families for the top dressmakers can be intense, since they are only able to take on so many dresses in a given year. Calls may be made to a dressmaker even before the actual invitation to participate in Coronation is issued.

The current dressmakers learned the necessary skills either through an informal apprenticeship with one of the previous dressmakers or through work on the trains worn in the Lutheran Coronation. Most of the dressmakers hire seamstresses to do much of the actual sewing, although they do at least some of it themselves (Figure 5). The ones who only take two or three robes may do all of their own sewing. The husbands of the married dressmakers are often involved to some degree. One does some of the actual sewing, but others help in the masculine arena of physical labor. Two of them make or help make headpieces (which take some metalworking ability to bend and form the wires), and most end up helping load and carry the gowns

Figure 5. Dressmaker Minna Bel Oland with some of the seamstresses who worked on the many Coronation robes she was responsible for in her forty-year career. Courtesy: Institute of Texan Cultures, San Antonio *Light* Collection.

and trains when they must be delivered to the auditorium the day of the Coronation. There are also other men and women who specialize in making the headpieces or high-standing deMedici-type collars for the queen and the princess.

There are usually five to seven officially sanctioned dressmakers, who have exclusive permission to construct the gowns and trains. With one exception the current dressmakers are not of the inner elite circle; however, they are comfortably middle-class, and one former dressmaker is the great-aunt of two recent duchesses. Historically, most of the dressmakers have been Anglo, as are most of the current seamstresses, who do much of the actual handwork. The only dressmakers available for interviews who have hired Hispanic seamstresses are themselves Hispanic – one emigrated as a small child with her family from Mexico during the revolution of 1910–21. The other emigrated from Cuba with her husband during the 1960s. All of the current dressmakers have their workrooms within private homes, most often using a converted garage but sometimes an extra bedroom. The only specialized equipment is the worktable, long enough to hold the fifteen-foot-long queen's train and high enough to be worked at for hours without too much discomfort. The walls are covered with racks holding fabrics and jars of beads, and there must be storage for the thousands of glass stones. The two current dressmakers who make the majority of the royal robes both hire friends who like to do handwork and who like the flexibility of part-time work. Much of the intricate beading is done directly on the fabric of the train, but elements of the design may be created separately and then appliquéd onto the train. The beaded appliqués may be worked on at home on a piecework basis and some are subcontracted to specialists. Some of the seamstresses work in groups on a given train and may engage in conversation as the work allows. Their workday generally ends at 3:00 p.m. when it is time to pick up the children. The domestic atmosphere in the workrooms reinforces the femaleness of the labor of constructing dresses designed by the cultural producers, the mistresses of the robes.

A dressmaker is not seen as a seamstress in a garret but as a woman whose expertise and opinions are respected by parents and by the mistress of the robes. The dressmakers, as the technicians who transform the conceptual designs into material form, are in a unique position of control and influence even though they are outsiders in terms of social class. They all view their work as demanding creative and artistic skills, not simply technical ones. "We don't think of this as craft. It is an artistic expression." The experience and expertise of the dressmakers can save a poorly designed train or an unflattering dress. Modifying a design can be a delicate maneuver, since a mistress of the robes or court artist may be sensitive to implied criticism of her work; and yet the royal customer must be happy with the results. It is also in the dressmaker's self-interest to make the royal robes as beautiful as possible. The financial return is important, but the women find great satisfaction in the work itself. Several of the dressmakers in the past were single women who relied on their sewing skills for their support, but now most see the income from the royal robes as discretionary.

Many of the royal customers develop strong bonds of affection for "their" dressmakers, and often there will be a continuing relationship between several members of a family and one dressmaker. The mistress of the robes usually rents a suite at the Menger Hotel for the night of the Queen's Ball, and invites all of the dressmakers to a reception. Some dressmakers have also been invited to the ball itself, but such inclusion depends on the individual mistress of the robes. The dressmakers occupy a liminal space socially. There appears to be no social contact between most of the dressmakers and their clients outside of the Coronation context, but during Fiesta week the dressmakers are drawn at least partially into the inner circle. This inclusion is based on their artistic abilities, which make them coproducers of cultural status.

President and Queen

The Coronation chairman automatically assumes the highest office available, that of president of the Order, the year following "his" Coronation. Conversely, the mistress of the robes makes a lateral move into "patroness," a category created for all former mistresses, princesses, and queens that entitles them to lifelong invitations to the reception and a luncheon for former mistresses. However, becoming a patroness is a recognition of something completed; it is not an advancement.

The parallel female role to the president is that of the queen. During Coronation they each are referred to as "Excellency" but are not consorts: the titles are "His" and "Her Excellency," not "Their Excellencies." They each are official representatives of the Order of the Alamo. The queen chooses a prime minister, but he acts only as an escort. The president stands in the receiving line with the queen, princess, and their escorts at the reception following the Coronation.[13] Most importantly, the president and the queen bestow on one another the symbols of their respective offices. The high point of Coronation is when the costumed president places the crown upon the head of the queen and administers the oath of office. "Do you promise to bring mirth, melody and sweet music to the Kingdom . . . to preserve gladness and banish sorrow and . . . to make each passing day brighter?" It is the original wording from 1909 and depicts the female representative of the Order as responsible for the happiness of her subjects, emphasizing the importance of woman as caretaker.

During the "Little Coronation" that takes place during the Queen's Ball three days after Coronation, the queen awards the president his insignia of office. She places a gold medallion on a ribbon over his head while he kneels at her throne. Although the president was voted into office by the entire board of directors, he has no visible symbol of his status as Order president until he is given the medallion by the queen. Past presidents wear their medallions at the social occasions that require formal wear, while all other members wear a purple ribbon, baldric style, across their chests. One former president claimed that all the work was worth it just to get to wear the medallion instead of having to fuss with getting the ribbon pinned on correctly. Former queens are given a gold pin, shaped like a crown, set with tiny diamonds, which they may wear at any time. The actions of the two representatives towards one another clearly demonstrate the interrelationships of the men and women involved in Coronation. The president and queen are mutually dependent on one another for the acknowledgement of their respective status, just as the royal women and the members of the Order are mutually involved in re-creating and perpetuating the boundaries of their social class.

The president takes part in Coronation but is usually not involved in the actual production of it. He takes no formal oath, but he is charged with maintaining all traditions involved in Coronation. At the past presidents' luncheon the day following Coronation, the current one is "roasted" and told of any misdeeds. Once a local television station filmed one of the dressmakers for a feature story. The mistress of the robes thought the dresses had not been filmed, but they were clearly visible in the broadcast. The president was roasted for breaking the tradition of never showing the dresses prior to Coronation. He was responsible for the robes when they were in the public domain of television. The publicity was acknowledged to perhaps be beneficial to ticket sales, but still tradition had been broken so the "criticism was legitimate." Even if the chairman or the mistress of the robes caused the break in tradition, the president is still held responsible. A president specifically stated that the "ultimate goal is to make it so much fun for the girls that they will want their children to do it . . . to perpetuate the tradition." It is fitting that the President of the Order of the Alamo has as his chief duty the preservation of traditions for, as Eric Hobsbawm points out, invented traditions may be used to symbolize social cohesion, to establish or legitimatize status in addition to socialization (1983: 9).

The president's concern with tradition, particularly in relation to the public arena of the media, contrasts with the essentially private nature of the position of the queen, paralleling the private/public roles of the mistress of the robes and the Coronation chairman. The queen's most important appearance is at her Coronation, an event open to the public but whose audience is primarily composed of relatives and friends of the Order members. The only other public event that the Queen of the Order of the Alamo appeared in for forty years or more was the Battle of Flowers parade. But even the parade had a familial feeling to it since many of the women in the Battle of Flowers Association were relatives of the royal participants. Although the queen was referred to as "the queen of Fiesta," she never took the active public role that King Antonio did. The queen still does not take part in the opening ceremonies of Fiesta, which include the rest of the female Fiesta royalty and King Antonio and Rey Feo. The queen and the princess now ride in the River Parade, but again, there is a private party feeling to it since there is a high degree of overlapping membership between the Order and the Cavaliers.

In the 1950s the queen and the princess began to accompany King Antonio on some of his official visits. The royal visits are appropriate to the private domain of the royalty of the Order, however, since they are made to children in schools and to the sick or infirm in hospitals and nursing homes. The queen makes appearances that emphasize the female qualities of caretaker and mother. The visits occur throughout Fiesta week, beginning early in the morning. Prior to Coronation night the queen and princess from the previous year make the school visits, then the first duty of the new royal pair on Thursday morning is to be ready for the 6:00 o'clock arrival of the royal car and its escorts. The king wears his uniform and the two young women wear dresses or suits plus beaded baldrics in the colors of their royal robes and their day crowns.

Each school prepares for the royal arrivals, and the children are gathered either outside or in a gymnasium. The visits last about ten minutes and are fast paced. The scream of the siren (carefully turned on just as the cars pull up to the school) announces the arrival of the royal party. The hands of children and teachers are shaken as the royals move to the front of the gathering to greet the waiting principal. The king makes a few remarks about Fiesta and then presents awards for good citizenship or grades (predetermined by the individual principal and teachers) to several of the students. The king then does a bit of sleight-of-hand trickery and makes comical remarks about the ineptitude of his aides and finally brings forth a bag of "gold King's coins" to be distributed to all the students.

The royal women do not have a verbal part in the presentation, and they stay in the background or on the sidelines while King Antonio goes through his routine. However, often the focus switches to the young women as they hand out the awards, because they usually kiss the children, who then giggle or offer a hug in return. When commenting on a queen's qualities, many refer to someone being a "good queen because she is so down to earth and will be good with the kids." "Being good with kids" echoes the underlying purpose of Coronation as a debut: endogamous marriage and reproduction of the next generation of the social class. One queen spoke of how important it was to her to be really "up" for the visits and ready for interactions even though she was exhausted from lack of sleep. Another said, "I loved going to the schools. The kids were such a blast. I can remember King Antonio when I was in grade school, and it was such a big deal. You thought they were real royalty up there. One little girl asked if Marie, the princess, were my daughter. Children said, 'Are you really the queen?'"

Once the new queen is crowned and takes over the royal visits, the now-former queen has no formal or informal duties after her year, although some have become mistresses of the robes many years later. The contrast between the achieved status of the male and the ascribed status of the female seen in the Coronation chairman and his mistress of the robes is also applicable to the president and the queen. The queen is always chosen on the basis of her lineage. A royal family background is even more important in the selection of princess and queen than for the duchesses. The 1987 queen had twenty-six family members, both male and female, who had taken part, as children or adults, in previous Coronations.

The stated requirement for a queen is to be unmarried and a resident of Bexar County for three years preceding the election. In an effort to democratize the position of queen, there is a direct election with the winner determined by the highest number of points. Nominees for queen are selected from the previous year's in-town duchesses and are voted on by the entire Order. Each member votes for three young women in order of preference on a secret ballot, presented in person (with the exception of non-resident members) to the president. The meeting at which the ballots are received is held in August in the chapel of the Alamo, the only fitting site for the most important act of the Order of the Alamo. The Order reproduces the social order through Coronation so the queen must be "born" in the Alamo, the "cradle of Texas liberty" (Brear 1995: 77–80). After a brief meeting, the members retire to the Menger Hotel for sustenance, while the privy council (the president and Coronation and in-town court chairmen) and treasurer go to a reserved hotel room. After verifying that all ballots have been submitted by members in good standing (no unpaid dues), the council counts the votes, with first choices receiving five points, three points for second choices, and one point for third choices. "The three young ladies receiving the highest number of points, regardless of whether a majority or not, shall, in the order of the number of points received, be candidates for the Queen-ship" (Order of the Alamo 1990). The runner-up becomes princess (although in the past the queen selected her princess), but discourse focuses on the shared quality of the two positions in order to lessen the compensation-prize feeling. When asked what percentage of the membership actually votes, one board member said, "In a good year we might get 60 percent turnout."

The privy council members then visit the home of the first candidate to ask if she will accept the honor. The visit is rarely a surprise, for usually families let it be known that they are willing to "run" for queen. Although ostensibly the young woman is the candidate, actually the whole multi-generation family runs for queen. The former queens interviewed fully realized that they were not elected as individuals. In recognition of her father's well-known, long-term Order activities, one daughter said that essentially "Dad is running for queen." However, families do give credit to the daughter herself. A father stated that he was "thrilled when she was elected. After all, she is my only daughter. I have worked hard for the Order and it was a great honor to the family, and for her. She made a great queen."

Beautiful and charming queens (and duchesses) are considered a pleasant bonus, but it is well known that "if you are from the right family you could be cross-eyed and have three legs and still win." The "election of the queen" is an oxymoron for the Queen of the Order of the Alamo is always an ascribed position. She is the young woman with the oldest family line, the most female royal relatives, and the father who has been the most active in the Order. If all those qualifications are met, the primary consideration for both princess and queen is whether the family can afford the reported $50,000 or more necessary to cover the cost of being queen. Included in that figure are the royal robes, the other clothes needed for the social events, the cost of the queen and princess's luncheon for two hundred guests, and the cost of the gifts presented as part of noblesse oblige. "The girl who was invited to be queen, oh, of course you wanted a lovely queenly person, but you also had to look at her father's bank account – you had to guess at it – to see if her parents were capable of taking on that kind of thing."

Just as in the case of nominations for membership in the Order, relatives and friends now write letters on behalf of a particular girl urging the recipient's consideration when voting. In the past, queens were elected only by the board of directors without direct input from the membership. The identity of the queen and princess was a closely guarded secret, with private bow rehearsals and dressmaker fittings scheduled so that there would be no possibility of the queen or princess running into one of the duchesses. "It was really secret. And it was more fun frankly. Ninety percent of the audience, and back then 90 percent of the audience really knew all about Coronation, really didn't know who the queen was until she started down the ramp." The newspaper ran teasers about the possible identities although only the Coronation families would have any idea of the identity. Some of the campaigns have been marked by intense competition and bitterness, a situation the Order tries to avoid. It also tries to bypass having two equally qualified families run against one another. The latter problem has been avoided in the past by asking one of the families to run the daughter a year early (skipping the duchess year) or to wait a year.

The results are not predictable when two families of reasonably good credentials run against one another, but if an old family runs against one with only one royal generation the outcome is inevitable.[14] Although this may be seen as a detriment to newer families, it actually provides an entree into the higher echelons. Even a first-generation duchess can be princess in a year when a young woman from one of the core families runs for queen and no one of lesser status wants to run against her. The newer family then can let it be known that they are willing to undertake the expenses of the princess position. By the next generation sufficient precedent will have been established for the princess's child to automatically be a duchess and possibly even fill a higher rank.

The Court Members

The aristocratic character of Coronation can be seen throughout the makeup of the court. Many of the old families intermarried, and cousins are often members of the same court. It is said that at any one time at least ten of the people on stage are interrelated. The small children who make up the queen's and princess's entourages are usually their nieces and nephews, and pages are often related to someone on stage or on the board of directors. Many informants have strong memories of being a ramp page at seven or eight and dreaming for weeks of wearing "beautiful big dresses" when they are grown-up. Some practiced the bow when young, either with other girls or as a form of entertainment for their parents. A princess remembered making trains for her Barbie dolls to wear on their shoe-box floats.

Most women from the old families have grown up knowing that they would be duchesses. "It was never a question of 'if' but 'when.'" Being a page and then a duchess is simply part of the family tradition. The activities of the children and the strong emphasis on tradition create an atmosphere in which attainment in hierarchical ranking seems normal. Edward Shils notes the importance of tradition in creating normative behavior. "There is more to it than the mere givenness of Tradition. Human beings become attached to the given. It becomes to them the 'natural way' to do things" (Shils 1981: 200). It is natural to become royalty and to enjoy the benefits therein. A woman who recently moved into one of the Coronation neighborhoods pointed out the effects of tradition-invoked normative behavior.

> Somehow I am not offended by _____ talking about the real ermine on her train because she was not showing off. The whole thing is just part of who she is, it's just how she grew up. There's almost an innocence about it. It's not said to impress or to shock. It's not like when some of the women who married into the old families talk about Coronation. Then it's "I can and you can't." It's the difference between something that is part of who you are versus who you wanted to be.

Naturalness or normativeness is part of Bourdieu's habitus, that generative principle that leads to reproduction of difference. Bourdieu asserts that habitus is even the basis of the transfer of motor habits within a social class (Bourdieu 1984: 175). An older Order member loves to tell the story of a visitor to the

Coronation who asked how the girls could be so graceful in the heavy gowns. The Order member responded, "Our girls are born knowing how to walk into a drawing room."

Duchesses and Dukes

The ideal court is made up of twenty-four duchesses and dukes, equally divided between the in- and out-of-town courts. However, numbers may be changed according to existing circumstances, since the guiding principle of court selection is aristocratic: the young women with the oldest family connections to the Order always have priority. The only formal requirements for an in-town duchess is that "each be an unmarried lady who has been a resident of Bexar County, Texas, for at least one year immediately preceding her selection," while there are no formal requirements for the out-of-town duchesses (Order of the Alamo 1990). Members of the in-town court are primarily daughters or granddaughters of members. If there are too many candidates in a given year, adjustments are made so that all old family daughters get to be duchesses. Either the balance is changed (i.e., ten out-of-town and fourteen in-town), or some of the girls simply wait and do it the following year. Both demographics and the economy in general affect the number of potential duchesses. Mothers have been known to count how many potentially royal peers their seven-year-old daughters have in order to plan ahead and forestall any conflicts by putting their daughter up as duchess either a year earlier or later. Several recent court chairmen mentioned the recession as a factor in receiving fewer applications for the royal ranks. If there are not twelve available and willing daughters in a given year, daughters of friends who are closely connected, but not actually Order members, are asked. Residency in one of the three older neighborhoods is one of the most important qualification for becoming a duchess when family members do not belong to the Order of the Alamo, just as it is for becoming a member of the Order. Long-term relationships with Order members or their families are necessary: wealth alone will not garner an invitation, although the family certainly must be able to afford the costs of the robes and attendant expenses. However, some of the most recent duchesses have not strictly followed this pattern. These new developments will be covered in the last chapter.

Out-of-town duchesses theoretically represent different towns, generally from Texas although occasionally from other states and even other countries.[15] Apparently the out-of-town court was initially used as a device to promote San Antonio. One chairman pointed out that the Order's primary obligation is to make sure that the "girls have a great experience. We want the out-of-town girls to have a great time here and to really like San Antonio."

However, most of the visiting duchesses actually have family connections to San Antonio, generally through the maternal line. Many San Antonio women who marry and move away want their daughters to be duchesses in order to spend time in the mother's home town and get to know some of her old friends. If there are not enough out-of-town "insiders," then the word goes out that the Order is willing to accept an "outsider" if someone in the Order will sponsor her. This is the one situation in which an invitation to be an out-of-town duchess can almost "buy her way in." All three of Texas billionaire Ross Perot's daughters have been out-of-town duchesses, although he had no San Antonio familial connections. One of Perot's friends knew someone in the Order and recommended that the first daughter be included since she was "lovely" and her father was "a nice man." Once a sister has been a duchess, a precedent has been set and invitations are invariably sent to other eligible sisters.

There are subtle differences in the presentation of the in-town and out-of-town courts that reveal the importance of being from San Antonio. The out-of-town duchesses enter from side entrances, while the in-town debs have a long walk down the center ramp in addition to the time on the stage, making their time in the spotlight longer. The in-town duchesses make their bows singly before climbing to their seats, while the out-of-town duchesses usually make their bows in pairs as they leave at the end of the Coronation. The distinction was clearly marked by the out-of-town duchesses wearing identical dresses in different colors in the 1930s, acting more as a background for the individualized dresses of the in-town girls. Sometimes they did not even stay on stage when the in-town duchesses appeared. Photographs of the out-of-town duchesses were not included in the illustrated programs published by the Order until 1958.

The aristocratic families have so many royal connections that Coronation is an integral part of family history. When asked if she knew how many family members had been in Coronation, one woman replied, "Six queens, seven princesses, four mistresses of the robes, and one past president. I can't tell how many duchesses because there are just tons of cousins. There is no way . . . I would just have to go back forever. The first queen and princess were daddy's cousins in 1911, so they've been in since then." Similar statements can be made by many royal women. Other aristocratic families downplay all of the royal relatives, but, when the daughter's friends start talking in high school about someday being in Coronation, the parents acknowledge the probable future involvement. Still others who are not from the old families, but who live in the proper neighborhoods and whose friends are, may attend Coronation when in grade school to see friends as pages. When asked if she had been jealous, one woman responded, "I don't think I was . . . I just felt proud. 'That's my friend up there.'" By the time her godmother was in the court, she started "really getting . . . Oh, I hope I get to do all of this" even though her father was not a member. When she was the appropriate age, she was invited to be a duchess because her godmother, neighbors, and friends were all involved in Coronation and there was an available spot for a new participant.

In contrast to those who always knew they would be, or at least wanted to be, part of the event, other young women have conflicting feelings about participation in the decidedly elitist and costly event. Some only accept the invitation after much thoughtful consideration or after sufficient familial pressure. Many young women do see it simply as a big party, but others approach the decision most seriously. A duchess whose family connection was through a stepparent had great doubts about accepting her invitation. She was worried about the cost since she had siblings in college and could not imagine herself doing all of the social things or being in the public eye so much. After intense discussion over a twelve-hour period with an older friend, who felt that it had been "the greatest experience," she did consent. At the time of the interview (prior to the Coronation), she was nervous about doing the bow and made numerous kidding remarks about the disastrous topple she expected to take, but she loved her dress and was surprised at how much she was enjoying all of the parties.

Some young women are asked to be duchesses but choose not to because they have serious boyfriends and do not want to take part in the extended round of parties. Others would rather have a new car or a trip to Europe, typical alternatives offered by parents who do not feel that having a daughter be a duchess is necessary for the family's social standing. "There is a certain power in knowing that you could have done it and chose not to," stated a woman who attended a prestigious West Coast girls' school and turned it down for political reasons. Some are committed to graduate school or beginning a career immediately after college and do not have the time to play dress-up. And some would-be duchesses recognize the inherent elitism and question their own participation. The most introspective Old Guard informant was deeply concerned about the political implications of Coronation. She also hesitated to make the time commitment and postpone pursuing a graduate degree. However, she did accept the invitation because "I think that it was decided for me, but not necessarily in a negative way. I am very close to my parents and this was something they really wanted me to do . . . mostly my father. I knew that he would take such joy and pride out of being able to do that."

Family, directly or indirectly, greatly influences a daughter's participation. Grandmothers often have strong feelings about seeing a beloved granddaughter wearing the royal robes. Stories are told of hospitalized grandmothers being wheeled in to Coronation in wheelchairs or even on gurneys. The great-granddaughter of one of the presidents of the Order of the Alamo had grown up knowing of her family's participation, but since she did not attend the same schools as most of the future duchesses Coronation was not a preoccupation. By the time she was duchess age, she had been an active war protester for several years and "a serious student since Kent State." On graduation her mother gave her a choice: she could make a traditional debut through the German Club or could do Coronation. She did not want to do either but complied with her mother's wishes, just as her father participated in social events. "Father did it for mother, as I did. I chose Coronation as the lesser of two evils" because it was possible to participate just for Fiesta week, not the six-month period required of the German Club debutantes. She was dating someone seriously and "was not interested in participating in it as a marriage market." She tried to keep her distance at first, remaining in Europe as long as possible even when the dress designs were passed out in September. Much to her surprise, by the time it was all over she ended up "having a wonderful time."

Royal memories last: a ninety-one-year-old woman who was a duchess in 1919 remembers seeing her sister in the 1916 court and feeling "so proud." She remembers her own dress and the names of the queen and her escort. She "loved it . . . going out to all of the parties," and, on being asked about the bow, immediately smiled and said, "Well, I did all right." Such long-held royal memories are viewed by many of the royal families as evidence of the lifelong importance of participating in Coronation. Others, however, are careful to point out that, while they loved being in it themselves and were delighted that their children took part and enjoyed it, "It should not be the most important thing in life." "Being a duchess is fine as long as you don't make too big a deal out of it." One informant told of a duchess who tearfully said, "I've waited twenty-two years for this night," as she waited for her entrance. The informant was distressed that the young woman had no sense of perspective on the relative importance of being a duchess for a week. She went on to voice her concern over duchesses of recent years who "cannot seem to get on with their lives," but who continue to go to round after round of parties and reminisce about their royal year.

Some members, even of the most aristocratic families, sardonically tell of middle-aged women who still work their royal titles into conversations with new acquaintances, or who continue to display large photographs of themselves in their royal robes in their living rooms. Headlining an obituary with a reference to a court or title is considered by some to be the ultimate in a lack of perspective. The mother of a recent duchess talked about how much fun her daughter had during the social season and Fiesta week. The daughter became a graduate student at a northeastern university the semester following her debut, but always got together with some of the other duchesses when she came home for a visit. After several semesters, the young woman stopped looking up the friends. When asked why, she replied that they just did not have much in common anymore. She felt that many of her friends were just stagnating – that they had not gotten on with real life after Coronation. The mother said that she was proud of her daughter and quoted the note she had attached to a gift for her daughter when she was a duchess. "I hope your life is so successful that they do not mention which court you were in until the third paragraph of your obituary."

Obituaries of Order of the Alamo members may mention their membership, and perhaps the offices held, but being a duke does not warrant a headline. Dukes do not seem to have many memories of conflicts or longings since their participation is more restricted and their roles are quite different. The duchesses are usually selected as representatives of their families, not as individuals, and their personal characteristics are not of primary importance. Like queens, beautiful and personable duchesses are desirable but these qualities are not required. The dukes for the in-town court are all members of the Order. While membership in aristocratic families is quite important for membership in the Order, the young men are not familial representatives as are the women. Family is the basic unit of elite identity, and the form of introduction of the duchesses emphasizes that the royal women are representatives of the family. Each duchess is introduced by her name and court title: "Her Grace Margaret Ann McCloud of the House of Smith, Duchess of the Sacred Chapel of Les Invalides." Breaking the name into two sections, the first and middle names followed by the surname preceded by "house of," emphasizes the middle name, often the mother's maiden name.

In addition to the emphasis on family names in the introductions, the parents of all of the royal women wear miniature trains, tying them visually to their royal daughters. The "tags" are about six inches long, made by the dressmakers of the same material and jewels, with one of the motifs from the full-scale trains worked in smaller stones. They are instantly recognizable on the formal black coats of the fathers, and most mothers wear gowns in complementary colors to draw attention to their bejeweled identification tag. They are worn at all Fiesta events, even to the informal events, creating a visual reminder that the wearers are members of the Coronation set and that they have both the lineage and the economic ability to participate. There is no equivalent signifier for the dukes' parents.

The dukes are simply introduced as "Mr. Edward James Jones" in accordance with their role as escorts, not as representatives of their families.

Although the dukes are present at all of the official events to act as escorts, attention is definitely on the young women in the royal robes. The dukes often wore costumes related to the theme until after World War II, but since then have always worn formal dress, creating a uniform that partially obliterates individual characteristics (Joseph 1986) and emphasizes the supportive role of the males.

The duke's only duty during Coronation is to meet the duchess at center stage and escort her to the small pedestal. He then exits until the crowning of the queen, when he slips back onto the stage. An eighty-four-year-old former duke diplomatically stated that "It was no reflection on the girls, but I thought the whole thing was kind of dull. Had to do a lot of waiting while girls were showing off their dresses. We had to do a little nipping to pass the time behind the scenes." However, he too was influenced by family, for he felt that he had to become a member of the Order and to participate as a duke because of his royal female relatives. "As a son, as a brother, I didn't feel that I could just flat say 'no.'"

The primary duty of the unmarried Order members is to act as duke/escort for the in-town duchesses (out-of-town duchesses may choose their own escorts, usually from their own cities) throughout Fiesta week. Dukes sometimes escort their duchesses to the parties during the rest of the long social season, but, since one of the purposes of participation is for the young women to meet many different men, the duke and duchess are only paired officially during the one week. There are parties every night and several luncheons in addition to the parade, and the dukes make sure that the duchesses get to all of the events, carrying the trains whenever needed (Figure 6). Some men act as dukes repeatedly before finally ending their careers by marrying or declaring themselves overage. A few men have been dukes so many times that the final young woman is known as "his last duchess" even years later.

Young men become eligible to be dukes for the in-town court duchesses on the basis of their status as unmarried Order members, but they are chosen by the young women on the basis of their personal characteristics. The in-town duchesses are given a list of eligible Order members and draw numbers for the order in which they get to choose. Dukes, as well as princes and prime ministers, consorts to the princess and queen, are valued by the young women for their reliability and companionship, not for their appearance or romantic potential. Experienced dukes are generally considered more desirable because they can guide the young woman through the unknown. A sense of humor is highly desirable as well as the ability to make the duchess feel confident and comfortable. The mother of a duke told him, "Remember that your job is to make your duchess feel like a real princess in a fairy tale." Although many marriages result from the social season, duchesses do not

Figure 6. Mothers tell their sons that their primary duty is to make their duchesses "feel like real royalty." The train of the 1922 Queen of the Court of Aladdin is gallantly carried for her by a member of the Order of the Alamo. Courtesy: Witte Museum.

always marry their own duke, even though the qualities that they look for in selecting a duke are those many women see as necessary in husbands.

The emphasis is on endogamous pairing, but the long debutante social season does provide some opportunities for "outsiders" to marry into the core group, particularly for young men. All of the debutantes must have escorts to the evening parties given during the season, and there should be additional single men at dances to form a "stag line" to ensure that all of the honored women dance as often and with as many partners as they desire. Therefore, young men who are not of the immediate social group, but who do have good credentials, are put on a list of potential guests. According to one young man who was on the guest list for three years in San Antonio, "It is possible to eat and drink well for six months and to meet a lot of attractive women just for the price of a tuxedo and a nice suit or blazer." Female friends of the debutantes, usually from college, are invited to the social events, as well as local friends who are peripheral to the core group but are still perceived as sharing the same values and attitudes. However, males have a better chance of breaking through the group boundary because of the constant need for extra dancing partners.

An interesting variation in the male/female roles of the dukes and duchesses is in the emic interpretation of the formal court bow. A duchess bows at center stage facing her duke, presenting a profile to the audience so that the full effect can be appreciated. As she sinks onto her folded legs and lowers her torso into the desired parallel-to-the-floor position, she turns to look at the audience just at the lowest point (Figure 7). Although the bow appears to be to the duke, who bends slightly at the waist and extends his hand in case she needs help getting up, the duchesses do not view it as an obsequious act. Duchesses from the past to the present talked of the bow as a physical feat to be performed for their parents or for the audience as a whole. The bow does take strength and flexibility, particularly considering the weight and restrictions of the royal robes. The duchesses work at doing it well – gracefully, as low as possible, and rising without the need of taking the duke's hand. They exploit the physical difficulty of the exaggerated bow to demonstrate their personal abilities, not to create or mark asymmetrical relationships.

Youngest Participants

Children participate in the Coronation either as attendants to the president, the princess, or the queen, as pages, or as part of the entertainment. The president is attended by his children, even those in arms. The princess and queen each choose three or four nephews and nieces, godchildren, or children of close friends to be in their entourages. All of the children are dressed in costumes complementing those of the adults and must remain seated on the stage (although babies are taken backstage) for the rest of Coronation, usually about fifteen minutes. Even the tiniest girls wear long full skirts, while the little boys are usually in knee breeches and hose.

Pages are girls who either stand along the sides of the ramp to make sure that the trains do not get caught on anything or are on the stage to help arrange the trains.[16] The ramp pages are usually seven to ten years old, while the stage pages are in their early teens. The mistress of the robes chooses the pages from among her friends' and relatives' children and from letters sent to her asking that she consider including specific children. Both the ramp and stage pages are potentially needed, but as many as thirty-six pages may be used. The Order realizes that most of the girls love their small parts and they look forward to being part of the fairy-tale atmosphere when they are older. "I took my job very seriously and felt very important in my blue satin dress running around the stage fixing trains, getting water for the girls. Later I realized that my mother must have been dying and hoping that I would just stand still. But I loved it." The costumes are an important part of the appeal. They are identical and are usually fairly simple in design but long

Figure 7. The formal court bow is performed by one of the duchesses in the 1986 Court of Embellished Dreams. Courtesy: Institute of Texan Cultures, Zintgraff Collection.

and of dressy fabrics that the girls love. Women in their fifties and sixties often remember their page costumes with great fondness. "It had a band of gold lamé and a band around the bottom that had some pink sequins. It was shiny and it was beautiful! Our sandals were sprayed gold, and I have it [all] in the garage with my duchess dress." Still more costumed children may be included as part of the staging during the prologue or as part of the formal entertainment. The Court of Spanish Empire had fifty young children as part of the prologue because the mistress of the robes felt "it was important to continue life, continue tradition."

Conclusion

The Coronation chairman thinks about his Coronation for three or more years; the mistress of the robes spends two years in research and design; the dressmakers work on the royal robes over a six-month period; and the ballet mistress conducts bow rehearsals for eight consecutive Saturdays. The result of all this preparation is a two-hour event. The royal court will appear in their robes two more times during Fiesta, and the queen and princess continue their royal roles in visits to schools and hospitals. However, the effect of being in Coronation can last a lifetime. All female royalty are given gold pins by the Order as remembrances of their participation in Coronation, and many of the pins are worn annually during Fiesta until the end of the wearer's life. Even obituaries may be headlined with a reference to a royal position held decades earlier.

Participation in Coronation not only marks an individual's status, but also reproduces the status because the participant learns and internalizes her or his societal role, thus reproducing the class as a whole. Presentation in the royal court identifies the participant's family as part of the elite social class but also provides a space where they can make or maintain those social and economic connections that allow them to remain the elite. The institutionalized hierarchy found in the board of directors' "ladder" and the progression from ramp page to princess naturalize ascendancy.

Aristocratic daughters continue to make royal debuts because the event marks and creates ethclass boundaries under the auspices of supposedly superficial activities. In accordance with the ideology that the United States is "the land of equal opportunity," many members of the elite are not comfortable identifying themselves as such, but Coronation provides perceptible boundaries without verbalization. It creates a frame enclosing only those who belong to the sponsoring organization, the Order of the Alamo, or who wear the royal robes. The frame marks the elite's difference in accordance with Bourdieu's cultural capital, evidenced in the thematic text, music, setting, and royal robes of the ceremony that are carefully researched and include many esoteric references. "[A]rt and cultural consumption are predisposed, consciously and deliberately or not, to fulfill a social function of legitimating social differences" (Bourdieu 1984: 7).

The royal dresses and trains are the excuse for the display of cultural capital. They are also the most important part of Coronation because they are the means of transforming an average young woman into a child's idea of a fairy-tale queen. As young pages, girls wish for the day they can wear one of the glittering dresses. Parents share in the wish and willingly perpetuate familial participation in Coronation. While the stage setting is important, the live music impressive, and the entertainment may be enjoyable, the point of Coronation is the display of dresses and trains. The process of creating the robes and the ways in which they reify the royal aspirations are treated in the next chapter.

Notes

1. The traditional white dress worn for most debuts is often similar to a wedding dress. Some San Antonio young women have purchased wedding dresses to be used as deb dresses because they could not find an appropriate evening gown and they felt there was more choice among the bridal gowns. Usually some alteration is made so that they are not readily recognizable as wedding dresses. Often the young women plan to use the dress as a wedding dress later but rarely do so.

2. Mothers also present their daughters but to other females at the less expensive afternoon teas, not to mixed society. San Antonio has at least one elite women's social club that sponsors a social event for the debut of daughters and granddaughters.

3. "Debutant," meaning a male performer making his first appearance, was noted in 1824; however, the reference to male debutants was still used in the United States at least until the late 1870s (Ruth 1877: 22).

4. Many people, both members and nonmembers, think that San Antonio's German Club was named for the nationality of many of its founders. However, it probably was named for a "german," a form of cotillion or quadrille, an elaborate dance that involved the changing of partners under the leadership of the dance master. This type of dancing was popular at formal dances at the end of the nineteenth century (the German Club was founded in 1881) and into the next. By the 1920s etiquette books decried the difficulty of finding a capable cotillion master and so it slowly died out.

5. The openness of charitable debutante balls in terms of race and ethnicity undoubtedly varies from place to place. In San Antonio the Symphony Belles, daughters of financial supporters of the symphony, have included several young

Spanish-surnamed women recently, frequently the daughters of doctors, but no African Americans.

6. Many Hispanic young women have a quinceañera, a religious/social celebration for fifteen-year-olds. There are regional variations based upon the country of origin, but they all combine religious and social events. After a religious service in which the young woman reaffirms her faith, the honoree, her attendants and escorts, and many family members and friends go to a hall, where they are served a barbecue dinner followed by a dance. The honoree wears an elaborate dress, often reminiscent of a wedding dress, and the ten or more attendants usually wear matching colored dresses. There is always a presentation of the court and of the sponsors who helped pay for the event. The young woman's new adult status is most visibly marked by the boudoir doll clothed in a miniature replica of her dress, designed to be placed upon her bed or dresser, not to be played with.

Quinceañeras have become so widespread that a how-to book has been published. Michele Salcedo's *Quinceañera!* (1997) is subtitled *The Essential Guide to Planning the Perfect Sweet Fifteen Celebration* but is much more. She interviewed families and attended quinceañeras in cities with large Hispanic populations, including New York, San Antonio, and Chicago and includes a wide range of family stories and experiences throughout the book.

7. The school district does include a very low-income area and the schools, particularly the elementary schools, are ethnically mixed. Again, however, the public perception is that the students are all elite Anglos because those are the ones who receive public attention.

8. See Prudence Mackintosh's articles in the *Texas Monthly* collection (Mackintosh 1978a,b) for insights into the lifelong importance of shared experiences through Greek organizations and summer camp. The current top-ranked sororities, according to my informants, are Pi Beta Phi, Kappa Alpha Theta, and Kappa Kappa Gamma, and the fraternities are Phi Delta Theta, Sigma Alpha Epsilon, and Phi Gamma Delta.

9. The initial vote of the whole membership puts a democratic appearance on the membership process, but the board does still wield a great deal of power. Two members may agree to blackball all nominees until they are successful in getting their own candidates elected.

10. One of the new members is the mentally retarded son of a family held in high regard for their lineage and for their handling of their son's condition. The young man apparently has always been included in family activities, including being part of his sister's entourage when she was queen.

11. Several men pointed out current or past board members who were "first generation," but later I found out that most of those were married to former duchesses, therefore first generation for the male, but not for the female. However, an older member reported that the board of directors has often been made up of "people who have no connection, but made friends, were taken in, were interested in working, and did such a good job that they just moved right on up. That's gone on for years."

12. A Dallas scenic design company has made the sets for many years. Although the mistress, chairman, and set designer do consult on the design, there is no continued personal contact as there is with the female professionals – the artist, ballet mistress, and dressmakers. Therefore, I have not included the set designers in the analysis.

13. A favorite story told by several past presidents is that at the reception many people tell him how much more they liked this production than last year's, little realizing that the previous one was his as Coronation chairman.

14. I posed a hypothetical slate of two young women from old families, but one had a slightly longer royal lineage and the other's father had a longer history of active involvement in the Order. This seems to be the combination that causes the greatest consternation, and most said that their vote would depend on the individual families involved.

15. In 1921 the possibility of duchesses from Mexico was discussed but, "as it was thought the stage was too small, this matter was not gone into very fully" (Order of the Alamo [1925]). However, there were two duchesses from Mexico City in the early 1980s, relatives of an Order member, and one in the 1990s.

16. In the early years the footlights lined the ramp and trains and dresses could really get caught. A favorite "near disaster" story is of a train that had metallic threads in it and caused the old-style lights to arc, starting a small fire. The wearer is referred to as the duchess whose train "really caught the lights."

4

"Catching the Light" in the Royal Robes

In summarizing the elaborately designed and decorated clothing worn in the debutante pageants of Laredo, Tyler, and San Antonio, columnist Molly Ivins, asserting that she did know fabulous when she sees it, commented, "Texas debutantes are like Las Vegas or a thousand-pound cheese or a submarine sandwich as long as a football field. Doesn't matter whether you like it or not – you have to admit it's really something. Even if you can't define what" (Ivins 1991:196). She calls the events "sheer spectacles." The royal robes worn in San Antonio's Coronation are outstanding even within the exalted excesses of Texas. The gowns and trains are the central focus of the event since the identities of the queen and princess are no longer a secret, and the only drama is the possibility that a bow will be bungled or that a child on stage will behave unexpectedly. The royal robes are the real stars of the show.

The 1993 Coronation chairman acknowledged that there would be no Coronation without the gowns in his speech of thanks to the mistress of the robes at the conclusion of the Little Coronation at the Queen's Ball. The robes have their own aesthetic and can be quite beautiful, particularly when seen at a short distance when all of the intricate details and handwork may be appreciated. The royal participants, court members, and their families want to be in Coronation in order to mark their inclusion in the aristocratic elite, but more importantly because they want to wear the dresses and trains. Only the royal families, the aristocrats, may wear the dresses, and only the dresses so readily mark royal status. The dresses and trains may become more important than the individual wearer, a fact recognized by some of the participants. "If you debut at the German, the dress is just something you wear. If you do Coronation, the dress is the most important. You are inconsequential." Thus the royal robes became a dominant symbol in Victor Turner's sense of producing action and becoming the center of the interaction (Turner 1967: 47).

This chapter is full of Geertz's (1973) "thick description" in order to try to convey to the reader not only a sense of the importance of the dresses and trains, but also of their very physicality. They are large and heavy and dominate their space, whether on a worktable or on a body or in a storage box. The royal robes are multilayered: underneath are corsets, hoops, and petticoats. They are inherently three-dimensional since they must cover a moving body, but even the surface is multilayered, due to the decorative techniques of appliqué and beading. The robes are all-encompassing and pervasive: they cover not only the young women but also the stage. Conversely, they also supply the infrastructure of Coronation.

The royal robes are discussed as they change from being evening dresses into true luxury goods: "goods whose principal use is rhetorical and social, goods that are simply incarnated signs" (Appadurai 1986: 38). The gowns and trains signal specific class distinctions, just as did fashionable clothing and fabrics under the ancient sumptuary laws of Europe and Asia. The royal robes. with their tightly fitted bodices and long full skirts, also reinforce gender roles through their shaping of the wearer's body and their adherence to a gender-specific silhouette. Kopytoff's model of the biography of an object (1986) is used to trace the life of the light-catching Coronation robes from design to deposition. Finally, the apparent conflict, engendered by the increasing importance of the royal clothing, between keeping Coronation a "private party" and making the gowns and robes visually accessible to the public is discussed.

Parallels of European and San Antonio Royal Robes

Specialized clothing has long been associated with ritual events, particularly those involving royalty (Hayden 1987: 63; Kertzer 1988: 5; McCracken 1988: 11).[1] While royal clothing usually symbolizes power, Bernard Cohn discusses the phenomenon of clothing as literal authority among the Mughal. A leader would take off an article of his clothing (usually a long coat) and "place it on one of his subjects, as a particular honor" (Cohn 1989: 314).

The most important piece of specialized clothing is the crown, for it is a metonym for the monarchy and dates at least from the time of the Old Testament, when David is crowned after overcoming the Ammonites. Crowns of precious metals and valuable stones proclaim "the supremacy of the state and its titular head" (Clark 1986: 93–6). The Order of the Alamo queens have always worn crowns, although the Order did not purchase a set of crown jewels to be used annually until 1916. That set, used until 1926, featured rhinestones and glass emeralds and included a crown, a scepter with a mother-of-pearl handle, a necklace, and two bracelets. In addition, a girdle of rhinestones and glass emeralds, from which hangs a long narrow rhinestone panel, was worn by each queen from 1909 until the early 1920s. The new set of jewels featured faux marquisette and multicolored glass stones and included a scepter, necklace, bracelet, and a replica of a British crown. A much simpler crown and scepter with stars and crescent (a motif from the Order's crest) were purchased in 1948 but have now been replaced. Smaller "day" crowns are worn during royal visits to the hospitals and schools. The princess has always provided her own crown. Most princesses have crowns, usually of rhinestones, lamés and wires, made by people who specialize in the construction of Coronation headpieces. However, several years ago the mother of the Princess of the Court of Spanish Empire had a crown made of sterling silver mounted with amethysts, a copy of a crown worn by Queen Isabella of Spain.

In addition to crowns, Order of the Alamo royal robes and British court clothing are similar in that both are highly embellished with embroidered beadwork. Beads are among the earliest known ornamentation and range from those of bone or clay to pearl and semiprecious stones. The popularity and specific use of beads have varied spatially and temporally, but they have consistently been associated with ceremonial and royal occasions. Some of Henry VIII's clothing was "so heavily encrusted with diamonds, rubies and pearls that the underlying material was invisible" (Laver 1969: 86). However, Grant McCracken points to Henry's daughter, Queen Elizabeth I, with her girdles of pearls, necklaces of rubies, pearls, and gold, and gowns with golden embroidery, as the instigator of a new standard of consumption. Faced with difficulties from within and without the kingdom "Elizabeth exploited the expressive hegemonic power of things. . . . The supercharged symbolism of the monarch's court, hospitality, and clothing became the opportunity for political instruction and persuasion" (McCracken 1988: 11). Although the current Queen Elizabeth wears simple, even somewhat frumpy. daytime clothing, her evening clothes are elaborately embroidered with beads and seed pearls. But, more importantly, the sheer weight of her tiaras, necklaces, and earrings, "measured in pounds, not carats," proclaim her royal status (Hayden 1987: 76). The use of precious stones upon clothing and in jewelry has conspicuously marked royal power from Elizabeth I in the sixteenth century to Elizabeth II in the twentieth.

"Catching the Light"

Precious stones and metals connote power not only because of their inherent value but because of their reflective qualities – the ability to increase or intensify the highly desirable phenomenon of light.[2] Diamonds were not prized as precious stones until lapidaries in the thirteenth century learned to cut them to reflect the maximum amount of light and to create facets to refract light and separate it into discernible colors. Once that technological breakthrough was made, diamonds became highly valued for their fire and flash (Clark 1986: 76). Transparent precious stones, gold and silver, and pearls are all materials that reflect light and have been used for centuries to focus attention on subjects of value, from individuals to holy icons.[3] Light-reflecting royal clothing has been made of cloth woven with gold or silver threads since the time of the Assyrians (Lewis 1937). Gold leaf is extensively used in illuminated manuscripts and representations of holy figures, while precious metals and stones are used in reliquaries.

Similarly, San Antonio's royal robes have been enhanced with pearls, beads, sequins, and metallic threads since their beginning in 1909. Glass stones of varying sizes, shapes, and hues are used to outline or accent the designs on the San Antonio gowns and particularly on the trains to make the design more discernible to the audience. However, the most important quality of the stones is their ability to "catch the light." Dressmakers, mistresses of the robes, parents, and the royal women all talk about the need to catch the light. On stage at Coronation, the multiple stones refract the spotlights through the faceted glass so that the royal garments truly sparkle. As the women slowly climb to their pedestals, the undulations of the trains over the steps cause the reflecting lights to become animated. Photographs do not capture this miniature light show, for it is only under the stage lights that the rhinestones act as prisms. The trains do glitter in the sunlight during the Battle of Flowers parade, but the effect is somewhat lost in the daylight and against the shiny plastic paper used to cover the float. Although the heavy-handed use of stones can overpower the design, add undesirable weight, and cause accusations of ostentatiousness, the emphasis on catching the light and creating reflecting glory remains greatly important. Arraying important or sacred personages or icons in light-reflecting materials visually draws attention to them in the same pragmatic way that shining a spotlight on a featured player on stage does: it makes it easier for the eye to focus. More significantly, the use of light-reflecting materials creates an indexical relationship between the physical light and the stars or bright lights of the elite. James Amelang in his study of the development of patrician culture in Barcelona (1986) traces the use of light as a metaphor for the educated, the powerful, and the civic elite. He points out that the prehistory of the enlightenment vocabulary can be found in classical antiquity, particularly in the Platonic tradition. But the Bible, especially the New Testament, is the most important antecedent of this imagery. "Identification of sun and light with the revealed truth of Christian doctrine provided a firm intellectual grounding for the subsequent transfer of this imagery from divine to profane knowledge" (Amelang 1986: 137).

By the beginning of the eighteenth century, intellectuals had become "guiding lights," "clusters of stars," imbued with the "light of knowledge." "Not surprisingly, such splendid reflection was ... restricted almost exclusively to members of the elite. In fact, the urban nobility exhibited an insatiable craving for description in the imagery of sun and light" (Amelang 1986: 139). The imagery of lights and candles permeated poems and funeral orations and even descriptions of such brilliant and splendid affairs as the fetes and ceremonies of the patrician class in France as well as in Barcelona. "Metaphors of illumination continued to be used in the eighteenth century to set apart the distinctive knowledge and comportment deemed characteristic of elites throughout Spain" (Amelang 1986: 140). Amelang goes on to demonstrate the rise of the term *cultura* as the preeminent term to refer to the elite, but metaphors of light continue to be used to contrast the upper classes with those people of the shadows, the uneducated, the poor. Such figures of speech continue in importance for centuries and throughout Western nations and are symbolized by the use of reflective materials, both fibers and minerals, on the bodies or statues of the elite.

Costly fabric woven of metallic threads – cloth of gold – softly reflected large areas of light when used to clothe the elite. Precious metals and stones and materials from mirrors to insect wings have also been used to reflect light. *Abhla bharat*, or mirror-work embroidery, a technique of attaching small pieces of mica and, later, mirrors to fabric, was developed in India and Pakistan. India is also the source of the eighteenth-century concept of attaching iridescent beetles' wings to embroidery. In the following century and until the 1920s, the practice was also followed in England and America for fashion accessories and evening dresses (Thompson 1987: 21). Young women in Jackson County, Texas, in the 1880s are reported to have placed lightning bugs on the bodices of their black evening gowns between the lace and the lining (Taylor 1938: 192). No lightning bugs were used on the San Antonio robes, but iridescent peacock and pheasant feathers have both been used. A technique similar to the Indian mirror-work is also occasionally used on the San Antonio gowns or trains.

Light-reflecting lamés and sequins were frequently used on early Coronation gowns and trains, but the preferred embellishment has always been glass stones. Lamés and sequins reflect light, but they do not refract light as do diamonds and rhinestones – splitting it into different colors as it bounces from facet to facet.[4] Glass stones of innumerable shades, shapes and sizes are the preferred means of catching the light. Colored stones are frequently used in carrying out the design, but rhinestones – imitation diamonds – are the overwhelming favorite. Literally thousands of rhinestones may be used on a single train, for they not only catch the light but also animate it through faceting. Strings of rhinestones are used to outline every element of the design.

Embroidery, the act of embellishing fabric with threads or beads, has always marked leisure status because of the time involved, either of the maker, who must have servants to relieve her of daily chores and allow her the time for needlework, or of the craft specialist, who must be compensated (Schneider 1980: 329). Veblen states that, since hand labor is a more wasteful method of production than that of machine labor, "the marks of [it] come to be honorific" (Veblen 1934: 159). Marx, too, refers to the fact that human labor-power "creates value, but is not itself value" (Tucker 1978: 316). Glass stones are expensive and labor-intensive in terms of the handwork involved. All of the appliqué and beading is done completely by hand (although some of the stones are first glued into place to make the sewing easier). The dressmakers emphasize that the work has always been done in this manner and that it would be against tradition to cut corners.

Although the jewels used to embellish the San Antonio Coronation gowns are glass, not semi-precious stones, the intention is still to signal elitism through similarity to the clothing of European royalty and through the emphasis on extensive handwork. The encrusted gowns and trains mark the wearers as members of a specific socioeconomic group, and many declarations are made regarding the "unique" and "one of a kind" nature of the San Antonio robes.[5] The lavishness of the royal robes is in contrast to the relatively conservative lifestyle of most of the families of old wealth. Quietly expensive cars and clothing and comfortable older homes make up the general lifestyle of many court members. The royal robes seem to be an opportunity to ostentatiously provide evidence of family finances. They are also similar to classic European portraits in which the subject is swathed in yards of drapery that ennobles and dignifies the wearer (Hollander 1980: 79). The yardage demanded by the design of the gowns and trains surrounds the girls with evidence of abundance, of surplus. Veblen notes that the appearance of waste denotes ability to pay (Veblen 1934: 70). The limited number of times that the gowns are worn also can be read as wasteful.

However, there is more here than can be accounted for by Veblen, since most participants see the robes neither as conspicuous consumption nor as wasteful. Of course, this cannot be a categorical statement, for some families do use the robes as a medium through which they display their greater disposable income, but these seem to be a minority. Also, a few of the young women do feel that the money is wasted, but they participate anyway because of family pressure. More often, the decision to participate in Coronation is what Douglas and Isherwood (1979) term "normative consumption." Although the high cost is acknowledged, it is seen as another one of life's expenses. The cost of the robes is often compared to that of a "new car or a year's college tuition," a necessity for the aristocratic families. There is a stated concern that many of the old families who lost money in the 1980s Texas recession or who were never really wealthy will no longer be able to participate, but there is also disapproval expressed toward families who are suspected of going into debt over the price of a gown. Generally, parents or grandparents who pay for a dress and train (and all of the accompanying expenses) view the cost as both expected and worthwhile, for it marks the family's continued group identity.

History of the Royal Robes

Changes have occurred in both the form of the dresses and trains and in their decoration, but the royal robes have never been common or ordinary. The current state of glitter represents one end of a continuum of increasing sparkle on the royal robes.

Dresses

In the earliest years the dresses appear to be fashionable contemporary evening gowns and not costumes designed for the event, but most were still decorated with pearls, sequins, or other beads (Figure 8). Costume-type accessories were added in 1912, when the duchesses carried staffs decorated with ribbons and a theme-related motif on top. The first thematically based costume included harem pants worn in the 1922 Court of Aladdin (Figure 9). By the 1924 Court of Chivalry half of the duchesses wore medieval-style costumes. This new trend continued and was exemplified in the dress of the 1928 Duchess of Venice in the Court of the Mediterranean. The duchess's mother made the skirt of tulle and the newly popular cellophane, imitating the reflective quality of the Venetian canals. However, the dress still had a fashionable 1928 silhouette. Well into the 1970s, costumes that conformed to the theme and highly decorated evening gowns were both worn. The 1933 Court of India was made up of theme-related dresses, including tunics and pants, while the following year most of the dresses in the Court of the Midnight Sun appear to be similar to contemporary bias-cut evening fashions. The fashionably tight bodice and extremely full skirt silhouette of the 1950s and 1960s (Figure 10) was predominantly used until the mid-1970s when the skirt was somewhat reduced in width. The first designers who tried to pare down the bulk of the skirt were criticized for not following tradition. The tulle and chiffon popular in the 1950s and 1960s are fondly remembered

Figure 8. Queen Nana Davenport of the 1910 Court of Roses wears her queen's crown and girdle with an evening gown, not a specially designed court dress. Courtesy: Witte Museum.

Figure 9. While earlier trains had specially designed motifs, the Duchess of Aben in the 1922 Court of Aladdin was one of the first royals to wear a thematically designed costume. Courtesy: Witte Museum.

Figure 10. The silhouette of the full-skirted dress worn by Margaret Reynolds King
as Duchess of the Mysterious Night in the 1953 Court of Opera remained
popular until the 1970s. Courtesy: Margaret King Stanley.

by many older participants because the young women could move so much
more easily in the lighter-weight dresses. Velvet has been the fabric of choice
since the 1970s (because it can support the weight of increased beading),
and now it would be considered a break in tradition to go back to the lighter-
weight fabrics. The trains are backed with heavy satin.

In the last ten years, more variety has been introduced in the design of the
dresses themselves. Some dresses are based on historic clothing, as that of

the duchess in the Court of Spanish Empire (1991) who represented Spain's classic past and wore a softly draped, almost Grecian dress, while the Duchess of Tartessian Opulence wore a dress suggesting the long, fitted tunics of the tower of Knossos.

Trains

Royal garments from numerous origins include some form of train since excessive amounts of fabric have long denoted elite status. The long sleeves and trains of medieval Europeans trailed in the dust and could only be worn by someone with the resources to clean or replace the soiled garment. By the fifteenth century trains were so long and so heavily trimmed with stones and fur that they had to be carried by pages (Schnurnberger 1991: 128). The San Antonio trains have been decorated with sequins and paste or glass jewels from the earliest years. The San Antonio court includes pages, but they do not carry the trains; pulling the train is clearly the responsibility of the young woman herself except when climbing the stairs to the designated seat when the pages and dukes do help pull the trains. In the first decades the train length varied considerably according to the individual's preference. In the 1930s and 1940s and even into the 1960s, many trains were not separate pieces but were an extension of immensely full skirts (Figure 11). Separate trains are generally triangular in shape but may be rectangular or trapezoidal, and the lower edge may be rounded, scalloped, dagged, or cut into a variety of decorative shapes. The first queen's train (1909) had a standing high collar but was no longer than those of the duchesses. The following year the queen's train was far longer than anyone else's. The train of the 1912 queen had a crown embroidered on it as well as the decorative design along the edges. All trains are now six-and-one-half feet wide at the bottom but in the past were sometimes even wider. Current rules restrict the use of the official crest of the Order of the Alamo to the queen's train, and the length is set at fifteen feet for the princess and queen while duchesses' trains are limited to twelve feet. Such regulations are functional (wider trains are liable to fall into the orchestra pit) but are also similar to the sumptuary laws of Europe and Britain during the fourteenth to seventeenth centuries, "an attempt to preserve the distinctions in rank, reflected in dress" (Wilson 1987: 24). The restriction on the duchesses' trains visually maintains the court hierarchy. Additionally, the duchesses' trains always attach at the waist, while those of the queen and princess are attached at the shoulder via a standing Elizabethan or deMedici-type collar, which is part of a harness, boned and wired and attached around the wearer's waist under the dress. The princess and queen literally bear the weight of family representation upon their shoulders. The duchesses'

Figure 11. There is no separate train for Her Royal Highness Pauline of the House of Carrington, Princess of Ys and Maid of Honor to the Queen of the Court of Legends, 1941. Courtesy: Witte Museum.

trains may weigh up to thirty pounds, while those of the queen and princess may be seventy-five or more pounds each.

Themes

The dress and train are integral parts of the whole, but the trains create the ethclass identity. The trains are more than just glitz: through embroidery and beading they symbolically present the thematic models of attainment and beauty, the legacy of members of the elite. While the earliest trains always had some form of decoration and were made of a variety of fabrics, including tulle, satin, and chiffon, they did not contain the symbols of the theme until 1913. Only the titles of the members of the court, Duchess of Buttercup of the Court of Carnival of Flowers (1911), for instance, conveyed the theme. Slowly the trains began to have theme-related embroidered or appliquéd motifs highlighted with beads, such as a bouquet of flowers for the Duchess of Jonquil. Representation of the theme through the robes becomes increasingly important, and in the 1916 Court of Fairies everyone had wings and an appropriate motif on her train (Figure 12). The motifs gradually occupied a larger area on the train, and by 1927 the trains had become the focal point of the royal robes. The train of the Queen of the Court of the Butterflies (1917) was simply an enlarged three-dimensional butterfly (Figure 13).

With occasional flights of fantasy – Court of Fairies (1916) – nature-based themes reigned from the 1909 Court of Flowers to the 1932 Court of Light, after which it disappears until 1969, when it reemerges under the guise of science in the Court of Time and Space. The preoccupation with flowers and creatures from the world of nature parallels that of fancy dress balls or charity fairs, middle- and upper-class social events well established by the 1850s in England and the United States and continuing well into the next century (Gordon 1986: 61). Historical themes, however, are by far the most numerous. Even in the 1912 Court of Lilies, when duchesses were named for flowers, the dukes were named for figures in Texas history, such as Travis, Bonham, Crockett, and Austin. By the 1930s history became the dominant source of themes for Coronation robes, both mythical – Court of Olympus (1931) – and documented – Court of Imperial Russia (1937). Art and literature do occasionally emerge, for instance the Court of Legends (1941) and Court of Opera (1953), but historical themes, particularly those of Europe, form the basis of the majority of the courts to the present day (see Appendix).

The emphasis on historical or educational presentations reflects Coronation's beginnings at the height of the pageantry movement, whose basic premise was that pageants and tableaux were important means of

Figure 12. In the 1916 Court of Fairies the theme is carried out in the motifs on the train, in the wings, and on the staff of the Moth Duchess. Courtesy: Witte Museum.

constructing a popular view of history – an idealized view ignoring class and ethnic divisions and tensions in a community (Glassberg 1990: 1). Typical is the text from the 1936 Court of Adventure, a celebration of the Texas Centennial, which reads, "Alien peoples ... imbued with the spirit of

Figure 13. The train of the Queen of the Court of the Butterflies (1917) clearly embodies the theme. Courtesy: Witte Museum.

adventure and love of freedom have appeared from the east to claim the land . . . the hour of departure of the Indian has arrived" (Order of the Alamo [1939]). In the idealized historical account the nomadic tribes simply *depart* and the Texas of the white man is born. After unending toil in the wilderness and sacrifices by the settlers (but without shedding anyone's blood), a "new race is to be brought forth, a race whose character will be composed of the finer qualities and attributes of the peoples of their forefathers' countries" (Order of the Alamo [1939]). The ancestors of these royal participants are firmly established as the worthy conquerors, well deserving of their dominant position.

Coronation's pageantry does not disappear with the rest of the movement in the 1940s, but it does become somewhat more subtle or sophisticated in its handling of the Other. In contrast to the 1936 Texas history theme and its reference to the silent departure of nomadic Indians, three duchesses represented Indian groups in the 1967 Court of San Antonio de Bejar. The Duchess of Comanche Warriors combines a traditional view of Indians as savages with an almost revisionist understanding. The duchess symbolizes "the dignity and ferocity of a great Indian tribe. We see them as dreaded foes facing a growing white population threatening them with subjection and extermination. We also see them as a people fighting for their soil and their way of life trying to hold back the march of empire." The dress, with its various Indian symbols and a train "cut like a War Bonnet," "pays tribute to their rude virtues as men and unhappy fate as a people" (Order of the Alamo [1975]).

In the 1960s the themes and texts reference non-European countries and events in positive terms. The 1961 Court of the Americas, with duchesses representing countries from Chile to Canada, included the Duchess of Peru, "A fascinating composite of Indian and colonial past blending in the twentieth century." The positive influence of Mexico on the character of San Antonio is alluded to several times in the 1967 Court de Bejar as in the Duchess of Glittering Fiestas, "Glorifying the everlasting influences of the Mexican Republic." Mexico itself becomes the theme in the 1975 La Corte de la Tierra Mágica, which included duchesses of the Baroque Cathedral, Toltec Deities, and Lyrical Languages.

Historic themes provide a rich array of story lines and motifs to be worked into the designs of the royal robes, but they also lead to incongruities and bowdlerization. The Court of San Antonio de Bejar (1967) included a Duchess of the Mondragon Tree, but not as an example of nature. Instead, she represented vigilante justice under an ancient Spanish oak. The train was simple in design, clearly showing a jeweled bare-branched oak tree with a gold noose hanging from a bare limb (Figure 14). The text explained

Figure 14. The Duchess of the Mondragon Tree in the 1967 Court of San Antonio de Bejar is attended by her duke at the reception following Coronation. Courtesy: Institute of Texan Cultures, Zintgraff Collection.

"Vigilantes kept a lookout for horse thieves and cattle rustlers. When they found one, they strung him up without further ado from a Spanish Oak on Flores Street. The tree was known as 'The Law of The Mondragon Tree.'" Apparently neither the mistress nor the duchess felt uncomfortable with such a stark image of death decorating the train. The 1991 Court of Spanish Empire provided a more subtle reference to death in the Duchess of Empires Reclaimed. The mistress of the robes pointed out that the chain design on the train was an enlarged version of the gold chains worn as trophies and found on the bodies of the men who had gone down with a ship. She did not seem to recognize the incongruity of using chains associated with dead bodies on the train of the young woman. She only saw the chains as a beautiful design and not as a symbol of greed and death. A straightforward lack of recognition of the incongruity of putting images of death on a deb's dress seems to be the only explanation for these two examples. Perhaps the emphasis on research and the subsequent hundreds of hours spent poring over sources created the classic inability to see the forest for the trees.

The Court of Spanish Empire (1991) and the Court of the Age of Discovery (1997) provide examples of the almost naive bowdlerization of history by the creators of the designs and texts. The selection of Spain as a theme provided a particularly rich array of events and motifs, which allowed San Antonio elite to identify with a glorified Spanish history culminating in Spain as conqueror and abstracter of the wealth of the New World. The royal household members were named for periods of Spanish history, from the ancient Tartessos to the eighteenth-century "Age of Reason." As in the pageantry tradition, at no time was reference made to any war, disease, ethnic strife, or political conflict – elements of the history of most countries. Rather, the narration was filled with references to "zenith of power," "time of prosperity," and "new zest for creativity." Even the Visigoths were characterized as monarchs with artistic tastes, not as the barbarians and invaders that they were. The out-of-town court depicted "Spain's global dominions," the result of Columbus's arrival – "the greatest revolution ever effected in the history of mankind." Columbus's discovery is read as the beginning of attainment, not as the beginning of loss. The out-of-town duchesses represented all of the categories of wealth that the conquerors extracted: from precious metals, Duchess of Empires Reclaimed; to culture, Duchess of la Cordilla de los Andes; to the environment, Duchess of Jade-Green Depths.

The 1997 Age of Discovery court, tracing the development of Renaissance exploration, shows a similar desire to ignore, or simply to be unaware of, the implications of the text or costumes. While the Andean empire is honored with its own duchess, "glittering in the ceremonial robes of the divine Inca," the bloody European conquest is simply referred to as "Pizarro's conquest of the Inca brought undreamed riches to Spain." Mexico's Aztec empire is also honored with its own duchess and glowing descriptions of "magnificent capital city . . . intense beauty . . . majestic shrines and palaces." Again the bloodiness of Cortés's conquest is ignored. The only reference to Cortés's military actions is "his pillage of Aztec gold and treasure led to the downfall of an empire."

Obviously images on the train should not portray the bloody battle between Cortés and Moctezuma or the death and disease brought by Spain to the New World, but pageantry's idealization of history does seem rather naive in today's world. A traditional reading of history with an emphasis on conquest and change is, however, somewhat understandable in a mistress of the robes or Coronation chairman who last took a history course twenty years ago. Pageantry themes based on literature and art do not seem to have as many pitfalls, so why are the historical themes so prevalent? While glory and beauty can easily be presented in courts based on music or art, examples of power are most available in history, particularly traditional history. Perhaps power issues are, at least subconsciously, an inherent part of the class consciousness preserved by wearing the royal robes. The increased emphasis on heavily researched historical themes in the last thirty years does correlate with the gradual loss of Anglo political control in San Antonio.

The two years of research and the extravagance of the costumes and set make the presentation comparable to Renaissance court spectacles mounted to celebrate weddings, births, and the anniversaries of reigns. They included masquerades, pageants, dances, and tableaux. The spectacles were created to impress the spectators and to elevate the stature of the sponsors (Baur-Heinhold 1967: 7; Clarke and Crisp 1981: 126; Strong 1984: 3). Classical ballet originated in the court spectacles, and it, as well as classical song, is the favorite entertainment for the Order of the Alamo's Coronation. The Renaissance spectacles were often based on historical events, such as the one arranged by Charles V of France at a banquet for the Holy Roman Emperor and his son, which featured the capture of Jerusalem (Gascoigne 1968: 89). "Mythohistorical" themes are increasingly important in San Antonio's Coronation, just as they are at the celebration of real crownings. The themes "distort time and thereby accentuate awareness of it. They proclaim the continuity of past and present. This distortion identifies the Queen and her family with the traditions of the realm, that is, the timeless moral order" (Hayden 1987: 5).

Research

The historically based themes create a need for research on both the theme itself and the way in which it can be carried out through the royal robes. By

Figure 15. Real shells decorate the train of the Duchess of Abalone in the 1923 Court of the Sea. Courtesy: Witte Museum.

the 1960s an increasing amount of time was spent by the mistress of the robes in this research. Although many of the early Coronation texts did include arcane information, this characteristic was intensified when extended periods of time were spent in research. The text read by the lord high chamberlain is full of detailed factual information to demonstrate the erudition of the researcher and her audience. Many titles of court members became more rarefied – instead of the earlier Duchess of Dolphins there is the Duchess of the Bold Pursuits of Pizarro. Even when the themes are based on "lighter" subjects, the transposition to royal robes and titles usually contradicts the intent of the theme. The Court of Festivals (1968), apparently one of levity, included the Duchess of Gala Renaissance Celebrations, not a title to be taken lightly. Once the heavy hand of research touches a theme, attempts at frivolity are submerged. The Court of Never Neverland (1983) was based on children's stories and set in a nursery. This was to be a light-hearted return to childhood memories, but it became a lesson in symbols and history when the duchess representing Little Bo-Peep was introduced as "Immortalizing the Enchantment of the Gentle Lamb, Duchess of Faithful Obedience," and the narrator related that the source of the nursery rhyme was a poem written to Mary Queen of Scots. The seriousness was exacerbated by the white velvet train with its flock of sheep outlined in rhinestones. "Their faces had jeweled pearshape rhinestone eyes, ears of crystal roquale beads and pink crystal jeweled noses" (Order of the Alamo [1975]).

Thematic Display

Once all of the research is completed, the problem is to transfer that esoteric information onto the trains. The question of how to represent the topics of the Court of Mysterious Worlds (1966) or Court of the Tudor Rose (1973) upon the trains becomes more difficult than for the earlier courts of nature or myths. The Duchess of Abalone in the Court of the Sea (1923) simply attached shells to netting to create her thematic train (Figure 15). The Duchess of Egypt, portraying the legend of the Ptolemys in the Court of Legends (1941), had pyramids embroidered in sequins on her train. The current trains are laden with carefully researched motifs individually outlined with the reflective stones, making them heavier in both iconography and weight. Virtually the entire surface of the train is now densely embellished.

What design could personify the Duchess of Hispania Nobilissima or even the simple sounding Duchess of Stories of the Stouthearted? Several different approaches to thematic design can be seen through the years. Most common have been clearly understood symbols, a Chinese dragon on the train of the Duchess of Jade in the 1926 Court of Jewels or keys and the Tower of London for the Duchess of Guarded Towers in the 1960 Court of Theatre (Figure 16). Many trains in the 1950s and 1960s had pictorial narratives. The Duchess of Brazil in the 1961 Court of the Americas depicted virtually all of the geographic and cultural highlights of that country on her train.

In the shimmering mirrors and jewels of the train was seen the incredibly beautiful harbor of Rio, with Pão de Açúcar mountain, the huge sentinal in moss green lamé, at the entrance of Guanbara Bay. One could follow Copacabana Beach and the glittering avenues of the lighted metropolis to the summit of Corovado, where the renowned figure of Christ the Redeemed seems to be perpetually blessing the city (Order of the Alamo [1975]).

By comparison the Duchess of Persian Gardens in the Court of Phantasy (1962) was shortchanged with only mountains and cypress and almond trees depicted on her train (Figure 17).

The most recent design approach is what art historian Judith Sobre terms "invented iconography with a surfeit of motifs with no apparent meaning" (pers. comm.). The hours of research result in knowledge of many motifs taken from architecture or the fine arts, personal appearance, historical events, and geographic space, which are combined to create the design of the train. The 1991 queen's train included motifs based on the Chains of Navarra, the Stripes of Córdova and Aragon, the Castle of Castile, the crown of the Queen of Spain, and the Bourbon fleur-de-lis: a weighty train indeed (Order of the Alamo 1991). Depending on the combined skills of the mistresses of the robes, court artists, and dressmakers, the designs may be pleasing to the eye and readily inform the audience of the relationship to the title and theme or may be unattractive in terms of balance and proportion and leave the viewer wondering why the motifs were picked in the first place. Several of the recent mistresses have been careful to explain the meaning of the design elements to the duchesses so that they will fully understand what they are representing. The Duchess of Splendid Palaces in the Court of Venice (1965) wore a dress with typical medieval voluminous sleeves and her train had an architectural design of columns and windows (Figure 18). The text includes the information that the design elements were from the façade of the Cà d'Oro, a palace on the Grand Canal, but the viewer did not need to know that to see the thematic connection. A court artist felt highly complimented by an Order member's comment that it was the first time in years that he could see the relationship of the train's design to the theme without hearing the explanatory text. However, his appreciation of clarity does not appear to be a widely held aesthetic. The designs on some trains are so obscure that the narration must explain the significance. The train of the Duchess of Gods Dwelling in Nature in the Court of the Floating Kingdom (1979) had numerous forms that looked vaguely like large oriental mushrooms outlined in pearls and rhinestones. According to the narration these embellishments were "snow-laden pine trees, homes of Shinto spirits."

The increasing historicity and research make Coronation an excellent marker of class distinction for it is built on the attainments that make up Bourdieu's (1984) cultural capital: education, knowledge of the arts, and

Figure 16. The train for the Duchess of the Guarded Towers in the 1960 Court of Theatre relies on easily recognized symbols for its connection to the theme. Photo by the author.

Figure 17. The train of the Duchess of Persian Gardens in the 1962 Court of Phantasy has a narrative design. Courtesy: Witte Museum.

Figure 18. The train of the Duchess of Splendid Palaces in the Court of Venice
(1965) uses architectural elements to symbolize the title and theme.
Photo by the author.

social skills. Details in the setting, text, and royal robes create elite identity for they rely on a certain degree of specialized knowledge for a greater appreciation of the "authenticity" of the presentation. For instance, in the 1991 Court of Spanish Empire, against a background of the overture from *Carmen*, the curtain opened on an elaborate set depicting a plaza in Segovia. Heraldic banners were suspended from the balconies of the buildings, and the backdrop showed the countryside complete with a Roman aqueduct. The stage was filled with court pages posed in a tableau from a Goya painting and dressed in velvet dresses based on a Velázquez court painting. The setting can be read fairly easily as a representation of a plaza or public place in Spain, and the heraldic banners suggest a historic period. However, the inclusion of the Roman aqueduct presupposes knowledge of Spain's history, and the titles of the duchesses, with references to Visigoths and Rio de la Plata, assume historical and geographical knowledge on the part of the viewers.

The costumes and staging of the pages, with their origins in Goya and Velázquez paintings, reflect the art history background of the mistress of the robes. The text writers were careful about the accuracy of their facts, but the narration is filled with flights of hyperbole and heavily loaded with adjectives: "brilliant synthesis of all that is bold and glorious" or "each treasure is gilded with lacy filigrees, encrusted with heavy jewels, inlaid with vibrant enamels." The text, as read by the historically costumed narrator, sounds authentic with its preponderance of place and personal names and somewhat archaic style, thus adding to the effectiveness of the displayed cultural capital. The historicity and obscurity of the references in both titles and trains create a frame in which the elite may stand and catch the light.

In addition to the emphasis on European historicity in themes and complexity and abstraction in design, the trains have become increasingly embellished, an effect achieved by using both more stones and more complex techniques. Even the earliest royal robes did have some beading, and by the 1920s some of the dresses and trains used hundreds of glass stones or sequins to create the designs. While overall there has been an increase in the number of stones or other reflective materials used, the change has not been at a constant rate. In all decades prior to the 1980s there were fluctuations among the courts and within any court in the actual amount of reflective stones or lamés used. Since the early 1980s there does not appear to be as much variation among courts as a whole, but there is still variation within each given court. There are always one or two dresses that have significantly fewer stones than the others. This is often due to economic considerations but sometimes it is because the family does not believe in what they perceive as excessive expenditure or because a simpler approach fits its aesthetic sense. "Oh, gosh, that is a lot of stones. Are we going to be tacky looking?" One former Coronation participant critiqued several dresses saying, "She might as well have just pushed a wheel barrow full of her daddy's money across the stage."

When asked about the increasing embellishment and resulting increased cost, most people do offer an explanation since the situation creates concern. Often "other people" who supposedly want to conspicuously consume are blamed. "The out-of-town duchesses overdo it because they feel that they have to in order to compete." "You know that it is usually the fathers who want to make their little girls outshine everyone else." "It's the mothers who want to glitz it up." "It's not the old families, it's the newer money that thinks that it is necessary to show that they can afford more."

The explanation for the overall increased complexity in design and embellishment has several elements. While some mistresses have created beautiful courts on their own, there is a discernible trend towards better designs after the addition of court artists. The increased research time spent on the rich historical themes also provides many more elements and motifs to be worked into the design. Most of the trains in the 1950s and 1960s were made of velvet with the major design elements in gold or silver lamés trimmed in glass stones. A greater variety of fabrics became available and was used by the early 1970s. Of equal importance is the explanation given by several mistresses of the robes: the increased complexity is due to the "expertise of the dressmakers."

> There is no comparison between the trains of 1960 and ones of today. They weren't even lined then. It sounds odd but the handwork has increased. Even in the last three years, there are many more fabrics to work with, more lamés, more glitzy fabrics since they are now fashionable. It opens a whole world of possibilities that just were not there before. That's what these dressmakers love to do.

The mistress of the robes provides swatches to indicate color and fabric with the design, but the dressmakers actually acquire the textiles and actively seek out new fabrics to create different effects. New synthetic fabrics provide a much broader spectrum of raw material for the dressmakers. "Now you have all kinds of weird stuff like tissue lamé that is iridescent, and you can lay it over another fabric. Layer a piece of gold mesh over this and get a completely different texture." Seven different gold lamés were used to create just one small branch of leaves on a duchess' dress. "I really do think that it is the expertise of the dressmakers. And the fact that they are artists as well. Their willingness to try to make the very best of whatever design they are given is unbelievable. They work as hard as they can to make it as beautiful as they can."

Plate 1. Maharani of the Lotus and Maid of Honour to the Queen (Court of India, 1933). Courtesy: Witte Museum.

Plate 2. This sketch for the royal robes of the Duchess of Scythian Antiquities in the Imperial Court of Fabergé (1982) was presented to the duchess at a party given for the Coronation royals by the mistress of the robes. Courtesy: Margaret King Stanley.

Plate 3. Notice the differences between the artist's sketch and the finished royal
robes. Dressmakers often make changes, based upon their years of
experience, that will compliment the duchess' figure or improve the
design. Courtesy: Billo Smith.

Plate 4. Dressmaker Ardyce Erickson (I) and her part-time seamstress, Mae Martin, work on a train. Erickson has been an official dressmaker for over twenty years and undertakes eight or nine royal robes yearly. Courtesy: Wilanna Bristow.

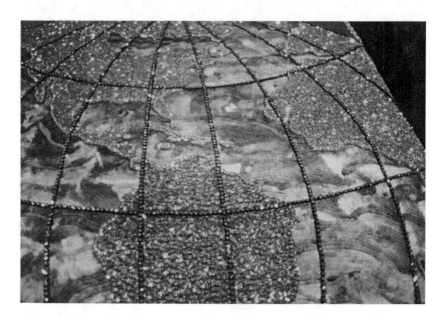

Plate 5. The artistry of Javier Castillo has renewed interest in the use of sequins. He used reversed matte finished sequins to simulate ocean currents in this map, which was featured on a train from the Court of the Age of Discovery. Photo by the author.

Plate 6. The Duchess of Symphonic Elegance of the Court of the Imperial House of Hapsburg (1987) makes her way down the runway to the stage. The pages are always told not to touch, but one succumbs to temptation anyway. Courtesy: Institute of Texan Cultures, Zintgraff Collection.

Plate 7. A stage page adjusts the train of the Queen of the Court of Embellished Dreams (1986), a celebration of needlework. The queen's train was based on medieval Opus Anglicanum embroidery and the duchesses' titles included "Treasures from Kashmir" and "Delicate Drawn Threads." Courtesy: Institute of Texan Cultures, Zintgraff Collection.

Plate 8. The Queen of Soul and other Fiesta queens are each crowned in a pageant or other ceremony, but they spend most of their time during Fiesta week enjoying as many Fiesta events as possible. The Order of the Alamo court spends more time at formal private events. Photo by the author.

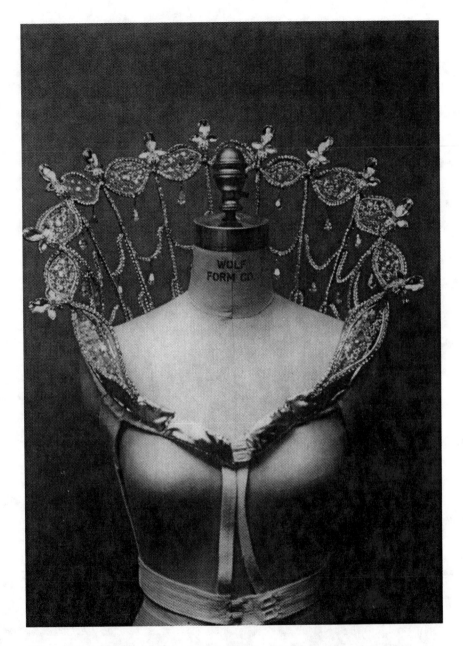

Plate 9. The queen's standing collar is attached to a harness constructed of wires and heavy webbing and worn underneath the royal dress. The fifteen-foot-long train is attached in the back to the lower edge of the collar. The harness not only supports the collar, but also helps distribute the seventy-five or more pounds of the heavily embellished train. Courtesy: Wilanna Bristow.

Plate 10. The Court of Spanish Empire (1991) is replete with numerous arcane references to Spanish history and literature in the set design and icongraphy of the royal robes. Courtesy: Jim Zintgraff.

Plate 11.   The thousands of rhinestones and beads "catch the lights" so well that
sometimes the flashing refractions of light obscure the design.
Courtesy: Institute of Texan Cultures, Zintgraff Collection.

Plate 12. The princess and the queen of the Court of the Imperial House of Hapsburg (1987) and their escorts in a formal portrait at the reception following the Coronation. Above them on the dais are the lord high chamberlain, Rey Feo, the president of the Order of the Alamo, and King Antonio. The kings do not appear on stage during Coronation. Courtesy: Institute of Texan Cultures, Zintgraff Collection.

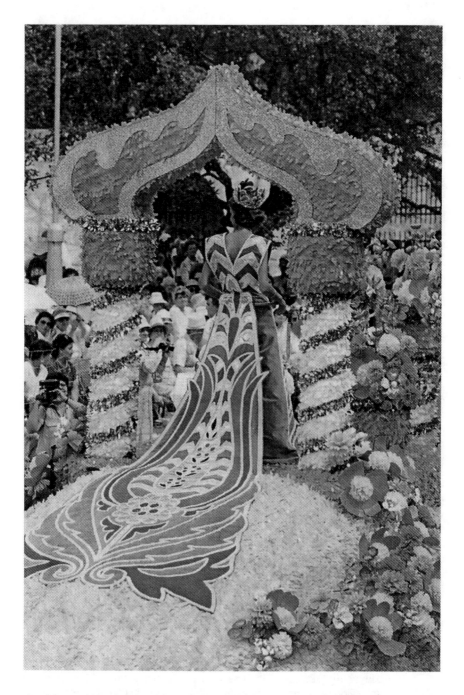

Plate 13. The bright colors of the plastic petal paper used on the floats diminish the glitter of the rhinestones and beads under the bright sunlight. Courtesy: Institute of Texan Cultures, Zintgraff Collection.

Plate 14.   The Duchess of Triumphant Discoveries of the Court of Heraldic Britain (1996) playfully responds when the parade crowd shouts its traditional demand of "Show us your shoes!" Courtesy: Mary Ann Bruni.

Plate 15.   The royal robes can be beautiful when seen from a distance at
Coronation or the Battle of Flowers parade, but only a close-up view
reveals the minute details that make them unique. The use of tiny gold
beads to create the textured antlers is typical of the extensive
handwork. Photo by the author.

Plate 16.   At least one row of rhinestones is typically used to outline each of the elements in a design. There seems to be no limit to the number of sizes, shapes, and shades of beads used to create the desired effect. Photo by the author.

Plate 17. Three-dimensional effects are often seen in addition to a flat application of embellishments. Photo by the author.

One informant reported that the dressmakers may specifically suggest an increase in jeweling to the clients. A dressmaker may say to one family that the train of the girl whom their daughter will be sitting next to is more highly jeweled than their daughter's. She then suggests that they would be happier if she added "just a row here and a few stones over there in that empty looking spot." Since the price is usually set at the beginning, adding extra jewels would cut the profit. However, it is to the benefit of the dressmaker that the parents of the future duchesses see her work as outstanding. Another informant believes that the biggest influence in "piling on the stones" is the rumor mill. All dressmakers are extremely careful to prevent their clients from seeing anything but their own dresses and trains. The robes of other customers are covered with sheets or are put away. Attempts are made, however, by some duchesses to get a peek at other trains by arriving unexpectedly at the dressmaker's house. Maybe something is seen or maybe not, but rumors begin to be heard that, "Peggy saw Ramona's train, and you won't believe the size of the rhinestones" and variations thereof. Some of the duchesses begin to wonder if their trains really will catch the light enough and start to add more embellishment. "One girl was so worried because she didn't think she had as much stuff on hers as someone else. Now that it has been done and she sees it in real life, she knows that she has just as much stuff."

Perhaps the most important factor in the escalating complexity and cost is the apparent irresistibility of using reflecting fabrics and glass stones to catch the light. Participants, past and present, talk about the need to lower the costs, even to simplify the royal robes in design and decoration. Mistresses of the robes and court artists are careful to design several of the trains in ways that do not call for heavy embellishment. People in the audience remark that the design on the train cannot even be seen when there are too many rhinestones because of the reflecting lights. And yet most trains have as much embellishment as space, design, and finances will allow.

Biography of Royal Robes

Kopytoff notes that "Biographies of things can make salient what might otherwise remain obscure" (1986: 67). A biography of the royal robes starts with the design and construction process that brings the robes into existence. Then the role of the robes in differing contexts is examined, and finally the royal garments are followed as they change from commodity to singularized object and as they move from spotlight to storage.

Construction of the Robes

Although some of the royals have been dreaming of their court dresses since they were quite young, they do not know what their gown will specifically look like. The royal robes exist first as abstractions in the minds of the mistress of the robes and the artist during the early period of research. They gradually are set down on paper as ideas, sifted through, and drawn to scale by the court artist after final selections are made (Figure 19). After the actual design work is completed, the assignment of dresses to the individual duchesses begins, probably the most important role of the mistress since the creation of a bond between the young women and the dresses is so necessary. All of the recent mistresses refer to the need to "sell the dresses."

The mistress may or may not know most of the young women. If she does not know the duchess, she has only an information sheet of basic measurements and color preferences on which to base her dress assignment. Sometimes a photograph is attached, but not always. She makes the assignments primarily on the duchess's choice of color, but some consideration may be given the family's estimated budget. The royal robes are designed so that they may be executed as simply or elaborately as the family wants; however, there are always a few that the mistress and the artist feel would be particularly effective at one end of the scale of adornment or the other. Therefore, an attempt may be made to assign a design that would still be attractive with a minimum of stones to a family with less disposable income, while those dresses that could bear a great deal more embellishment are given to wealthier duchesses. Although the mistress is responsible for assigning the dresses, many confer with the Coronation chairman and his wife before the final decision.

The mistress holds a sketch party in August to present the designs to the young women, but individually, not as a group. Pressure is applied to keep the designs a secret; the girls are asked not to share them with one another. One of the mistresses explained her reasons for upholding the practice of secrecy, saying that, if the young women view the other designs before any of the dresses are actually made, it is too easy to automatically want what someone else has. Even at the dressmakers', where six or seven trains may be under construction at the same time, the dressmakers cover all other dresses and trains during fittings. "The focus should be on them [the girl being fitted] and their design and not on this or that table." One or two additional designs are prepared just in case someone is extremely unhappy or simply refuses her dress, but this fact is not publicized. The sketches are presented as being especially prepared for that individual (even though they are actually completed even before the duchesses have been invited to participate). "But in my mind it is because it was given to them, that it is special for them."

Figure 19. The artist's sketch for the Duchess of Spinning Satellites in the 1969 Court of Time and Space typifies the only court to have any futuristic elements. Courtesy: Witte Museum.

Amazingly few dresses are rejected outright (although considerable modifications may be made to a design), and the vast majority of royal women end up with strong positive feelings about their robes. "I love it! It's just beautiful." "I can't believe how perfect it is." Even the most skeptical royal players are emotionally attached to their dresses.[6] One recent duchess fantasized about someday having a house where she could use her train as a wall hanging because it was "so fantastic." In spite of the facts that she was not from one of the old families, had been working outside the country, and was present only for the final weeks of preparation and Fiesta itself, she still had strong emotional ties to her dress. Even the young woman most concerned about the social implications of Coronation and who questioned her children's future participation had strong feelings about her royal robes. She would not remove stones from her duchess's robes to be used on her princess's robes for she could not bear to "ruin" her first dress, even though the cost of the second set of robes was something of a financial strain on her family. She recognized her lack of logic, but her emotional attachment to the dress and train was too great.

Additional evidence of these strong feelings is provided by the case of a woman who had been an out-of-town duchess thirty years earlier and was driving through San Antonio during her state-wide political campaign. She suddenly thought of her Coronation dress, which had been donated to San Antonio's Witte Museum. She took time from her highly contested race to call the museum to check on the dress and later wrote a thank-you note to the curatorial assistant who had taken the call and assured her that her dress was still there.

Many of the young women who become emotionally attached to their dresses simply find the dresses and trains aesthetically pleasing, but some find emotional or intellectual ties to specific aspects of the design. One duchess was thrilled when she saw that her dress represented the work of her favorite artist; another immediately liked her dress because it had tulips, her favorite flower, on it. A dress with religious symbols was given to a young woman on the basis of the color. The mistress knew that the family was Catholic but was surprised when the mother "was practically teary-eyed because they belong to a religious organization that uses that same symbol, so it meant very much that the daughter got to wear the dress."

These examples were the result of fortuitous coincidence. Other royal members create attachments – one used a few stones from her mother's dress on her own, one had the dressmaker put her grandmother's initials into the trains' design, another incorporated an animal from the logo of her father's company in a hidden place on the dress "since that's what paid for it." A loyal graduate added the Texas A&M University letters, and several have added family crests. Such additions are incorporated into the design and are not always immediately visible. The dressmakers usually are the means by which such personal touches are added, both in terms of actual construction and in terms of knowing how to modify the mistress's design so that the desired new motifs can be included. The dressmakers provide the technical ability but, perhaps more importantly, are more willing to modify a design in order to satisfy a customer. The mistresses see the robes as part of a whole, while the dressmakers deal with individuals.[7]

Dressmakers are contacted and lined up sometimes even before an invitation to be a duchess has been received. Each of the current seven dressmakers takes only a limited number of clients, and families often have strong feelings about their choice of dressmaker. Sometimes it is a matter of tradition; the dressmaker made the mother's dress and perhaps a sister's. Sometimes there is a definite preference for one dressmaker's style or personality. Each dressmaker is known for a specialty: fabric flowers, beading, or use of color. Many parents who either know, or hope, that their daughter will be a duchess pay close attention to the royal robes in the preceding years and note the maker of their favorite dresses.

After a dressmaker is chosen the duchess and her family take the design to her and ask for a cost estimate and a verbal description of how she thinks that it should be embellished. The dresses and trains are drawn to scale but often undergo considerable changes in the hands of the dressmakers. As discussed, the influence of the dressmakers may be enormous for they, in consultation with the family, determine the amount of beading, the specific fabrics, and even details of the design. The rules of participation in Coronation specifically state that all changes in dress design have to be approved by the mistress of the robes, but adherence varies. Some mistresses know precisely what they want the court to look like, from the youngest entourage member to the lord high chamberlain, from the headpiece to the shoes. Another mistress may simply feel that, if the parents or girls want small changes, sleeveless versus sleeved or a specific headpiece, it doesn't matter. "It's their money and their dress . . . why not?" Just as the mistresses, the artists vary in the amount of control they feel that they should have. One not only did the designs but also picked all the fabrics and colors. She knew exactly the effect that she wanted and pointedly told the dressmakers, "I don't want you to mess around with the design. Don't change it. My sketch is exactly what I want you to do." Two mistresses mentioned that their artists had become upset by some of the changes the parents and dressmakers made to the designs and they, the mistresses, had to rely on their diplomatic skills to smooth over the ruffled feelings. Perhaps the artists were more concerned because they view themselves as professionals (and are recognized as such by the Order since they are paid) and feel that their designs should be respected, unlike the mistresses, who are volunteers and therefore amateurs.

There are usually three fittings for the dresses, but there are many more visits to the dressmaker to check on the progress of the train and to make adjustments in the amount and type of ornamentation. The trips to the dressmaker are family affairs, almost always including at least the young woman and her mother. But they frequently include the father, siblings, grandmothers, or other relatives. There is a rather domestic atmosphere in the workrooms, with multiple women discussing or working on projects, and most of the clients develop affectionate feelings for their dressmakers and their homes. The physicality of dressmaking invites a level of intimacy, for the dressmaker knows her client's measurements and can easily discern any changes that occur as a result of overindulgence of any sort.

The first fitting is done with a muslin pattern and is quite mechanical, allowing for technical adjustments. By the second one the future duchess can begin to see what she will look like. The dress is completely done by the third fitting except for hems and other hand finishing. Most dressmakers have a room set up with several full-length mirrors and sometimes even track lighting to give the full effect of the lights on the reflecting materials. The royal woman-to-be may arrive for a fitting in shorts and a sweatshirt, but in front of the mirrors she can see the transformation that the dress creates. The dressmaker has now become the fairy godmother who provides the fairy princess with a dress to wear to the ball.

Contexts in Which the Robes Are Worn

The royal robes are specifically designed for Coronation; however, they are worn in four different contexts, each of which has its own implications and affects. The royal robes are worn at the Coronation, the reception immediately afterwards, the Battle of Flowers parade and the Little Coronation at the Queen's Ball.

The first official appearance of the robes is at the Coronation itself.[8] There is no dress rehearsal, for, by tradition, the dresses are not to be seen publicly until the royal performance. The queen and princess do practice with their trains in the afternoon after the rest of the court has finished its rehearsal, but the trains are covered with black casings (rather like huge pillowcases). The duchesses rehearse only with older (and lighter-weight) trains used at bow practice. Small beanbags are placed on it to try to duplicate the feel of pulling the actual train.

Comments are often made about "how amazing it is that the show goes smoothly even without a rehearsal." When asked why there is none, the answer is either that the Order cannot afford to pay the symphony for rehearsal time, or that the girls do not have enough time for a longer rehearsal. The reality is that there are relatively few variations that can be made in the order of the production due both to practical considerations and the overriding need for tradition. The talk about "the show going on" creates an impression that this is just a small, amateur production and obscures the amount of money and professionalism actually involved. Even when the Order members were the crew, there was a professional stage manager in charge of the backstage area. The emphasis on the lack of rehearsal and supposed amateur theatricality reinforces the presumed "naturalness" of the elite and their activities.

The evening of Coronation the young women in the dressing rooms are filled with both nervousness and excitement. The prospect of performing the court bow creates the most trepidation. Parents and friends drift in and out while other parents or volunteers keep the children occupied and try to make sure their costumes do not get dirty or torn. The dukes usually remain in the backstage area closer to the beer coolers. They get into their formal clothes at home and have little to do until the production begins.

Each young woman has a specified space at the long rows of tables and mirrors where she sits while being transformed by her hairdresser. The royal robes are delivered in the morning by the dressmakers, who return in the evening to make sure that there are no problems with the dresses or accessories. The young women arrive at the auditorium wearing casual, often loose-fitting, outfits, but as soon as they start getting dressed their bodies begin to be reshaped. They are first zipped or hooked into Merry Widows (the modern equivalent of a corset), which change not only the outline of the upper body but also posture. Petticoats are added next, often over a hoop skirt. Then they are zipped into the close-fitted floor-length dresses weighing as much as twenty pounds. Finally, the train is attached at the waist for the duchesses and at the shoulders for the princess and queen. When the headpiece or crown is in place the wearers are transformed into regal young women.

The sheer weight of the gown and the length of the train radically affect physical movement, reinforcing the traditionally controlled and decorous movement of women. The young aristocrats must be helped up the stage steps by their escorts, and the pages have to help arrange the train. While the construction of the dress and train reinforces the gender role, it also emphasizes class roles due to the excess fabric used in the full skirt and the long train. The increasing historicity of the themes and, even more importantly, the weight of the gowns and trains seem to create an effect of great solemnity. The young women are usually nervous as they come down the long runway and, therefore, are a bit tremulous in their movements, but the weight of the train and gown is the biggest factor. A former court artist felt that the girls moved "like draught horses" because of the great weight, and she tried to design her court for greater ease of movement, using lighter-weight fabrics and less beading. Ironically, the court was criticized for its lack of tradition. Many do realize the disadvantages of weighty royal robes, but little change ever occurs for the reasons stated earlier. Reportedly, several trains in the past had to have ball bearings attached to make making them possible, but the story is always told as being an example of excess.

It is difficult to tell how much attention is actually paid to the text accompanying each dress as it is read by the lord high chamberlain, but it is full of facts and dates and is intended to be informative. The most obvious effect is that of demonstrating the cultural capital of the Coronation crowd. The emphasis on classical music played by the San Antonio Symphony also strongly marks possession of cultural capital, for "nothing more clearly affirms one's 'class,' nothing more infallibly classifies, than tastes in music" (Bourdieu 1984: 18). The audience is warm and appreciative of outstanding trains and well-done bows, but most members behave decorously. An occasional father or friend will whistle or vocalize loudly, but according to some informants this happened more frequently in the past. The court members are equally as well behaved as the audience, but in the past, perhaps twenty years ago, duchesses were known to pull hidden caches of confetti or flowers from under the upper portions of their trains and then throw them at the audience.

Many Order members and their wives contend that Coronation should not be so formal. "Coronation is just for fun." "It is not a life-changing event." "If people take it too seriously, something is wrong." Such statements are made with conviction, but are contradicted by the formality of Coronation with its English court titles, the presence of the symphony, the historicity of the themes, and the elaborate set and royal robes. At the beginning of her term, a recent mistress of the robes asserted that Coronation should not be so formal, but she chose Napoleon for her court theme and her royal robes became heavily historicized and extremely formal.

However, any break in the formality of Coronation is immediately noticed. The most common surprise moves come from the extremely young children who are part of the entourages of the princess and queen. In 1992 the audience was charmed when the queen's three-year-old nephew, in velvet knee breeches, began his walk back down the runway at a deliberate syncopated march in time with the music, a skill probably learned in nursery school. Nothing deterred him from his measured march, even though the queen had to wait several extra minutes to make her exit. In contrast, the audience reaction to the princess who removed a lace insert in her bodice to create an extremely low decolletage was primarily one of astonishment. The court members on stage tried to act as if nothing were amiss, but it was the chief topic for several days afterwards.[9] The neckline of the dress would cause attention in any social situation, but within the carefully constructed and controlled atmosphere of the Coronation it was particularly noticeable. Even if the change in neckline were done just for fun, such an act takes on more serious interpretations because of the importance of the royal robes. In 1978 a hunting dog was smuggled onto the stage by a debutante portraying the Duchess of the Hunt. It is still talked about, much to the delight of some listeners and the chagrin of others, two decades later.

The largely homogeneous makeup of the audience contradicts a common assumption that dominant groups present elaborate public performances to an audience of nonmembers as a means of empowering the performing group through ostentatious display. The coronation of royalty in San Antonio is more important for the performers themselves as a means of reaffirming or validating their hierarchical position and group identity. Like Renaissance court spectacles that took place within the castles and great halls, Coronation is presented to an audience of the elite. Only the audience at Coronation, made up largely of the friends and relatives of the participants, gets the full effect of the embellishment of the gowns, for it is under the theatrical lighting on the stage that the gowns and trains fully catch the lights. They twinkle and flash as they undulate up the steps and the only time that the entire court is brought together in their full royal robes is just before the court retires for the official photograph. The visual effect of all of the royal robes displayed in their full splendor is quite impressive, but it is seen primarily by the elite themselves, not the people on the streets.

Exactly at 10:00 p.m. after the last bows are made to the newly crowned queen, the court retires to the private reception at a nearby hotel. This is the most private of the parties, with guests limited to the membership, the court and immediate families, and specially invited guests of the board, such as the widows of members (until remarriage) and the patronesses, former mistresses of the robes, queens, and princesses. As soon as each duchess steps off the ramp at the back of the auditorium, the train is unhooked from the dress, folded up, and handed to her duke, who is responsible for getting it to the next event. Formerly, the court walked to the hotel, the dukes following each duchess carrying the trains, visually emphasizing the supporting role of the males. Twenty or more years ago, it rained on Coronation night, and one of the Order members, who owned a moving company, sent a van to transport the court since it was the only vehicle large enough to hold all of the duchesses and their full-skirted gowns. The humor of the thousands of dollars of gowns in a moving van is appreciated by most participants and is held up as part of the tradition complex.

At the reception the queen, princess, and president of the Order and their attendants and escorts form a receiving line on a raised platform at the front of the room. The duchesses form another reception line, with the trains carefully arranged in front of each royal woman so that guests going through the line are able to view the train at close range and to associate the royal robes with the individual being greeted. The women's job is to be seen in their royal gowns, while the men serve: they stand by waiting for requests for food or drink or anything else that is needed.

The opportunity to closely examine the robes is the most important consideration in the minds of many who attend the reception, for only then can the detail and the handwork involved in the construction of the robes be appreciated. "It is hard to sit for so long but you have to. The whole reception is so that members can see." After an hour or so, the young women disengage their trains, leaving them in place, and go into the adjoining rooms to move about more freely. People continue to go past the trains to get a closer look. The trains themselves are metonyms for the duchess, who is in turn a metonym for her whole family. One informant refers to the event as "viewing the bodies." The trains are even more specifically identified with the family because of the tag, or miniature version of the train, worn by all parents of court members.

Although the reflective qualities of the trains are most fully exploited during Coronation, the use of multiple layers of fabric, of shadings in a beaded flower, of the different beads for a textured effect, can only be appreciated at close range. These are not fancy-dress costumes dependent on illusion created with dyed or painted osnanburg and ornaments cut of tin. The only people who can see and appreciate Veblen's "honorific handwork" are insiders. In explaining the need for the hours of expensive handwork, a dressmaker stated that the quality is expected. "The general public doesn't see, but people who matter see it and want quality work." Admittance to the reception is highly prized, and even people who do not attend Coronation itself will go the reception to see the gowns at closer range. The royal robes are magnetic, for the viewer is pulled closer and closer in order to see the smallest details of the handwork. The desire to own or wear one of the robes primarily comes to those who have closely observed royal robes in the past. Such proximity is gained either through membership in the Order and attendance at the reception or through friendship with a member of the court when the gowns can be looked at in the home.

Two days later, on Friday of Fiesta week, the young women put on the robes to wear them in the Battle of Flowers parade, the only really public appearance of the royal court of the Order of the Alamo. The young women all receive invitations to ride in the parade, and the Battle of Flowers organization provides the floats. The princess and queen have individual floats, while the twenty-four duchesses share eight floats. The floats are multileveled in order to provide a standing space for each duchess and an exhibition space for her train.

The effect of the trains is quite different in the natural light against the plastic paper covering the moving floats. The stones do glitter in the sunlight, but the effect is subdued because of the competing shine of the plastic. The colors of the floats are chosen to complement those of the gowns, but float paper is available only in limited colors. Therefore, the floats are always bright, almost neon, and the trains are not in the spotlight as they are in the formal Coronation presentation or even at the reception. Additionally, young women on other floats compete for attention. Some of the regional queens, such as the Citrus Queen from Mission, Texas, wear evening gowns and trains. None of the regional royal robes are as elaborate as those of the Order of the Alamo, except those of the Lutheran Coronation, virtually indistinguishable at a distance.

Over the years the court section has occupied different positions in the parade, interspersed through the parade or treated as a unit at either the beginning or the end. In 1991 the entire court was at the end, and people had begun to leave by the time the queen finally rolled out. A more equal distribution has been used since then.[10] The only identification of the royal women on the floats is provided by two private-school students who precede the float carrying a banner with the names of the duchesses and their titles, but the information is not always easy to read since the banners often get creased or folded over as they are carried.

Riding on the floats is physically uncomfortable. The young women are atop the floats for more than three hours without access to any facilities or even shade. They are placed on the tall floats by a hydraulic lift and cannot get down until the parade is over. They must be lifted into place because the robes restrain their movements and because the surface of the float is slippery. The image of the mechanical placement of the royal women on a high surface strongly suggests that they are literally being placed upon the classic pedestal. Although the royal women have learned not to wear petticoats and other underpinnings, the velvet and lamé dresses get very warm on an average April afternoon in Texas.

Somewhat surprisingly, the young women often report the parade to be the favorite part of the entire Coronation process. An Order member told of the importance of the parade to an out-of-town duchess who had agreed to be in Coronation only because of her mother's insistence. When rain began pouring down on the parade, the mother worried that her daughter would be "absolutely mad, livid that I had gotten her into something like this." Later, the daughter walked into the hotel, dripping wet and said, "I've never had a better time in my life!" The parade had continued even in the rain, and a bond formed between the participants and the remaining spectators, a development still talked about by several of the participants.

The smiles of the children on the sidewalks were the most important element in the parade experience for many. A woman who had been in the parade more than twenty-five years earlier said, "There are these little kids with smiles bigger than you have ever seen. It is just really neat to think that I am making them smile." Another duchess remembered "The kids . . . these beautiful little faces looking up at you. They just yelled and screamed my name and yelled 'Wave to me!' It blows you away. You can't imagine the rush it gives you. It is just like 'wow.' That is what I remember. Those kinds of things." Two more recent royals reported, "I love it because there are so many people there to see you and they make your ego this big." "All the way down the street, on both sides, people are calling to you, telling you how great you look. You really do feel like a celebrity." The tones in their voices indicated that they had not known they would get that kind of reception from the viewers.

The royal robes as costume also give the wearer a beautiful appearance. A middle-aged woman who did not feel that she was considered particularly pretty as a young woman remembers the parade as a time when she could have the luxury of being seen as attractive. "This one little boy came up to me 'Oh, you are so beautiful' and I was just like . . . I cried every time I thought about it. I just loved it." Another duchess, who is quite shy, felt that the parade was fun, but she was amazed at how people reacted. "They are not just spectators. They like to participate in the parade. Lots of people shouting different comments 'Oh, how pretty.' or 'Are you getting tired?' or 'Aren't you hot?' All along the route people were verbal and involved. It really surprised me." After the Menger Hotel crowd made the traditional call for a glimpse of the tennis shoes one duchess commented, "I just stuck my foot out and I've never had such a reaction from a crowd in my life. It was great. They went berserk."[11]

Women do tell of the misgivings they had before the parade either because of their own shyness or because they were concerned about the public's perception of them in their "big dresses." There is some concern among more recent royals that the spectators will take offense at the apparent cost of the gowns. During the Depression there was hesitancy for the daughters of bankers to appear in the parade but there were no incidents.[12] However, the "big dresses" actually become protective costumes; that is, clothing put on in order to portray an assumed role. They are not even worn in the same way as at the Order-sponsored events. The dress is not worn over proper underclothing, and the trains are attached to a metal support stand and tacked to the float so that they will not blow about. It is impossible to see the detail and the handwork of the trains. They are theatrical costumes as far as the spectators can tell.

Erving Goffman speaks of clothing as part of the personal "front" that an individual uses during a performance as well as "manner" indicating the type of interactive role the performer expects (Goffman 1973: 24). The royal robes allow the young women to portray their dual roles in the parade – embodiment of family and group identity to their peers on the parade route and that of beauty queen for the people on the streets. The peer role is easy to carry out, but as the previous comments indicate many of the young women are hesitant about how they are to react to the spectators, particularly to the young Mexican American males, who wolf whistle and call out the women's names they have read on the banners. The women apparently do not feel physically threatened since they are above the reach of the crowd, but many of the predominantly blond Anglo women do implicitly recognize the symbolic positioning between themselves and the darker-skinned, black-haired spectators on the streets.

The royal robes as costume provide Goffman's front that allows them to be vulnerable to the public despite differences in class. They can wave and blow kisses and acknowledge the reactions of the people.

> It could have been a frightening thing and I knew that I had to take control of it before it took control of me. Particularly the crowds of people who were not going to be my old friends at the Menger or at the Gunther [hotels] and how they were going to respond to me. So what I did was I went to them by my behavior. I was out there for them.

The royal robes as costume indicate the manner in which the young women on the floats and the spectators should interact. They create a fantasy quality through their characteristic exaggerations in size and elaborate decoration when read against the background of the street. The people on the street seem to see the young women not as elite debutantes, but as beauty or fairy-tale queens, women whose artifice is acknowledged and accepted. The glitter of the gowns is familiar to the spectators through experiences with similarly "glitzy" costumes at the circus, the Ice Capades, and acts in Las Vegas. The heavy use of rhinestones denotes status as an entertainer, someone from the world of make-believe, not the neighbor or the daughter of your banker.

However, when worn inside at the Coronation, reception, or Queen's Ball the robes are articles of clothing with specific information encoded in the motifs in the design and in the amount of detailed handwork. In this context the information is perceived as reality, not fairy-tale artifice. Kopytoff calls the ability of luxury goods such as the royal robes to give multiple messages "semiotic virtuosity, that is, the capacity to signal fairly complex social messages" (Kopytoff 1986: 38).

Saturday is the Queen's Ball, part of Coronation since 1909 and the last time the royal robes will be worn. The Queen's Ball guest list is limited to ensure a feeling that this is a private and restricted event and, pragmatically, to prevent it from becoming too crowded. Still, it is a large party with multiple bands, an open bar, and breakfast served around midnight. It is always held at a downtown hotel and has been at the Menger hotel, across from the Alamo, for at least forty years. The highlight of the evening is the Little Coronation, a simpler reenactment of the earlier performance with a key difference: the young women are presented by their fathers rather than escorted by their dukes. It has been a "traditional" feature of the ball since the 1950s. It currently is staged around the swimming pool located within a quadrangle formed by the old and new sections of the hotel. A small arched trellis surmounted by the crest of the Order of the Alamo creates an entrance for the young women, and a platform with two thrones on it is placed at the far end of the pool. Rows of folding wooden chairs are set up on two sides of the pool, leaving a path wide enough for the trains. Royal mothers take front row seats, and other guests fill the remaining spaces. Many of the contemporaries of the court members crowd onto the balconies of the adjacent hotel suites. The friends gathered in these rooms yell, whistle, and hoot for particular participants. The families of the queen and princess usually have suites overlooking the pool area and hang banners with the name of the queen or princess over the balconies.

The Little Coronation is shorter since most of the text is eliminated, there is no long ramp, and there are no children or entertainment. A combo plays a selection of semiclassical music for each procession around the pool, not the carefully selected classical pieces used in the full Coronation. There are no professionals involved (other than the musicians), and two spotlights are run by Order members. The space is much smaller and there is a more intimate feeling overall. In contrast to Coronation, attention is somewhat more focused on the young women themselves rather than on the trains since they are not as easily seen by the seated spectators and, after all, are making their third appearance. Although the young women seem somewhat nervous, there are definitely more smiles and enjoyment in the more relaxed atmosphere. However, the presentation maintains something of a formal air. In addition the sheer materiality of the royal robes still seems to hold down any possibility of real levity.

The order of presentation is inverted with the queen and her father being introduced first, followed by the princess and her father. They take their respective thrones with their fathers standing to each side. Each of the duchesses is then introduced using the name of father, daughter, and her title. The father looks appropriately proud as he carefully helps his daughter negotiate the turns, walking on the inside between daughter and pool. They hold left hands and he keeps his right hand on the train to help pull the weight, undoubtedly also with an eye to preventing any possibility of that expensive garment accidentally flipping into the swimming pool. Most girls acknowledge their mothers, either by a kiss, a curtsy, or nod of the head and big smile; but the mothers are in the audience. They are not in the spotlight as are the fathers. This is the time for the daughters to reflect glory on their fathers, who ostensibly have provided them with their glittering finery. The mothers remain in supportive roles as befits an event with Edwardian origins.

After each duchess is introduced and performs the court bow, father and daughter climb the stairs to a balcony area where the trains are removed and placed over the railing. The fathers and the daughters and their trains are arrayed together above the audience so that there is no doubt as to the paternity of the young women. When the trains are hung over the railing the spacing is not gauged properly, and everyone, and every train, has to be shifted in order to make room for the last of the duchesses. Reportedly, this happens each year and is in marked contrast to the formal Coronation where each court member has a precisely set place upon the stage to create the desired final visual effect. The Little Coronation is a family event with small slips and adjustments, and the emphasis is on the interrelationships associated with kinship, fictive or real.

The origin of hanging the trains over the railing is unknown, but it was begun in the 1960s when the Little Coronation moved out into the pool area where the balcony is located. The effect again recalls the Renaissance for richly designed banners were strongly associated with nobility, from the doges of Venice to the knights of England. Banners were markers of authority and of relationship to those in authority and were used in processions, tournaments, and on buildings to designate the occupants (Martin 1985: 45). The twenty-four trains draped over the railing are visually impressive and mark both group identity and that of the individual. After photographs are made the trains are quickly pulled off the railing and rolled up to be put into rooms for the night, before being returned to the homes of the owners the following day. The royal women put on shorter and lighter evening dresses and dance away the last night of their fairy-tale experience.

Life after Fiesta

Theoretically, at least 2,096 royal robes have been created for Coronation since its inception in 1909. Where are they? They can be found in many places, but most are stored away in boxes: tossed into white wooden boxes with the Order's crest on the top, sealed into boxes used by dry cleaners to store wedding gowns, carefully folded into long plastic storage boxes, stuffed into cardboard boxes that formerly held various potables, and tucked into florists' styrofoam boxes. The majority of robes have been donated to museums or simply kept by the families. Many have disintegrated because of age and the fragility of the fabric (particularly the chiffon dresses from the 1920s), fifty or more were damaged in a museum warehouse fire and later flood, several were donated to various theatre departments, and a very few have simply been thrown out. A local college student told of walking down the alley in her apartment neighborhood and finding a jewel encrusted velvet train obviously put out for the trash. She took it home, cut it up, and used it in a variety of ways for decoration and in theatre projects at school.

A great deal of time and energy, as well as emotion, are invested in the design and construction of the royal robes, and they have an explicit value for they come into being as commodities: items with use value as well as exchange value (Kopytoff 1986: 64). The price of the dress and train is the topic of much concern but little public discussion. Frequently, the young women themselves are not told the cost; however, all participants are quite aware of the financial investment. An initially reluctant duchess who agreed to participate only because her grandmother wanted it so much (the mother having passed it up for graduate school) remarked, "Who wouldn't love doing all of this. You would be really spoiled if you had this kind of money spent on the dress and didn't enjoy it." The limited public discourse regarding the price usually focuses on the contrast between the current costs and those of the past. Older informants often point out that their dresses cost a fraction of the current ones. Less expensive fabrics were used, fewer rhinestones were required, and mothers occasionally made the costume to save money.

Coronation robes as commodity seem to contradict or conflict with the premise of royal status based on genealogy. The impossibility of simply "buying" a place in Coronation is widely proclaimed, but the fact is that the gowns to clothe the royal personage must be purchased. Only in the very earliest years were they ever made by family members. The increasing cost and the required use of specified dressmakers comes perilously close to commoditizing the position itself. However, as soon as the families take ownership of the robes, they remove the royal garments from the sphere of exchange for they are immediately singularized, an intrinsic move in the sacralization of items. "Power often asserts itself symbolically precisely by insisting on its right to singularize an object, or a set or class of objects" (Kopytoff 1986: 73). There is a limited market for resale of the gowns, but it is rarely exploited, partly because the gowns are seen as being unique to San Antonio and to the Order of the Alamo's Coronation. They should not be worn by unknown persons in unknown places. Kopytoff refers to terminal commoditization by cultural fiat (1986: 75).

Kopytoff's model of a biography of an object as applied to Coronation robes reveals not only changes in their physical condition but also the changes in their singularized value through time. Many of the robes remain spread out on dining room tables or on spare beds for weeks after Fiesta is over, almost as if they could extend the pleasures of Coronation beyond its boundary by their very presence. The royal women often speak of the difficulty of "returning to the real world." They miss the constant companionship and the busy social calendar. When the dress and train are finally put away in a box it is usually done with great care, layering tissue paper or a sheet or other fabric over the train so that the stones will not indent the velvet when it is folded.

The rectangular shape of the boxes visually suggests coffins. When the staff carries the large boxes around in the Witte Museum in preparation for display, someone, usually a child, always asks, "Is there really a body in there?" The tongue-in-cheek references to "viewing the bodies" at the reception do reflect the reality that the gowns are the visible representations of family lineage. The corporate body of kinship is manifested in the clothing of the royal robes. Family crests upon the trains make the statement even more explicit. The blurring of boundary between family body and dress makes suitable treatment necessary. The large box into which the folded garments are placed will often be stored under a bed, often that of the parents. Pragmatically, the bed is the best location since the box fits underneath and it can be hidden from sight. However, it is highly appropriate that the robes live under the most personal piece of furniture in a house. Beds represent family for they are the site of the creation of a family either as a nuptial bed or as the location of procreation. In the past beds were often the site of both births and deaths, and many family heirloom bedsteads carry with them the legend that "great aunt so-and-so was born in that very bed."

The box usually stays in the family home until the house is sold or the mother decides that she has to clear things out before someone is forced to do it for her. At that time the daughter becomes the custodian of her own dress in her own home. The box is usually opened several times over the years to show to friends or relatives or to a young daughter. Over time the dresses lose their hold on the former wearer, and in the past they sometimes became dress-up clothes for daughters or a favorite niece or godchild. One dress from 1928 worn by a quite petite duchess later became her young daughter's favorite costume for her grade-school theatricals. However, since the 1970s the royal robes have either been too heavy or too costly to be used as dress-up clothes. A few gowns and trains lose their singularity status and safe spot under the beds when they are given away to charitable causes. Many years ago one reportedly was put into a "missionary box" bound for foreign lands and another duchess gave her robes to the Good Samaritan Center. Later she received a photograph of children in a costumed production. "One lad wore the front panel of the dress as a flowing cape, the skirt became a dress for a small girl and another child wore a combination of the black velvet and the diamond skirt pattern. The background of the picture showed the train as a wall decoration" (Corning 1987). At least one was donated to the local Junior League rummage sale.[13] In the first two decades some of the royal robes were rented or loaned to local royalty in smaller towns surrounding San Antonio. And a few are sold years after their debut as royal robes. One duchess sold her gown to a costume shop, and for years the dress was used as a Little Bo-Peep costume. One older dress and train were recently sold to an antique shop. The train ended up being used as part of a costume in Cornyation, the satirical version of Coronation that will be discussed in the next chapter.

As the years pass the daughter becomes the custodian of more dresses, for eventually her mother's dress also ends up under her care. Even if she has dealt with her own dress, the care of a mother's is more difficult, for over time the gowns and robes become heirlooms: objects that are in some sense part of the person who wore them and therefore inseparable from the wearer (Kopytoff 1986: 80). One woman who, after almost thirty years, finally divested herself of her own robes in their cumbersome white box still finds a corner where she can tuck the small box containing the remnants of her mother's dress. The fabric has deteriorated and the box now holds mostly loose beads, but even though she herself did not share her mother's love of Coronation she "cannot part with the box for it represents her mother and her mother's value system." Heirlooms never exist without strings attached.

Although most of the gowns and robes spend their lives in dark boxes, the desire of most Coronation personnel is to place the robes where they will still be able to catch the light. "It's too beautiful to be put away in a dark box somewhere." "I just wish I could figure out a way to keep it around all the time so I could still see it and enjoy it." One family hung their daughter's train, featuring a stag in its center, over the bar in a ranch/hunting house in south Texas. A father displays his daughter's robes on a mannequin in one of the many rooms in his large house. Several are used as wall hangings in two-story houses. One mother uses her two daughters' trains as Christmas tree skirts. Trains from previous Coronations may be hung over second-floor railings as decoration during each Fiesta week, and the royal robes of multiple generations may be the feature of a party for a new duchess in the family. But the last two examples are only temporary solutions to the problem of what to do with the gowns.

At one time the preferred solution was to donate the royal robes to the Witte Museum, the local history and science institution. It seemed perfect. A museum was the ideal context for the gowns for it implies immortality. After checking on the status of her robes, a former duchess commented, "I am so pleased that it is still there." Donors expect their donations to receive perpetual care and yet still be displayed occasionally. Acceptance by a museum also validates the importance of the gowns and, by implication, their owners. "[T]he traditional cultural role of the museum has conditioned us and thus has implicitly given value to the objects inside" (Skramstad 1978: 180). Additionally, and not inconsequentially, for many years there was an accompanying tax write-off. A tax credit does not imply commoditization but rather, in this instance, support for the concept of a donation being altruistic and a sharing of a valuable object for the greater public good.

The Witte Museum received its first gown in 1939, a duchess's gown from 1927. Currently the museum owns 163. The gap of thirty years between the first Coronation and the first donation reflects the time needed for the owners to perceive the gowns as singularized items that should be conserved. Obviously the women sentimentally saved their gowns, but it took fifteen years or more for Coronation to become institutionalized enough for the participants to realize that the clothing associated with it should be kept for non-family viewing.[14] Over the years the museum has mounted many exhibitions of the gowns so that their beauty could be publicly seen (and the names of the families involved brought to the attention of the public once again). The exhibits are usually opened during Fiesta week and remain up for varying lengths of time. Text panels giving the history of Coronation and Fiesta are included, and often royal photographs of earlier decades as well as the court jewels are exhibited. An entire hall devoted to the Coronation gowns was established in the 1950s, financed by a local philanthropist. It was open for twenty years and was eventually removed to make room for newer exhibits and needed storage space. For years afterwards, visitors would come into the museum and demand to know where the Fiesta robes were because "Aunt Minnie from Minneapolis wanted to see them."[15] Many Coronation participants express disappointment or frustration that there is no institution with a permanent exhibit of gowns and unlimited storage space. For several decades the Witte annually received a percentage of each year's gowns. The curatorial staff became concerned that they did not have the funds to adequately care for and properly store so many. In the early 1980s the museum board began to require a donation of $1,000 for the care and maintenance of newly donated robes, and the number of donations declined significantly. When the board raised the donation to $5,000, donations ceased almost entirely, and the museum owns only one robe from the last ten courts. However, earlier dresses and trains have been accepted without the large endowment and have been carefully restored by a group of expert needle-workers who volunteer at the museum weekly. The previous administration was not particularly interested in the Coronation robes so the policy, and lack of current donations, stayed in place for years. The current administration does find exhibit value in the gowns, and a new collection and exhibit policy is being developed.

In contrast to the museum venue, which validates the cultural worth of the robes, they have also been exhibited in what seems to be a highly commercialized venue, that of department store windows. The two oldest and most prestigious downtown department stores displayed the current court in their front windows during the week following Fiesta for many years, beginning in the 1920s. Reportedly, there was always some conflict over which store got to display the princess's robes and which the queen's. The practice was discontinued in the 1960s, perhaps as a response to the general movement of commerce to the suburbs. One store did display some of the courts in their windows at North Star, San Antonio's most upscale mall, in the 1970s, and small specialty stores occasionally displayed single gowns belonging to long-time customers. However, no annual displays were mounted by department stores between the late 1960s and 1992. That year a department store in a new downtown mall, Rivercenter, displayed part of the previous year's court in their front windows during Fiesta week. There was no identifying text of any kind and several people, possibly tourists, were overheard wondering what the unusual costumes were.[16]

The next year a marketing specialist from Rivercenter mall who now works for North Star mall asked the Order if they would help organize an exhibit of both historical and current gowns. Forty royal robes from previous years, including those of pages, lord high chamberlains, and presidents of the Order, were displayed during Fiesta, and the entire 1993 court was displayed the following week. The gowns were displayed in store windows, in free-standing Plexiglas cubes in the center of the mall, and inside some of the stores. Each costume was identified on a professionally prepared placard indicating court title, year, role title, and wearer's name. The mall also made available a brochure containing the above information and a short interpretation of each gown's design, for example, "The dress is inspired by the new architectural art form that became the Magic of Manhattan – the Skyscraper." A short series of text panels with photographs was installed at one of the anchor stores, giving a brief history of Coronation and the making of the gowns. However, it was easy to miss the text panels, so there was little contextual information for the exhibit as a whole.

A past president who was instrumental in securing the loan of the costumes for the 1993 display reported that the Order is happy with the public attention generated by the mall exhibit. The exhibit was publicized in conjunction with a scholarship cosponsored by the mall and the Order. He felt that the "public interest had been served" through the historical display of the robes and the scholarship. He reiterated the feeling that the gowns should not just be hidden away in boxes "to be swallowed up by history." The mall spokes-woman reported that the mall was pleased with the response and was planning an exhibit for 1994 that would be twice as large. She did not have figures to prove an increase in attendance but felt that the exhibit did arouse a lot of interest and, again, that the public interest had been served. The mall exhibit continues with both a selection of older dresses and the current court.

Display of royal robes in the context of the most commoditized of venues, the shopping mall, seems contradictory to the singularized characteristic of the robes. However, department stores have a long history of displaying art and costly goods intended to educate the public (Harris 1978: 154). Museums and department stores rose to prominence in the same decades at the end of the nineteenth century and shared many architectural and display character-istics. Malls are now the site of many forms of public service, from "health fairs" to arts and crafts shows. Perhaps the contradiction between museum and mall displays is not as great as it superficially seems.

Conclusion

However, the other contradiction between the private aspect of Coronation and its parties and the apparent deeply felt desire to display the gowns still must be addressed. Why would the members welcome an opportunity to place the gowns in a very public arena, which might lead to charges of elitism or conspicuous consumption? The explanation to the apparent paradox lies in the materiality of the royal robes themselves, in the perceived beauty, and in the desire for it to be shared.

Public mall versus museum displays epitomize the contradictory nature of Coronation. It began as a private affair involving a small number of families to select a queen to reign over Fiesta. In 1909, the date of the founding of the Order, much of Fiesta was largely a private party that took place on the streets of San Antonio. The Battle of Flowers parade and the selection of monarchs and subsequent social activities were all controlled and enjoyed by the elite. The businessmen did have trades-day parades and the carnivals did give the people a place to party, but Fiesta in 1909 was not the broad-based city-wide affair that it is currently.

Once the Order of the Alamo was established, the crowning of the queen took place within sanctioned halls, first in Beethoven Hall, the German cultural center, and then in movie theatres (but not during regular hours), and finally in the Municipal Auditorium. Coronation was not closed to the public, but it was never a street activity. The majority of the audience at Coronation has always been made up of Order members, family, and friends. As Coronation has become more elaborate, and as sensibilities are alerted to charges of elitism or even racism, Coronation seems to become more inwardly directed, with minimal advertising of ticket availability. Although the court always has ridden in the Battle of Flowers parade, it is not a royal procession, for there are too many other entries in the parade for the public's focus to be on the royal court.

Coronation as ritual is a means of renewing bonds of social identity, of distinguishing those who are on the inside through the wearing of unique examples of material culture. The royal gowns as material culture provide ways of publicly marking cultural categories under the guise of appreciation of their beauty. The participants, though members of an exclusive and private organization, want the public to see the gowns, though whether the motivation is to conspicuously display or to share the beauty of the dress probably varies with the owner.[17] Dresses designed to catch the light must not be hidden under bushelbaskets or in boxes under the bed.

Notes

1. Highly decorated clothing is also associated with non-European leaders, such as the *chilkat* Tlingit blankets worn by chiefs (Inverarity 1950). Beading is used by many non-Western, unstratified societies, but this discussion focuses on the European royal tradition.

2. See Sidney Perkowitz's *Empire of Light* (1996) and David Park's *The Fire Within the Eye* (1997) for excellent histories of the search for understanding the nature and meaning of light in science and in art.

3. George Hamell in writing of Native Americans' use of European trade beads suggests the widespread acceptance was partially based on the concept that such reflective substances as shell, crystal, and copper are expressions of a "metaphysics of light," a "metaphorical conceptualization for semantic domains of highest cultural value or significance: Life, Mind, Knowledge and Greatest Being" (1983: 2).

4. Lamés and sequins are also considered less desirable, probably because they are usually less expensive than glass stones. However, sequins are being used more frequently since a local designer of haute couture sequin embroidery has begun working with several of the dressmakers. He has made extremely beautiful sequinned appliqués for the trains of duchesses and queens in recent years. He says that sequins were not in favor previously because people were just not aware of the potential of the imported sequins he uses. They come in a much wider range of colors and finishes than the more familiar domestic sequins.

5. As far as I have been able to determine, the Coronation robes are unique. Other events may have courts, themes, trains, elaborate dresses, and embellishment, but none seem to combine them in the same way: Mardi Gras has trains and large collars, but no court; Waco's Cotton Ball has a large court, but no theme; Corpus Christi's Buccaneer Days has a court, theme, and individually designed dresses, but, as San Antonians are quick to point out, they use more sequins than rhinestones and often the stones are glued on. Ironically, the closest royal robes in terms of design and elaborateness are those in the Lutheran Coronation. However, they are not nearly as costly.

6. Wedding dresses are the only other gowns that hold similar places in the heart of the wearer. Both royal robes and wedding dresses are associated with ritual occasions and become highly personalized through either modifications or selection. More importantly they both make the wearer feel beautiful and extremely special. One woman pointed out, however, that wedding dresses have a slight edge because there is only one bride but there are twenty-three other duchesses.

7. Different alliances often come about. The family may wish to make a number of changes and the dressmaker diplomatically presents them to the mistress as improvements. The dressmaker often is able to adjust elements of the design to better fit the parameters of the train or is able to modify the design of the dress to be more becoming, for she is the one who has the experience. The mistress is sometimes seen as the adversary of the dressmaker, but she and the dressmaker may also unite sympathetically in dealing with a difficult family. The family and mistress rarely form a dyadic relationship in opposition to the dressmaker, for the dressmaker usually makes herself agreeable to the family, even if she is known to the mistresses to be a terror to work with.

8. However, all royal robes must be finished in early March in time for the formal photographs to be taken. Since there is still almost a month of parties left, the big concern for the young women is to maintain their weight, since it is difficult, if not impossible, to make alterations at this point.

9. Several stories went around the royal gossip circle as explanations for the revealing bodice. It was suggested by some that she did it to draw attention to herself and away from the queen, more specifically by others because the queen was dating her former boyfriend. Another version suggested that she actually did not want to be in Coronation at all but had been forced to by her family.

10. One Battle of Flowers member said that the floats began to be spread out in the 1970s because of fear of some sort of attack, presumably based on the obvious

ostentatiousness of the gowns. However, other members denied that, saying that it would be boring to have all of them together. A sniper did fire on the spectators during the 1979 parade, and that may have led to the fears by some members of the Battle of Flowers Organization that the court was in danger.

11. In recent years spectators at the parade have begun yelling "Show us your shoes!" to all the young women wearing long formal dresses on the floats, much to the surprise of some first-time participants.

12. One middle-aged former duchess reported having had spitballs flung at the horses pulling her float when riding through "Mexican town," but other duchesses and newspaper stories reported that young boys with spit-wads for the horses did not single out the duchesses as targets.

13. I purchased the dress at the Junior League sale. It comes from the mid-1930s and I paid $15 or so for it in the late 1970s. The train cost either $25 or $50, and I did not buy it because it was too expensive. I have regretted that many times. I have worn the dress twice, and it now sits in a bag in my attic.

14. The age of the museum must also be considered. The Witte was instituted in 1923 and began officially accessioning articles in 1926. It takes time for the public mind to begin to think of a museum as a depository for valuables, just as it took time for the gowns to be perceived as valuable and worthy of the immortalizing of a museum. The Witte does have gowns from the first decade, but they were not donated until many years later.

15. Individual gowns and trains reportedly have also been displayed in several museums in Texas to which they were donated. However, Fiesta gowns have been displayed as a group outside of San Antonio only twice: in 1991 at the Kent State University Museum in Ohio is association with the School of Fashion Design and Merchandising and in 1996 at Neiman-Marcus in Fort Worth, Texas. The Order and the donor families were pleased by the "outside" interest.

16. One informant said duchesses used to love to go downtown and stand in front of the windows where their dresses were displayed just to listen to the comments.

17. Only the names of the actual wearers of the gowns were used on the identifying placards at the mall exhibit. One mother was somewhat upset because she had remarried and her surname was different than her daughter's. The mother wanted the placard to read "so and so, daughter of Mr. and Mrs. such and such." This indicates to me that it was quite important to this mother that the public know the identity of the parents who paid for the gown.

Judgements and Justifications

The elaborate Coronation gowns of Duchess Margaret and her friends are displayed on mannequins in the mall and in the museum and are worn through the streets of San Antonio in the Battle of Flowers parade. The local newspapers carry full-color supplements with individual photographs of each court member. Despite this public display of the elaborate dresses, Coronation, an elite event involving a very small percentage of the city's Anglo population and an even smaller percentage of the demographically dominant Mexican American population, continues with relatively little protest from political or interest groups. Its essentially private nature and the symbolic multivocality of the royal gowns are the primary reasons it continues to enjoy its reign.

Cornyation and some entries in the King William parade satirize the idea and the form of Coronation, but not the personnel. The elaborate gowns and overdone royal titles are played with in both venues for comical effect, not for social change. In contrast, the few, but vocal, newspaper columnists who in recent years have annually written about Coronation and Fiesta criticize both Coronation itself and the participants. In 1990 a demonstration mobilized by local artists was held at the San Antonio Museum of Art to protest a display of Coronation gowns, an exhibit usually mounted at the history and science museum. While comments were made about the elitism of Coronation, the protest actually was based on an ongoing conflict regarding the lack of exhibit space for local contemporary artists. The two most political and pointed attacks on Coronation are found in a video and a newsletter, both produced to bring political awareness to Fiesta as a whole. In 1991 the video deeply criticizing Fiesta was made by two film students for a New York public-access satellite network. In 1993 a newsletter from the Esperanza Peace and Justice Center, an organization advocating social reform for disenfranchised groups, was also devoted to a critique of Fiesta.

The Coronation parodies and the serious critiques have had relatively little effect, however, and Fiesta royalty continues to appear in all of its glory with little notice from their supposed subjects. Similar events in other parts of the country – the Veiled Prophet Ball in St. Louis and the parades of the krewes of Comus and Rex in New Orleans – have come under heavy criticism for their exclusionary practices. The Veiled Prophet organization was forced to integrate its membership in the 1980s, and in 1992 the New Orleans city government passed an ordinance forbidding use of public streets for the private parades of krewes with restricted membership policies.[1] As stated in chapter 2, there was some political dissent over San Antonio's King Antonio at the City Council level in the late 1970s and early 1980s, but the only real result was that the Cavaliers, rather than the city, now pay off-duty police officers to act as escorts for King Antonio: a quite minor change in comparison to those in St. Louis and New Orleans.

Why have Fiesta San Antonio and Coronation in particular continued into the 1990s? The politically negotiated addition of Rey Feo, the official representative of the League of United Latin American Citizens (LULAC) and the Mexican American population, at the highest level of Fiesta royalty has largely been an effective defense against charges of racism regarding King Antonio. Undoubtedly Fiesta as a whole has escaped enforced reformation because it did broaden its activities in the 1970s and 1980s to include most communities within the city. The hundred or more current Fiesta events make Coronation increasingly less important to all but its participants. Most San Antonians either do not know anything about Coronation royalty, or they simply like to look at the dresses and know little or nothing beyond their appearance. Limited public knowledge of the elite and their practices prevents criticisms and calls for change. A brief questionnaire distributed to four classes at the University of Texas at San Antonio (UTSA) in the spring of 1993 supports this observation.

The satires and protests are briefly described in this chapter, followed by a discussion of the varied reasons for the continuation of Coronation, despite the view of a number of both participants and observers that it is too expensive, anachronistic, and elitist. The recent small, but significant, increase in Spanish-named duchesses is also discussed.

From Satires to Protests

Cornyation

Cornyation stands out amidst the many historic, ethnic, athletic, and gustatory attractions of Fiesta, for it is the only official event that currently embodies the carnivalesque of Mikhail Bakhtin (1984: 7–11). It is a parody of Coronation with exaggerations of the costumes, titles, and format. The current version of Cornyation is quite ribald, making the 1950s and 1960s versions mild by comparison. The theme of the first Cornyation was the Court of the Cracked Salad Bowl, and its monarch was King Anchovy who ruled over his court including Duchesses of Scallions, Radishes, and Parsley. King Anchovy remains the title of the male monarch, but the other royal titles depend on the current theme.

Cornyation has several predecessors from the first decades of Fiesta. In 1917 the Rotary Club sponsored a burlesque parade with floats satirizing politics, city fathers, bankers, and businessmen. An all-male coronation was also held by members of the Rotary Club honoring King Vitus and Queen Loco with performances by local 200-pound businessmen as queens of the Hawaiian ballet.

Cornyation was first presented in 1951 as part of the Conservation Society's "Night in Old San Antonio" (NIOSA) as a fund-raiser for the San Antonio Little Theatre. Early Cornyations were light-hearted spoofs, with such themes as the Court of Cosmetic Subterfuge, featuring Her Well-Preserved Majesty wearing a panniered skirt with a built-in dressing table (Anon. 1953). The participants were members of the theatre group and included some "real" Coronation participants. By the end of the 1950s the themes had turned to politics, and duchesses represented the "Castle Hills Speed Trap," a neighborhood known for the high number of speeding tickets issued within its borders, and "the Chughole," a reference to the condition of the streets. Cornyation continued as part of NIOSA until the mid-1960s. There is no official reason why the event was dropped by the Conservation Society, but its increasingly pointed political satire probably was an important factor. After Cornyation lost its spot in NIOSA, it was presented unsuccessfully in a new location the following year. It was revived in 1982 by two men who had been involved in the original production, and the San Antonio Little Theatre continued to sponsor it until 1990, when Cornyation was incorporated and acted as its own sponsor. A larger segment of the arts community participates in its revived version since it is no longer tied to the theatre group. It was held in a large unused space at the Bonham, San Antonio's largest gay bar, for eight years but now is performed at Beethoven Hall, coincidentally the site of the 1909 Coronation. Although the Bonham has both gay and straight customers, some spectators did not start attending until it moved to Beethoven Hall. Since 1992 the proceeds have been designated for Arts for Life, a group that supports AIDS education and research.

Although many gays are involved in both the production of Cornyation and in its audience, the director and writer do not want it to be seen as a primarily gay event. They stress that everyone is welcome to share in the fun. Cornyation still satirizes King Antonio and the idea of Coronation through its use of titles and the costumes, but the target of the satire is politicians and political situations, not the Coronation class per se. The scriptwriter feels that trying to satirize the Coronation class as individuals would simply not work because it would be too narrow. One of the crew members stated, "It wouldn't be funny if you tried to satirize the Coronation people because nobody would know who they were." Although the political satire is important, the primary purpose of Cornyation according to the director is to give the designers "a chance to let go. To be wild and crazy."

The 1993 Cornyation, presented by the Order of the A-Corn, was based on the theme "The Court of Faux Fast Foods Representing New Beginnings and Disastrous Endings." Royalty included "The Queen of Macho Cabana representing the American Gladiators." The titles are as absurd and often as seemingly unconnected to either the theme or the costume as are those of Coronation. The script is written before specific royal figures are assigned to the designers, and the results may or may not be cohesive. The costumes themselves are constructed of fabric, styrofoam, plastic tubing, black plastic sheeting, or anything else available to the designer. There used to be a specified limit on how much money could be spent on the costumes, but that restriction has been dropped. Many of the costumes include clever plays on the trains of the royal robes of Coronation, but a few Cornyation costumes come perilously close to becoming as weighted down by decorative detail and seriousness of the intent as those of Coronation. Sponsors are now sought for the duchesses to help with the costs of the costumes and various souvenirs thrown to the spectators in the tradition of Mardi Gras beads.

Nonetheless, of all Fiesta events, Cornyation comes the closest to being carnivalesque in Bakhtin's sense (Bakhtin 1984: 7–11). Alcohol is consumed before and during the performance, the recorded music is loud and pulsating and has personal meaning to many of the listeners, and the general atmosphere is one of great expectation of fun. A major factor in the lack of a carnivalesque atmosphere in the rest of Fiesta is that there are no masks, no mechanisms by which ordinary citizens can take on other personas. Although literal masks are not worn in Cornyation, the absurd costumes and the satirical narration create a figurative masquerade that allows the performers to behave in unrestricted ways. There is a lot of exaggerated sexuality, from bumps and grinds to apparent nudity. According to the long-term director, "The duchesses escape into a plateau. It is a time to be free, to be festive." The division between the audience and performers is constantly bridged as the royal women throw candy, confetti, condoms, and assorted other items to the audience members, who reach up and over the stage to grab the goodies. Bakhtin's grotesque body (1984: 18–27) is seen in the extreme size of the costumes in one dimension or another. "A sign of an experienced designer is one who asks 'How high is the proscenium?' or 'How wide is the loading dock?'" Some of the royal women are costumed with grotesquely exaggerated body parts: usually huge breasts or buttocks. Inversion is present in King

Anchovy, who misbehaves, making lewd remarks and gestures throughout the performance and wearing a costume similar to King Antonio but with reversed colors and additional decorative pieces.

Gender inversion is not typical of Cornyation, however. For the last three years one of the acts performed for the royal entertainment has been played in drag, but all of the duchesses are women. Recently rumors circulated that some of the Cornyation duchesses were drag queens; however, the director says that information is incorrect. "We have always used real women and always will. It is a tradition." Some of the costumes are purposefully ambiguous, but the scriptwriter points out that Cornyation has always had some "real" royal family participation and that might change if some of the duchesses were played in drag. Cornyation itself, despite its avowed belief in artistic license, tempers its freedom in the name of tradition and recognizes the importance of at least minimal elite participation. Some members of the Coronation crowd attend Cornyation, particularly those of high-school age, reportedly feeling that it was rather daring to do so. Primarily, however, the Coronation crowd ignores Cornyation, either realizing that it satirizes the idea of Coronation, not the personnel, or knowing little of its content since they are absorbed by their own parties and crownings.

King William

The King William neighborhood, with its large, late nineteenth-century homes, was home to many of the most successful German immigrants and their descendants, early participants in the development of Fiesta. Most of the original families moved away by the 1940s, and now it is a designated historic area inhabited by successful professionals from a variety of backgrounds. The one-day-long King William Fair started as a small neighborhood Fiesta event with food and drink booths, lots of music, and a play area for the children. After twenty years it has grown so much that it is difficult to push a stroller through the crowds. It still retains a relaxed, family feeling, however, and attracts a varied crowd, ranging from Mexican American families from the adjacent lower-income neighborhood to members of the Coronation crowd.

The King William parade includes flatbed trucks covered with children, garbage trucks bedecked with ribbons, dog clubs, vintage Volkswagens, and a sprinkling of assorted royalty. King Anchovy and at least one of the Cornyation duchesses ride in the parade, as do the Mud King and Queen (representatives of the San Antonio River Festival held when the river is drained every January). Residents of King William also take on royal titles. The organizers of the parade, known for their culinary abilities, once sat at a formally decorated table in the back of a flatbed truck and, wearing suitable dress and cocked tiaras, presented themselves as the "Duchesses Lynn and Lola of the House of the Hostesses with the Mostesses." A truck full of dressed-up children had signs with references to "heirs apparent." A former Coronation duchess appeared as the Duchess of Recycled Memories as part of the Court of Trash on a garbage truck.

The parade reflects the relaxed attitude of the event as a whole, and the references to royalty are readily seen as spoofs. Perhaps the spirits of the previous royal residents or the occasional appearances of more recent royalty prevent the development of sharper barbs.

Newspaper Columns

The comments about Fiesta events and Fiesta royalty that have appeared in recent years in various columns in the San Antonio newspapers are not spoofs, but range from fault finding to serious criticism. One columnist, who focuses on issues of social justice in many of his columns, frequently calls on the Cavaliers to broaden their membership. He also decries the costs of the Coronation robes. Charges of racism and elitism are made by various writers during the run of Fiesta. Over the next week or ten days, a few letters to the editor are printed in response to the columns. Then it all seems to be over for another year.

Interestingly, Rey Feo was the cause of an increase in royal criticism recently. In 1993 the column inches devoted to a discussion or dissection of Fiesta royalty rose to new heights due to the conflict within LULAC Council No. 2 over sponsorship of Rey Feo. After several years of court cases, competing LULAC factions, each claiming exclusive use of the Rey Feo position, ran separate Rey Feo scholarship campaigns, resulting in two monarchs. The ensuing bitterly competitive atmosphere elicited numerous critical remarks from the columnists not only regarding Rey Feo, but also questioning the concept of Fiesta royalty in its entirety. Cartoonists also contributed their interpretations. One columnist, who usually does not discuss the question of royalty and is herself a former duchess, suggested that all royal trappings should be eliminated from Fiesta and the focus should be on children and their enjoyment.

Some former royal participants express their discomfort or dislike of the columnists' comments. However, since most critical columns appear during Fiesta week, the current court and Coronation participants usually do not even read them because they are so involved in their own activities. Most royals, if they do become aware of the criticisms, seem to just ignore them.

Art Museum Protest

The protest staged at the Museum of Art as well as the video and newsletter are quite different from the satires or parodies and the newspaper columns. They are much more political in nature and have a biting quality not seen even in the most critical newspaper column.

Coronation gowns have long been exhibited at the Witte, a history and science museum, for several weeks during Fiesta season. From 1981 to 1994 the Witte Museum and the San Antonio Museum of Art were two components of the San Antonio Museum Association. They were housed in separate buildings but shared administrative and educational staffs. In 1990 the museum administration decided to display the Coronation gowns at the Museum of Art to try to bump up the attendance figures. Displaying clothing as decorative art in art museums is not without precedence, and the most prestigious costume collection in the United States is housed at the Metropolitan Museum of Art. In 1989 Fiesta gowns were displayed without criticism at the McNay Art Museum since there was no room at the Witte because of a traveling dinosaur exhibit. The display at the Museum of Art, however, incurred the wrath of a small, but vocal, number of people.

About forty people gathered on the steps of the art museum on the evening of 17 April 1990. Two male performers, dressed as "Duchess of Ostentatious Display" and "Duchess of House of Inane Splendor" and escorted by costumed dukes, left a twelve-foot paper train at the entrance. The train/petition signed by local artists read, "Put the trains in the Transportation Museum, the dresses in the mall and Contemporary Art at SAMA!" As the last phrase points out, the basis for the protest lay in the longstanding argument between the museum and the art community over recognition of local contemporary artists (Figure 20). An exhibit of contemporary art had been moved from the downstairs gallery to a larger one on the second floor to make room for the gown display. However, a rumor was started that the art exhibit had been completely removed. This added fuel to the feud regarding local exhibition space for contemporary art.

The performance was short, but the columnists and a cartoonist in the local paper intermittently argued for several weeks over the legitimacy of displaying the gowns in an art museum while others focused on the implications of the line in the petition that stated, "If these robes are art, then so are the KKK [Ku Klux Klan] robes." The thrust of most of the critique was that the art museum had succumbed to pressure from its Anglo, elitist board to present the gowns in the more prestigious art museum. "It was almost tolerable for the Witte Museum to trot out the Coronation dreck every year. The Witte never pretended to be a legitimate museum, anyway"

Figure 20. A parody of Coronation trains is worn during a protest held at the
Museum of Art. Courtesy: Institute of Texan Cultures, *San Antonio
Express- News* Collection.

(Greenberg 1990). Charges of racism and elitism, both in Coronation itself and the makeup of the board of the museums, were also repeatedly made. The museum issued press releases referring only to the original reason for the decision and later claimed that attendance had increased. Some members of the board were involved with Coronation, but the staff denied that the board had any input on the decision to move the exhibit.

One change did result from all of the coverage. The organizer of the protest had pointed out that the makers and designers of the royal robes were never credited on the title cards, only the wearers and the providers. The director of the museum agreed that it had been "an oversight" and promised that in the future they would be identified when possible.[2] Reportedly, the museum uproar did cause distress among some of the Coronation participants as well as members of the museum staff. The reaction of the Coronation group is probably due to the arena of the protest, museums and art. The royal robes, those reflectors of light and beauty, were censured because they represented elitism but, more painfully, were not deemed worthy of exhibit in an art museum, the rightful domain of their owners.

Video and Newsletter

The last critiques to be discussed point to racism and elitism in Coronation but extend the charge to Fiesta as a whole. In 1991 a video critical of Fiesta was made for a New York public-access satellite network, Deep Dish TV, by two film students, one of whom was from San Antonio. *Puro Party: Celebration of a Genocide* has been run several times on the local community-access channel, but it is not listed by name in the published schedule so it is seen purely by chance. It has been aired nationally and in Mexico. It was shown once at the Esperanza Center to an audience of about forty people. The audience was made up largely of Mexican Americans and Anglos associated with the center. Reportedly, two blond women who "looked like they were from '09" attended and took notes.

The maker of the video also had an article in the April 1993 issue of the Esperanza Center newsletter devoted to a criticism of Fiesta. Not coincidentally, the satiric illustrations accompanying the articles were drawn by the organizer of the art museum protest. Both the video and the newsletter specifically decry the "elitism and racism" of Fiesta royalty. The newsletter included four articles, three that are general exhortations to forgo Fiesta activities, which the authors assert are based on the overthrow of Mexico and on false concepts of fun. "But do they [tourists] (and we) really want to know the truth or do they want to continue as our own citizens do during fiesta week 'todos miados y babosos' (reeking of piss and acting stupid)?"

(Codina 1993: 3). The authors also called attention to the closed nature of membership in the Order and Cavaliers. In contrast, the author of the last article calls Fiesta a "democratic Bacchanal. More or less." She charges that the fantasy aspect of Coronation plays on old gender stereotypes found in pagan myths. She states in her article that her mother was a duchess in 1938 and thus positions herself as an insider who has rejected the hierarchy of her background. "Conclusions? – ha! I do not pity the 'excluded' ones any more or less than I pity the 'included' of fiesta san antonio" (Newton 1993: 6).

Like the video and the newspaper columnists, and unlike the King William parade or Cornyation, the criticism in the newsletter is directed specifically at the people involved, not just at the idea of royalty. Both the video and newsletter were strong denunciations of Fiesta and Coronation but had relatively few viewers or readers.[3] The limited visibility of the video and the newsletter, and the marginal nature of the sources, made it easy to ignore the criticisms.

Given the ninety-three years of Coronation's history, particularly during the social upheavals of the 1960s and 1970s, these are remarkably few public or formal critiques of Fiesta or the elaborate debutante presentation with its pretend royalty. Significantly, none of these spoofs or criticisms came from the streets or even from the average San Antonio citizen, outside of the letters to the editor. The King William parade takes place in the neighborhood that was the original home of the German members of the Order. Many of the current residents are middle- and upper-class friends of '09ers. The artists and designers of Cornyation and the art museum protest make their living within the arts. They may be marginalized, but they are not typical citizens of San Antonio's westside. A red Porsch was used as the royal carriage for the royal pairs at the art museum appearance. The video, although representing the voice of the westside, was made by a young woman who grew up in Alamo Heights and her fellow student at a prestigious university. The four articles in the Esperanza newsletter were written by two professionals, the video maker, and the daughter of a former duchess. None of the above, from Cornyation to the video, fits into the model of expressive discourse, such as verbal plays and visual jokes, created by the dominated as discussed by José Limón. He explores Frederic Jameson's political unconscious: "the socially produced, narratively mediated and relatively unconscious ideological responses of people – scholars and 'folk' to a history of race and class domination" (Limón 1994: 14). Coronation and Fiesta have not been the sites of ideological response by the dominated of San Antonio.

An important point that must be emphasized is that most citizens of San Antonio have positive feelings about Fiesta. A lower-middle-class Mexican American college student remarked after being given a copy of the critical newsletter, "I almost wish I had not read that. I never thought about the meaning of Fiesta. I just have always loved it." San Antonio is touted by many of its citizens as being "a party town." "San Antonio will find any excuse to have a party." People who have been going to the parades or NIOSA or any of the other Fiesta events for years do not want to have their Fiesta traditions broken. The tradition of taking the whole family to the Battle of Flowers parade and sitting in the same location year after year is just as deeply instilled for some people as is the tradition of being in Coronation for others. The results of a survey conducted in classes at UTSA reveal some of the reasons that Coronation dresses do not come under attack more often.

UTSA Survey

The questionnaire filled out by students at UTSA was a limited effort to elicit responses to Coronation from a more general audience than those represented in the critiques just discussed. While the questionnaire is not a scientifically developed survey instrument distributed to a large cross-section of respondents, the results are revealing. Essentially, most people not connected with the Coronation crowd either are interested in the dresses as material objects, not as reflections of class, or simply do not care. Two anthropology classes, one graduate history seminar, and one American studies class participated. The questions asked how long the students had lived in San Antonio, if they knew anything about Coronation, and if so how the information was gained. The last question was, "What are your feelings about the event and/or the dresses?"

Of the seventy-eight returned questionnaires, seventeen reflected positive feelings about Coronation or the dresses, sixteen were negative, but the majority (forty-five) were indifferent or knew nothing about it. Some people had strong responses, either positive or negative, but more had little specific knowledge of Coronation or were indifferent to it. As expected, the negative responses focused on the costs of gowns, wasted resources, and elitism. Two of the sixteen critics had enjoyed the glittering robes as children at the parades but later in life saw it as "pretentious and very Euro-american." The student who gave the most detailed answer spoke of "imagining when [she] was young that the queens and princesses were real," but her mother let her know that "she could never be in it" and now she tells her young daughters exactly the same thing. "In this country – where we are taught that anything we might desire is possible through hard work or maybe even through money – It has always seemed like an interesting 'Old World' statement – It's not what you have or have accomplished, but who you are and specifically who you come from."

The perceived beauty of the dresses was the prime reason for most of the seventeen positive remarks, while several people mentioned the importance of Coronation and Fiesta to the economy of San Antonio. Two women mentioned knowing girls who were in it, one specifying that she herself lived in Alamo Heights. One of the most vehemently anti-Coronation students referred to the female exploitation, wasted money, and lack of democracy but still said that she liked the dresses. However, 58 percent (forty-five of seventy-eight) of the respondents stated that they knew nothing of Coronation and the dresses or were indifferent to them. Significantly, nineteen of these forty-five students had lived in San Antonio for four years or fewer, presumably during their academic careers (as opposed to the positive and negative respondent groups, of which more than 80 percent had lived in San Antonio for most or all of their lives). Living in San Antonio only as a student would explain the lack of knowledge about Coronation. However, that still leaves twenty-six people living in San Antonio for a minimum of five years and a maximum of thirty-four years without recognition of, or response to, the event.

Private and Public Faces of Coronation

The inherently private nature of Coronation is the primary factor in the limited knowledge the general public has of the event. If you are not part of the social group, you have to read the newspaper stories during Fiesta week and carefully read all of the text panels at the museum exhibits to learn about the existence of the Order of the Alamo and the limited access to royal stations. That kind of effort is usually only made when someone already has some knowledge and, therefore, interest in the event and its process.

As stated earlier, while Coronation is actually a public event, many people who are not connected with it either assume that it is private or may not even know of its existence. Similar to European court spectacles, Coronation is primarily an event for the peers of the court. The majority of the available seats in the Municipal Auditorium are purchased by members of the Order, parents of the royal women, or patronesses for themselves, friends, business connections, and family retainers.[4] Although the remaining tickets are sold at the same locations where tickets to other Fiesta events are handled, most San Antonians do not even know that Coronation is ostensibly a public event. However, the homogeneity of the audience seems to be less a matter of deliberation than of neglect. The Order formerly advertised its tickets in the newspapers but has not for some time. When questioned about the lack of advertising, several of the older members said that they had not realized that it was no longer done. Current directors felt that the Order could not afford advertising costs, although they would like to sell out the auditorium to offset the costs of the event. The range of ticket prices ($10 to $36) implies that the Order does not deliberately set up barriers to keep out nonmembers, but neither do they make a concentrated effort to attract new audiences.

The homogeneity of the Coronation audience may not be intentional, but it does preclude larger numbers of outsiders from witnessing the spectacle of the gathering on stage of the entire court in their glittering royal robes. Only in the context of Coronation itself or at the associated parties do the royal gowns act as full signifiers of an aristocracy with all of the implied requirements of lineage in addition to sufficient disposable income. Only at the Coronation and the following parties are the intricate designs and carefully detailed beading really visible. One UTSA survey respondent perceptively interpreted the relative privacy as, "For a public event, they're very discreet. They don't so much lord it over the lower classes, as ignore them." The cost of the gowns is concealed as much as possible, not flaunted.

The audience at Coronation is limited and the guest lists for the associated parties where the royal robes are worn are restricted, but the entire court is publicly paraded through the center of San Antonio in the Battle of Flowers parade. There has never been a reported incident of public outcry over this very public appearance of the gowns. Why not? Gowns costing thousands of dollars and worn almost exclusively by Anglos can be paraded through town without fear of denouncement because the royal robes are symbols and, as such, multivocal. They are read as symbols of group identity and lineage by the participants and their families but have different connotations to other viewers. They can be read by outsiders to fit into their own frame of reference or social schema, that mental filter through which people can sift the continual onslaught of new information into recognizable categories (Kertzer 1988: 80).

Most interestingly, the common promotion of San Antonio as a bicultural city and the widespread knowledge that San Antonio's citizens of Hispanic descent are in the demographic majority create a schema for some people that allows them to interpret Fiesta as a whole, and Coronation gowns specifically, as related to Mexican culture. One student stated that he thought that Coronation dresses "reflected San Antonio's various cultures," and one Anglo female believes that "it is a hispanic custom." Most surprisingly, a thirty-one-year-old Hispanic female reported, "The dresses to me are a part of the radiance of not just the Coronation but part of the hispanic culture and part of the city itself. The colors of the dresses are bright, dynamic and beautiful." To these observers, it may not make sense that the Anglo elite would parade through town in expensive gowns in the late twentieth century, so it is reinterpreted in a more acceptable way. Coronation robes survive because of their ambiguity, their multivocality, which enables "a wide range of groups and individuals to relate to the same signifier-vehicle in a variety of ways" (Turner 1975: 155).

Additionally, as suggested in chapter 4, the spectators at the parade do not realize the amount of detailed, and expensive, work that goes into the royal robes simply because they are not close enough to see the details. Nor do they realize that the gowns are paid for by the parents, not by a group of sponsors. The people on the streets view them as costumes, similar to others worn in the parade, with rhinestones and sequins shining in the afternoon sun. Young women in beautiful dresses have become part of the expected visual pleasures of parades. By the time the three-hour parade is over, all of the crowned heads and their clothing become blurred in the memory of the hot and tired viewers.

Even the public displays at the mall and the museum do not blatantly convey information regarding elitism. Usually older robes are also shown in both venues, and often viewers do not realize that Coronation is an ongoing event. Additionally, the information regarding the importance of family lineage is embedded in text panels not read by all viewers. Recently, two young visitors to the museum exhibit called excitedly to their parents, "Oh, come see the Barbie doll dresses!" If the young girls do not learn more about them, the Coronation dresses may remain in the easily accessed category of fairy-tale dresses for dolls. Without prior knowledge the general public usually sees the royal gowns as pretty or unbearably overdone, depending on individual tastes, and does not respond further. Additionally, many newcomers to San Antonio, even those with sufficient income to participate, have no interest in Coronation because it is not part of their tradition or their value system. Coronation apparently carries little valence factor, something that makes a viewer react strongly positively or negatively. The most abundant verbal criticism from the citizenry at large appears to come from those who are socioeconomically close enough to the participants to know costs and practices of membership. Often these are the people who would like to be members of the aristocracy, since they are close enough to see the benefits, but do not have the proper bloodlines.

Possibly the concept of an American aristocracy seems so contradictory to average Americans and their ideological beliefs that even a faux coronation is not perceived as being truly based on lineage. Or perhaps the glitter and glitz of the gowns fit the American ideological construct of rewarding those who are financially successful. Although the Order of the Alamo is particularly sensitive to criticism about the costs of Coronation, an attitude that is held by some people both inside and outside of the Coronation ethclass is that the Order is a private organization and receives no public monies; therefore, the families involved should be able to continue the traditional practices, no matter how expensive they have become. Christopher Columbus's quotation used in the Court of Spanish Empire (1991), in which he appeals to God for success in his search for wealth, is perhaps fitting: "[F]or gold is excellent, and he who has wealth may do what he will in this world and even send souls to Paradise" (Order of the Alamo 1991).

Recent Responses to Critiques

Coronation has continued through most of this century with relatively little change, although the rest of San Antonio and indeed Fiesta itself have changed dramatically. The inclusion of Rey Feo, Queen of Soul, and the LULAC Reina reflects the changing political structure of San Antonio. Coronation has been remarkably resistent to change, but recently a small, but significant, change in participation has occurred.

The 1994 court included three out-of-town duchesses with Spanish middle or surnames, including one from Mexico City. The following year there were three in-town duchesses and one out-of-town duchess with Spanish names. Names alone certainly do not always reveal ethnic or cultural identity, but they are one indication of heritage (Royce 1982: 145–52). Seven Hispanic duchesses out of forty-eight court members is not an accurate reflection of San Antonio's demographics, but it is still noticeable, given the preponderance of Anglo and German names that have filled the royal roles for years. There have been a total of eighteen Spanish-named duchesses in the history of Coronation. The first participated in 1948, but the second did not appear until 1967. Thereafter, a Hispanic participant appeared as an out-of-town duchess every three years on average. The first seven were all related to a South Texas family with roots in early nineteenth-century San Antonio, a longer lineage than that of many of the Coronation aristocrats. Up until 1994 there had never been more than one Spanish-named duchess in any one court, and until 1995 there had never been a Hispanic in-town duchess.

Is there any significance to these names and numbers? Names are only one element in the complex issue of ethnic or cultural identity. But Coronation, after all, is an institution based on family lineage, and lineage is marked by names so the recent appearance of more Spanish names must be notable. Undoubtedly there have been any number of duchesses in the past who had Spanish names in their family histories, which were lost when a Hispanic woman married an Anglo or German man. Typical of this phenomenon is the Coronation dressmaker who emigrated from Mexico as a small child with her family during the Mexican Revolution in the 1910s. Her niece married into a family with Order of the Alamo connections, and her two daughters became duchesses. No one has ever mentioned the Mexican background of the duchesses. The last name is Anglo, masking the Mexican heritage. More importantly, the mother's family was an elite Mexican family, so the ethnicity is overridden by the more important issue of class.

When issues of class and ethnicity are separated, class is more effective at creating boundaries based on shared values and common interests. "It is only natural that people want to be with those of their own kind." Elite Mexican Americans and elite Anglos have much more in common than either group has with those of other classes. In the absence of blatant racism, it is primarily when ethnicity and class are collapsed into stereotypes of "poor Mexicans" and "elite Anglos" that supposedly innate differences are perceived. Racism may have precluded Spanish-named duchesses in the past, but most of the people involved in current Coronations are educated, intelligent, and often politically astute. Most work and socialize in relatively restricted circles, but few members of the Coronation group can actually be labeled as racists.

Several factors seem to have led to this widening in the ranks of duchesses. Due to increased economic opportunities, there are more of "our own kind" who happen to have Spanish names. Additionally, there has been an increasing number of duchess slots available for semi-insiders, those close friends of Order of the Alamo members who go to the right schools and belong to the right sororities. More slots are available because there has been a small increase in old families who do not participate because of rising costs. Some years there also seem to be more daughters who have more pressing ways to spend their time. There also is an increasing awareness of the irony of an all-Anglo court in the San Antonio of today. Some members of the elite are self-conscious or even embarrassed about it, while others cry "unfair political correctness" when there is any public criticism. However, there is a clearly demonstrable increase in Hispanic participation, and it does seem to be the result of some quite politic selections. The recent participants are spoken of as being "lovely people." Some Coronation participants may not consciously pay attention to the names, but others certainly do. The Order of the Alamo is a private organization, but the charges of elitism (read as racism) have been heard.

The Coronation families of Anglo and German heritage have turned to Spanish-named families, at least in these cases, to help fill the ranks of duchesses. Increasing opportunities in this century, particularly in the last twenty-five years, have allowed Mexican Americans and recent Hispanic immigrants to prosper as lawyers, doctors, and to a somewhat lesser extent businessmen. Will the Hispanic population continue to grow in political and socioeconomic power so that the Anglo elite once again turn to the Hispanic elite for economic and social advantages as they did in the early years of Anglo settlement when both elites had to interact and intermarry for strategic reasons? Will Spanish-named elite families become increasingly embedded in the Coronation tradition? *¿Quién sabe?*

Tradition in a Postmodern World

The private nature of Coronation protects the participants from some potential criticism by creating feelings of indifference in outsiders. The ambiguity of the royal robes as symbol allows for a variety of readings that conform to the needs or available information of the observers. But some criticism, both private and public, does occur, and Coronation participants are sensitive to the criticisms in varying degrees. Some former royals are quite concerned about the social and political implications of the entire event. A young, introspective, Old Guard informant talked about the difficulties of trying to sort out some of "these conflicting feelings because there are beginning to be societal judgement calls on it [Coronation]. You can see some of the reasons . . . and even voice some of the same opinions, but you also feel like you are betraying something that is a central part of you." Some families, even those with the longest lineages, decry the rising costs of the royal robes and may decline to participate on principle. Others are not able to afford the higher costs because of heavy losses in the 1980s recession. Some sons and daughters of Order of the Alamo families choose not to participate because their beliefs concur with those of the newspaper columnists, while others are simply too busy with other interests.

Despite the questions and doubts, Coronation continues. However, most participants do not read their activities as related to role and class dominance. The American ideology of classlessness makes them uncomfortable with the concept that dressing up as pretend royalty is actually a conduit to continued elitism and class stratification. After reading the dissertation, the basis for this book, a woman whose family had participated in Coronation for several generations commented thoughtfully, "I never thought about any of it like that, but I suppose you are right." Ortner notes that Americans in general do not have a discourse of class (1991: 169–71). Similarly, Coronation participants have no public or private discourse regarding class; instead, issues of socioeconomic dominance are displaced by the concept of tradition. When a woman is asked why she was in Coronation, the almost inevitable answer is, "It is a family tradition." One former princess said that she could name her relatives who had been queens and princesses but could not list all of the duchesses because there were so many. Further discussion may elicit comments on the pleasures of participation and of wearing the gowns, but the predominant discourse is focused on familial tradition. The standard answer to many questions ranging from "Why were you in it?" to "Why is the bow done like that?" is "Because it is a tradition." Such a tradition-laden secular ritual is an important means of connecting the past and the present, whether the tradition is "real" or "invented" (Hobsbawm 1983: 1; Moore and Myerhoff 1977: 17). That connection to the past is of paramount importance because it implies a continuity with the nineteenth century when the ancestors of many of the Coronation participants began to dominate San Antonio.

In a Durkheimian manner the ritual reaffirms the elite's mutual identification and cohesiveness primarily through the emphasis on tradition (Shils 1981: 301). Like the Visigothic aristocrats in the narration of the 1991 court who "created an independent culture with its own personality" (Order of the Alamo 1991), the ancestors of the Coronation families, who came to San Antonio in the nineteenth century, gradually established themselves as the elite socioeconomic class. Their descendants perpetuate the entitlement to those privileges through the annual ritual of Coronation, which both models and reflects their elite culture. They can annually, and generationally, display their familial "superior distinctiveness" through Coronation, the kind of collective representation or rite that Marcus asserts is no longer available to the dynastic families of Galveston (1992: 182). The pageantry creates a poetic space where a mythical ethclass history and class consciousness are presented. The multigenerational participation conveys the importance of family tradition to the younger generation and is reinforced through family stories.[5] Most importantly, the overriding emphasis on tradition discourages inquiry into the validity or the appropriateness of participation in the elaborate event. The trope of "family tradition" functions as a true mask, for it both obscures the underlying elitism and provides an alternative face to justify participation.

The other important trope is that of the fairy-tale princess. The metaphor of Coronation as fairy tale is one repeatedly used by many of the participants, whether discussing memories of their dresses or valued attributes in a duke. Some of the young royal women will lead lives that follow classic fairy-tale story lines with stepchildren and evil conjurers and dragons to be slain. However, many others will lead variants of Walt Disney fairy tales, expurgated versions in which the lessons to be learned from the hunger of Hansel and Gretel or the avarice of the stepmother have been removed. Will Duchess Margaret live happily every after? Perhaps not in the fairy-tale sense, for being a member of royalty or of the Order does not protect against the realities of unhappiness, illness, and death; but the financial and social resources that abound among the social group do protect individuals from some of the vicissitudes of life. Giving a daughter an opportunity to be a Coronation fairy princess does bestow certain tangible benefits on her through Bourdieu's social capital.

The most salient element of the fairy-tale metaphor is that the genre is marked by the predictability of the closing line. There is comfort in listening to or reading a fairy tale since one can depend on the outcome. Fairy tales are models of order even if babies are snatched by dwarfs and evil spells are spun by witches in the body of the tale. One knows what the final words will be. Coronation not only continues, but gains in importance, because of its very predictability, its continuity, its repetition. Every year twenty-four duchesses are introduced, and the queen takes exactly the same oath promising to bring mirth, melody, and sweet music and to banish sorrow. Some members of the Order sheepishly admit that "the whole thing really is a bore" because it is always the same, while other members of the audience revel in the warmth of the known. "The repetitive insists and may even persuade that its messages are durably true, now and in the future. It gives information that affairs and states, attitudes and understandings are stable; we may count on them, make plans in terms of them. As such, rituals are promises about continuity" (Moore and Myerhoff 1977: 17). Traditional practices create connections for the current elite to their ancestors who enjoyed the golden age of late Edwardianism when life itself seemed to be more predictable.

Coronation is so predictable that a mother of a two-year-old can figure out who will be eligible for duchess when her daughter comes of age because the unwritten rules for participation are so entrenched. When a young woman receives an invitation to be a duchess, she knows what her social life will be for the next eight months because she has heard all about it from older friends and her sister or cousin. It is so bound by tradition that innovations do not occur. Themes change and minor variations in the blocking are made, but a duchess of 1927 would recognize Coronation even if she had not attended one since hers.

That duchess of 1927 would even recognize much of the three contiguous neighborhoods where most of the Coronation class still lives. The towering oak and pecan trees of the area are still there, shading the inhabitants from the class and ethnic divisions found throughout San Antonio. One informant, talking of the benefit of the community service required of Junior League members, admitted that "I saw parts of San Antonio that I had never seen before and will probably never see again." The world outside of the older neighborhoods and their royal residents is full of the realities of modern life. Current San Antonio newspapers may contain critical columns calling Coronation a "medieval ritual" rather than a hallowed tradition. The news is also full of stories of violence and crime rates. But inhabitants still enjoy the luxury of feeling that they are safe within their own territory, although the totally disconnected violence of today recognizes no zip code boundaries.[6] The comfort of the regularity of Coronation and all that it encompasses is an underlying reason that it persists despite the criticisms from without and the doubts from within. In the midst of the chaotic postmodern world that fragments societies and alienates individuals, the repetitive, predictable tradition of Coronation provides a frame within which participants may reaffirm the illusion of order within their world. Nothing is so comforting, or so restrictive, as a family tradition.

Notes

1. None of San Antonio's parades are private even though sponsored by private organizations. The Comus and Rex parades in New Orleans limit participation in their parades to their own members.

2. However, the identity of the dressmakers of many of the old gowns cannot currently be ascertained.

3. One member of the Coronation crowd did receive the newsletter, but her membership in the Esperanza Center clearly demonstrates that her political interests are broader than average.

4. There are few non-Anglos in the audience. I have not done much interviewing of audience members, but several African Americans and Mexican Americans to whom I spoke were household employees of duchesses' families. During the years that the Auditorium was segregated, one side of the balcony was set aside for household servants. I have noticed several ethnically mixed groups of well-dressed women whom I assume are co-workers, perhaps in banks or offices, and attend just for the royal robes; or perhaps they too are employees or co-workers of participating Order members. I have talked with a few older women who are not part of the Coronation crowd but who loved the beauty of the gowns and enjoyed a chance to get dressed up. I was told of two local women (not associated with the Order) who called the ticket chairman to get information about Coronation tickets. They wanted to know what the appropriate dress would be. He told them that some people would be quite dressed up since they were going to the reception afterwards, but that evening dress was certainly not required. The women thanked him and said they understood that there was no dress code but that "we will dress for the queen." The Order member felt that it was quite a compliment.

5. An eighty-year-old informant told his favorite family story about coronation.

> If you want a little humor I will tell you about Whitney, a four-year-old page to his aunt, my first cousin. [D]own [at] the family ranch . . . the disciplinary method was a little, light switch which was no longer than that, and the kids who were misbehaving would get a sting on the

legs. Sometimes the parent could just pick this thing up and wave it, and the kid would get the message.

Queen Sallie gets down the ramp and is just crossing the orchestra pit . . . as Whitney, some twenty feet behind her, got up close to the pit. And here was the conductor with that switch that he knew was no good for him. He looked at it with big eyes and all of a sudden he just turned and ran back down the ramp at full speed. Sallie, who was being very dignified, heard this great outburst from everybody and just didn't know what in the hell had happened. But it added a whole lot to an otherwise dull affair, as far as I was concerned.

6. Violent acts, including murders, do take place in the '09 neighborhoods. The most recent one was the killing of a young mother jogging with her baby in a stroller in Olmos Park on a street bounded on one side by a woodsy area. At first there were reports of seeing a stranger, a black man, on the street, but the newspaper soon dropped the story as no suspects were arrested. The widespread story/rumor now is that her husband either did it or hired a hit man. Apparently, residents would rather believe the worst of a neighbor than have to live with the knowledge that random violence by a stranger could take place in the morning on one of their streets.

Appendix: Coronation Themes

1909	Court of Flowers
1910	Court of Roses
1911	Court of Carnival Flowers
1912	Court of Lilies
1913	Court of Spring
1914	Court of the Year
1915	Court of Romance
1916	Court of Fairies
1917	Court of the Butterflies
1918	World War I (no court)
1919	World War I (no court)
1920	Court of the Birds
1921	Court of the Universe
1922	Court of Aladdin
1923	Court of the Sea
1924	Court of Chivalry
1925	Court of Sylvan Flowers
1926	Court of Jewels
1927	Court of the Seasons
1928	Court of the Mediterranean
1929	Court of Louis XIV
1930	Court of Seville
1931	Court of Olympus
1932	Court of Light
1933	Court of India
1934	Court of the Midnight Sun
1935	Court of Enchantment
1936	Court of Adventure
1937	Court of Imperial Russia
1938	Court of Italian Renaissance

1939	Court of Music
1940	Court of the Old South
1941	Court of Legends
1942	World War II (no court)
1943	World War II (no court)
1944	World War II (no court)
1945	World War II (no court)
1946	Court of Honour
1947	Court of Holidays
1948	Court of Empires
1949	Court of Gaiety
1950	Court of Islands
1951	Court of a Thousand Nights and a Night
1952	Court of Make-Believe
1953	Court of Opera
1954	Court of the Mystic Sea
1955	Court of Enchanted Dance
1956	Court of Old Vienna
1957	Court of Ageless Art
1958	Court of the Golden Journey
1959	Court of Courts
1960	Court of Theatre
1961	Court of the Americas
1962	Court of Phantasy
1963	Court of Beauty
1964	Court of Ages
1965	Court of Venice
1966	Court of Mysterious Worlds
1967	Court of San Antonio de Bejar
1968	Court of Festivals
1969	Court of Time and Space
1970	Court of Classics
1971	Court of Gardens
1972	Court of Our Heritage
1973	Court of the Tudor Rose
1974	Court of Musical Theatre
1975	Corte de la Tierra Mágica
1976	Court of the Lone Star
1977	Court of the Voyage Extraordinaire
1978	Court of the Sun King
1979	Court of the Floating Kingdom

1980	Court of Victorian Splendor
1981	Court of Lost Realms
1982	Court of Fabergé
1983	Court of Never Neverland
1984	Court of Shining Moments
1985	Court of the Italian Renaissance
1986	Court of Embellished Dreams
1987	Court of the Imperial House of Hapsburg
1988	Court of Classical Design
1989	Court of Eternal India
1990	Court of Artistic Splendour
1991	Court of Spanish Empire
1992	Court of Imperial Patronage
1993	Court of the Napoleonic Empire
1994	Court of International Celebrations
1995	Court of the Marvelous
1996	Court of Heraldic Britain
1997	Court of the Age of Discovery

Bibliography

Achor, Shirley (1978), *Mexican Americans in a Dallas Barrio*, Tucson: University of Arizona Press.

Almaraz, Felix D. (1993), "Merchant's Lifestyle: Store Gives Snapshot of Old S.A.," San Antonio *Express-News*, 17 January, 5M.

Amelang, James S. (1986), *Honored Citizens of Barcelona: Patrician Culture and Class Relations, 1490–1714*, Princeton: Princeton University Press.

Anon. (1953), "Corny-Ation Top Attraction at La Villita," San Antonio *Light*, 23 April, 5.

—— (1977), "Council Considers Changes in Fiesta," San Antonio *Express*, 15 September, 7A.

Appadurai, Arjun (1986), "Introduction: Commodities and the Politics of Value," in A. Appadurai (ed.), *The Social Life of Things*, Cambridge: Cambridge University Press.

Arch, Nigel and Marschner, Joanna (1987), *Splendour at Court*, London: Unwin Hyman.

Bakhtin, Mikhail (1984), *Rabelais and His World*, Helene Iswolsky (trans.), Bloomington: Indiana University Press.

Barnes, Ruth and Eicher, Joanne B. (eds) (1992), *Dress and Gender: Making and Meaning in Cultural Contexts*, New York: Berg.

Barthes, Roland (1983), *The Fashion System*, Matthew Ward and Richard Howard (trans.), New York: Hill and Wang.

Baur-Heinhold, Margarete (1967), *The Baroque Theatre*, New York: McGraw-Hill.

Bell, Catherine (1992), *Ritual Theory, Ritual Practice*, New York: Oxford University Press.

Birmingham, Stephen (1990 [1987]), *America's Secret Aristocracy*, New York: Berkley Books.

Bogatyrev, P. (1971), *The Functions of Folk Costume in Moravian Slovakia*, Richard G. Crum (trans.), The Hague: Mouton.

Bollaert, William (1956), *William Bollaert's Texas*, W. Eugene Hollon and Ruth Lapham Butler (eds), Norman: University of Oklahoma Press.

Booth, John and Johnson, David R. (1983), "Power and Progress in San Antonio Politics," in David R. Johnson, John A. Booth, and Richard J. Harris (eds), *The Politics of San Antonio*, Lincoln: University of Nebraska Press.

Bourdieu, Pierre (1984), *Distinction*, Cambridge: Harvard University Press.

Brear, Holly Beachley (1995), *Inherit the Alamo: Myth and Ritual at an American Shrine*, Austin: University of Texas Press.

Brischetto, Robert, Cotrell, Charles, and Stevens, R. Michael (1983), "Conflict and Change in the Political Culture of San Antonio in the 1970s," in David R. Johnson, John A. Booth, and Richard J. Harris (eds), *The Politics of San Antonio*, Lincoln: University of Nebraska Press.

Canty, Carol (1991), "History of Fiesta," unpublished notes a for museum exhibit, San Antonio: Institute of Texan Cultures.

Chodorow, Nancy (1974), "Family Structure and Feminine Personality," in Michelle Rosaldo and Louise Lamphere (eds), *Women, Culture and Society*, Stanford: Stanford University Press.

Clark, Grahame (1986), *Symbols of Excellence*, Cambridge: Cambridge University Press.

Clarke, Mary and Crisp, Clement (1981), *The History of the Dance*, New York: Crown Publishing.

Codina, Laura (1993), "The What, How *y Qué Más* of Fiesta," *La Voz de Esperanza*, April, 3.

Cohn, Bernard (1989), "Cloth, Clothes, and Colonialism: India in the Nineteenth Century," in Annette Weiner and Jane Schneider (eds), *Cloth and Human Experience*, Washington: Smithsonian Institution Press.

Collins, Randall (1992), "Women and Production of Status Cultures," in Michèle Lamont and Marcel Fournier (eds), *Cultivating Differences*, Chicago: University of Chicago Press.

Corning, Blair (1987), "Flotsam: Once a Duchess, Always a Duchess," San Antonio *Express-News*, *Sunday* Magazine, 12 April, 12–13.

Davis, Fred (1992), *Fashion, Culture, and Identity*, Chicago: University of Chicago Press.

Davis, John (1978), *San Antonio: A Historical Portrait*, Austin: Encino Press.

de la Teja, Jesús and Wheat, John (1991), "Bexar: Profile of a Tejano Community, 1820-1832," in Gerald E. Poyo and Gilberto M. Hinojosa (eds), *Tejano Origins in Eighteenth-Century San Antonio*, Austin: University of Texas Press.

de León, Arnoldo (1983), *They Called Them Greasers*, Austin: University of Texas Press.

—— (1991), *Mexican Americans in Texas*, Arlington Heights, Illinois: Harlan Davidson.

di Leonardo, Micaela (1984), *The Varieties of Ethnic Experience*, Ithaca: Cornell University Press.

—— (1987), "The Female World of Cards and Holidays: Women, Families, (and the Work of Kinship," *Signs*, 12(3): 440–53.

Domhoff, G. William (1967), *Who Rules America?*, Washington: American Council on Education.

—— (1971), *Higher Circles: The Governing Class in America*, New York: Random House.

—— (1974), *The Bohemian Grove and Other Retreats*, New York: Harper and Row.

Douglas, Mary and Isherwood, Baron (1979), *The World of Goods*, New York: W.W. Norton.

Eicher, Joanne (ed.) (1995), *Dress and Ethnicity*, Oxford: Berg.

Ember, Carol and Ember, Melvin (1990), *Anthropology*, Englewood Cliffs: Prentice Hall.

Evans, Sara M. (1989), *Born for Liberty*, New York: Free Press.

Everett, Donald E. (1975), *San Antonio: The Flavor of its Past, 1845–1898*, San Antonio: Trinity University Press.

—— (1979), *San Antonio Legacy*, San Antonio: Trinity University Press.

Feagin, Joe R. (1978), *Racial and Ethnic Relations*, Englewood Cliffs: Prentice-Hall.

Foley, Douglas (1990), *Learning Capitalist Culture*, Philadelphia: University of Pennsylvania Press.

Frese, Pamela (1991), "The Union of Nature and Culture: Gender Symbolism in the American Wedding Ritual," in Pamela Frese and John Coggeshall (eds), *Transcending Boundaries: Multi-Disciplinary Approaches to the Study of Gender*, New York: Bergin and Garvey.

Gascoigne, Bamber (1968), *World Theatre*, Boston: Little, Brown.

Geertz, Clifford (1973), *The Interpretation of Cultures*, New York: Basic Books.

Gilligan, Carol (1982), *In a Different Voice*, Cambridge: Harvard University Press.

Glassberg, David (1990), *American Historical Pageantry*, Chapel Hill: University of North Carolina Press.

Glassie, Henry (1983), "Folkloristic Study of the American Artifact: Objects and Objectives," in Richard M. Dorson (ed.), *The Handbook of American Folklore*, Bloomington: Indiana University Press.

Goffman, Erving (1973 [1959]), *The Presentation of Self in Everyday Life*, Woodstock, New York: Overlook Press.

Gonzales, Manuel (1989), *The Hispanic Elite of the Southwest*, El Paso: Texas Western Press.

González, Jovita (1930), "Social Life in Cameron, Starr, and Zapata Counties," Master's thesis, University of Texas at Austin.

Gordon, Beverly (1986), "Dress and Dress-up at the Fundraising Fair," *Dress*, 12: 61–72.

Gordon, Milton (1964), *Assimilation in American Life*, New York: Oxford University Press.

Graham, Henry (1976), *History of the Texas Cavaliers*, San Antonio: n.p.

Greenberg, Mike (1990), "In Like a Lion, Out Like a Loon," San Antonio *Express-News*, 8 April, H1.

Guerra, Mary Ann Noonan (1985), "Introduction," in Ruben Rendon Lozano, *Viva Tejas*, San Antonio: Alamo Press.

Hamell, George (1983), "Trading in Metaphors: The Magic of Beads," Typescript (revised 22 May 1983) of a paper presented at Glass Trade Bead Conference, Rochester, New York, 12 June 1982.

Harris, Neil (1978), "Museums, Merchandising, and Popular Taste: The Struggle for Influence," in Ian Quimby (ed.), *Material Culture and the Study of American Life*, New York: W.W. Norton.

Harris, Olivia and Young, Kate (1981), "Engendered Structures: Some Problems in the Analysis of Reproduction," in J. Kahn and J. Llobera (eds), *The Anthropology of Pre-Capitalist Societies*, London: Macmillan.

Hayden, Ilse (1987), *Symbol and Privilege*, Tucson: University of Arizona Press.

Herdt, Gilbert (1982), *Ritual of Manhood: Male Initiation in Papua New Guinea*, Berkeley: University of California Press.

Hinojosa, Gilberto (1997), "Diez y Seis Long a Part of San Antonio History, Celebrations," San Antonio *Express-News*, 14 September, 3J.

Hinojosa, Gilberto and Fox, Anne (1991), "Indians and Their Culture in San Fernando de Béxar," in Gerald E. Poyo and Gilberto M. Hinojosa (eds), *Tejano Origins in Eighteenth-Century San Antonio*, Austin: University of Texas Press.

Hobsbawm, Eric (1983), "Introduction: Inventing Traditions," in Eric Hobsbawm and Terence Ranger (eds), *The Invention of Tradition*, Cambridge: Cambridge University Press.

Hollander, Anne (1980), *Seeing Through Clothes*, New York: Avon.

Holman, R.H. (1980), "A Transcription and Analysis System for the Study of Women's Clothing Behavior," *Semiotica*, 32(1/2): 11–34.

Horn, Marilyn (1968), *The Second Skin*, Boston: Houghton Mifflin.

Inverarity, Robert (1950), *Art of the Northwest Coast Indians*, Berkeley: University of California Press.

Ivins, Molly (1991), *Molly Ivins Can't Say That, Can She?*, New York: Random House.

Jaher, Frederic (1973), *The Rich, the Well Born, and the Powerful*, Urbana: University of Illinois Press.

—— (1982), *The Urban Establishment*, Urbana: University of Illinois Press.

Jakle, John, Brunn, Stanley, and Roseman, Curtis (1985), *Human Spatial Behavior*, Prospect Heights, Illinois: Waveland Press.

Johnson, David R. (1990), "Frugal and Sparing: Interest Groups, Politics, and City Building in San Antonio, 1870–85," in Char Miller and Heywood T. Sanders (eds), *Urban Texas: Politics and Development*, College Station: Texas A&M University Press.

Johnson, David R., Booth, John A., and Harris, Richard J. (1983), *The Politics of San Antonio: Community, Progress, and Power*, Lincoln: University of Nebraska Press.

Joseph, Nathan (1986), *Uniforms and Nonuniforms: Communication through Clothing*, New York: Greenwood Press.

Kaiser, Susan B. (1990), *The Social Psychology of Clothing*, New York: Macmillan.

Kertzer, David (1988), *Ritual, Politics, and Power*, New Haven: Yale University Press.

Kopytoff, Igor (1986), "The Cultural Biography of Things: Commoditization as Process," in A. Appadurai (ed.), *The Social Life of Things*, Cambridge: Cambridge University Press.

Kuper, Hilda (1973), "Costume and Identity in Comparative Studies," *Society and History*, 15(3): 348–67.

Lamphere, Louise (1993), "The Domestic Sphere of Women and the Public World of Men: The Strengths and Limitations of an Anthropological Dichotomy," in

Caroline Brettell and Carolyn Sargent (eds), *Gender in Cross-Cultural Perspective*, Englewood Cliffs: Prentice Hall.

Laver, James (1969), *A Concise History of Costume*, London: Thames & Hudson.

Lewis, Ethel (1937), *The Romance of Textiles*, New York: MacMillan.

Lich, Glen E. (1981), *The German Texans*, San Antonio: Institute of Texan Cultures.

Limón, José (1994), *Dancing with the Devil: Society and Cultural Poetics in Mexican-American South Texas*, Madison: University of Wisconsin Press.

Limón, José and Young, Jane (1986), "Frontiers, Settlements, and Development in Folklore Studies, (1972–1985," *Annual Review of Anthropology*, 15: 437–60.

Lomnitz, Larissa and Perez-Lizaur, Marisol (1987), *A Mexican Elite Family, 1820–1980: Kinship, Class and Culture*, Princeton: Princeton University Press.

Lozano, Ruben Rendon (1985 [1936]), *Viva Tejas*, San Antonio: Alamo Press.

McCracken, Grant (1987), "Clothing as Language: An Object Lesson in the Study of the Expressive Properties of Material Culture," in Barrie Reynolds and Margaret A. Stott (eds), *Material Anthropology*, Lanham, Maryland: University Press of America.

—— (1988), *Culture and Consumption*, Bloomington: Indiana University Press.

McGimsey, Mary Etta (1984), *Battle of Flowers Association of San Antonio, Texas*, n.p.: n.p.

Mackintosh, Prudence (1978a), "The Greatest Experience of Your Life," in *The Best of Texas Monthly 1973–78*, Austin: Texas Monthly Press.

—— (1978b), "Sisterhood is Powerful," in *The Best of Texas Monthly 1973–78*, Austin: Texas Monthly Press.

Maguire, Jack (1990), *A Century of Fiesta in San Antonio*, Austin: Eakin Press.

Marcus, George (1983), "'Elite' as a Concept, Theory and Research Tradition," in George Marcus (ed.), *Elites*, Albuquerque: University of New Mexico Press.

—— (1992), *Lives in Trust*, Boulder, Colorado: Westview Press.

Martin, Rebecca (1985), *Textiles in Daily Life in the Middle Ages*, Cleveland: Museum of Art in cooperation with Indiana University Press.

Mauss, Marcel (1967), *The Gift*, Ian Cunnison (trans.), New York: Norton.

Maverick, Mary A. (1921), *Memoirs of Mary A. Maverick*, Rena Maverick Green (ed.), San Antonio: Alamo Printing.

Miller, Char and Sanders, Heywood (eds) (1990), *Urban Texas: Politics and Development*, College Station: Texas A&M University Press.

Miller, Daniel (1987), *Material Culture and Mass Consumption*, Oxford: B. Blackwell.

Mills, C. Wright (1959), *The Power Elite*, New York: Oxford University Press.

Montejano, David (1987), *Anglos and Mexicans in the Making of Texas, 1836–1986*, Austin: University of Texas Press.

Moore, Henrietta (1988), *Feminism and Anthropology*, Minneapolis: University of Minnesota Press.

Moore, Sally and Myerhoff, Barbara (1977), *Secular Ritual*, Amsterdam: Van Gorcum.

Mosca, Gaetano (1939), *The Ruling Class*, New York: McGraw-Hill.

Mukhopadhyay, Carol and Higgins, Patricia (1988), "Anthropological Studies of

Women's Status Revisited: 1977–1987," *Annual Review of Anthropology*, 17: 461–95.

Myerhoff, Barbara (1978), *Number Our Days*, New York: Simon and Schuster.

Nader, Laura (1964), "Perspectives Gained from Field Work," in Sol Tax (ed.), *Horizons in Anthropology*, Chicago: Aldine Press.

Newton, Luisa Inez (1993), "Fairy Tales y Reinas, Myths and Fiesta," *La Voz de Esperanza*, April, 5–6.

Order of the Alamo [1925], *Courts of the Order of the Alamo 1909–1925*, San Antonio: Order of the Alamo.

—— [1939], *History of the Order of the Alamo, Volume Two, 1926–1939*, San Antonio: Order of the Alamo.

—— [1975], *History of the Order of the Alamo, Volume Four, 1960–1975*, San Antonio: Order of the Alamo.

—— 1990, *Membership Roster*, San Antonio: Order of the Alamo.

—— 1991, *The Court of Spanish Empire* [Program], San Antonio: Order of the Alamo.

Ortner, Sherry (1978), "The Virgin and the State," *Feminist Studies*, 4(3): 19–35.

—— (1979), "On Key Symbols," in William Lessa and Evon Vogt (eds), *Reader in Comparative Religion*, New York: Harper and Row.

—— (1981), "Gender and Sexuality in Hierarchical Societies." in Sherry Ortner and Harriet Whitehead (eds), *Sexual Meaning: Cultural Construction of Gender and Sexuality*, Cambridge: Cambridge University Press.

—— (1991), "Reading America: Preliminary Notes on Class and Culture," in Richard G. Fox (ed.), *Recapturing Anthropology*, Santa Fe: School of American Research Press.

Ostrander, Susan (1984), *Women of the Upper Class*, Philadelphia: Temple University Press.

Pareto, Vilfredo (1935), *The Mind and Society*, New York: Harcourt, Brace and World.

Park, David (1997), *The Fire Within the Eye: A Historical Essay on the Nature and Meaning of Light*, Princeton: Princeton University Press.

Perkowitz, Sidney (1996), *Empire of Light: A History of Discovery in Science and Art*, New York: Henry Holt.

Post, Emily (1937), *Etiquette,* New York: Funk and Wagnalls.

Poyo, Gerald E. (1991a), "The Canary Island Immigrants of San Antonio: From Ethnic Exclusivity to Community in Eighteenth-Century Béxar," in Gerald E. Poyo and Gilberto M. Hinojosa (eds), *Tejano Origins in Eighteenth-Century San Antonio*, Austin: University of Texas Press for the Institute of Texan Cultures.

—— (1991b), "Immigrants and Integration in Late Eighteenth-Century Béxar," in Gerald E. Poyo and Gilberto M. Hinojosa (eds), *Tejano Origins in Eighteenth-Century San Antonio*, Austin: University of Texas Press for the Institute of Texan Cultures.

Poyo, Gerald E. and Hinojosa, Gilberto M. (eds) (1991), *Tejano Origins in Eighteenth-Century San Antonio*, Austin: University of Texas Press for the Institute of Texan Cultures.

Pringle, Margaret (1977), *Dance Little Ladies*, London: n.p.

Ramsdell, Charles (1959), *San Antonio, A Historical and Pictorial Guide*, Austin: University of Texas Press.

Roach, Mary Ellen and Eicher, Joanne Bubolz (eds) (1965), *Dress, Adornment, and the Social Order*, New York: Wiley and Sons.

—— (1973), *The Visible Self: Perspectives on Dress*, Englewood Cliffs: Prentice-Hall.

Rodriguez, Jose (1913), *Rodriguez Memoirs of Early Texas*, San Antonio: Passing Show Printing.

Rose, Dan (1987), *Black American Street Life*, Philadelphia: University of Pennsylvania.

Royce, Anya Peterson (1982), *Ethnic Identity: Strategies of Diversity*, Bloomington: Indiana University Press.

Rundquist, Angela (1995), "Presentation at Court in Sweden 1850–1962," in Mary Ellen Roach-Higgins, Joanne B. Eicher, and Kim K.P. Johnson (eds), *Dress and Identity*, New York: Fairchild.

Ruth, J.A. (comp.) (1877), *Decorum: A Practical Treatise on Etiquette and Dress of the Best American Society*, New York: J.A. Ruth.

Sahlins, Marshall (1976), *Culture and Practical Reason*, Chicago: University of Chicago Press.

Salcedo, Michele (1997), *Quinceañera! The Essential Guide to Planning the Perfect Sweet Fifteen Celebration*, New York: Henry Holt.

Sanders, Heywood T. (1990), "Building a New Urban Infrastructure: The Creation of Postwar (San Antonio," in Char Miller and Heywood T. Sanders (eds), *Urban Texas*, College Station: Texas A&M Press.

Santino, Jack (1995), *All Around the Year: Holidays and Celebrations in American Life*, Urbana: University of Illinois Press.

Schneider, Jane (1980), "Trousseau as Treasure: Some Contributions of Late Nineteenth-Century Change in Sicily," in E.B. Ross (ed.), *Beyond the Myths of Culture: Essays in Cultural Materialism*, New York: Academic Press.

—— (1987), "The Anthropology of Cloth," *Annual Review of Anthropology*, 16: 409–48.

Schnurnberger, Lynn (1991), *Let There Be Clothes*, New York: Workman Publishing.

Shils, Edward (1981), *Tradition*, Chicago: University of Chicago Press.

Skramstad, Harold K. (1978), "Interpreting Material Culture: A View from the Other Side of the Glass," in Ian M.G. Quimby (ed.), *Material Culture and the Study of American Life*, New York: W.W. Norton.

Stack, Carol (1974), *All Our Kin*, New York: Harper and Row.

Stone, Gregory (1965), "Appearance and the Self," in Mary Ellen Roach and Joanne Bubolz Eicher (eds), *Dress, Adornment and the Social Order*, New York: Wiley and Sons.

Strong, Roy (1984), *Art and Power*, Berkeley: University of California Press.

Sutherland, Anne (1986), *Gypsies: The Hidden Americans*, Prospect Heights, Illinois: Waveland Press.

Taylor, I.T. (1938), *The Cavalcade of Jackson County*, San Antonio: Naylor.

Thompson, Angela (1987), *Embroidery with Beads*, London: Batsford.

Thompson, Holland (ed.) (1929), *The Book of Texas*, Dallas: The Grolier Society.

Tucker, Robert (1978), *The Marx–Engels Reader*, New York: W.W. Norton.

Turner, Victor (1967), *The Forest of Symbols*, Ithaca: Cornell University Press.

—— (1975), "Symbolic Studies," *Annual Review of Anthropology*, 4: 145–61.

van Gennep, Arnold (1960), *The Rites of Passage*, Chicago: University of Chicago Press.

Varenne, Hervé (1977), *Americans Together*, New York: Teachers College Press.

Veblen, Thorstein (1934 [1899]), *The Theory of the Leisure Class*, New York: Modern Library.

Warner, W. Lloyd (1941), *The Social Life of a Modern Community*, New Haven: Yale University Press.

Watson, Rubie (1993), "The Named and the Nameless: Gender and Person in Chinese Society," in Caroline Brettell and Carolyn Sargent (eds), *Gender in Cross- Cultural Perspective*, Englewood Cliffs: Prentice Hall.

Weiner, Annette (1988), *The Trobrianders of Papua New Guinea*, Orlando: Harcourt Brace Jovanovich College Publishers.

Weiner, Annette and Schneider, Jane (eds) (1989), *Cloth and Human Experience*, Washington: Smithsonian Institution Press.

Wildeblood, Joan and Brimston, Peter (1965), *The Polite World: A Guide to English Manners and Deportment (from the C13th to the C19th)*, London: Oxford University Press.

Wilson, Elizabeth (1987), *Adorned in Dreams*, Berkeley: University of California Press.

Yanagisako, Sylvia Junko and Collier, Jane Fishburne (1987), "Toward a Unified Analysis of Gender and Kinship," in Jane Fishburne Collier and Sylvia Junko Yanagisako (eds), *Gender and Kinship*, Stanford: Stanford University Press.

Index

assignment to participants, 120
commodification of, 134–5
comparison to wedding dress, 51, 141–6
as "conspicuous consumption," 6, 97
construction of, 3, 6, 124
costs of, 6, 10, 97–8, 117–20, 134, 153, 155, 159
criticism of, 153–5
dresses, 98–100, **100–1**, 102
effect upon the wearer, 12, 130
embellishments on, 3–4, 117–19, 122, 141n4, **Plates 16–18**
"catching the light," 5, 95–7, 127, 136, 140, **Plate 11**
fairy tale or fantasy quality, 131–2, 156
feelings of wearers about, 3, 120–23
handwork on, 92, 97, 128
as material culture, 140
parade, 128–31
public displays of, 128–31, 138–40, 142n15, 143, 156
as reinforcers of gender, 12, 72, 93, 125
status markers, 12, 92–3, 97, 125
symbolic nature of, 3, 7, 13ft, 92–3, 131–32, 143, 155–6
see also Coronation themes
trains, 1, 102, **103**, 104–8, **111**, **114–16**
length of, 38
as metonyms, 128
miniature, 83, 128, 141n10
origins of, 38–9
on parade floats, 129
themes of, 104–8
use after Fiesta, 122, 134–9
weight of, 125–6, 136
Royce, Anya Peterson, 157
Rundquist, Angela, 6
Ruth, J.A., 89n3

Salcedo, Michele, 90n6
San Antonio history, 18–28
Canary Islanders and soldiers, 19–20
founding, 18
hierarchical relations, 18–20, 25–7
immigrants, 18–21
American or Anglo, 2, 18, 20, 22, 47
German, 2, 18, 25, 47
indigenous groups, 18–20, 29

inter-ethnic cooperation, 22–3, 27
intermarriage, 21, 23, 25, 27, 48n6
military importance, 15, 24, 30–1, 33, 41–4
political representation of Hispanics, 22–4, 27–8
Republic of Texas period, 23–4
Tejano and Anglo-American relations, 21–5
Texas Revolution against Mexico, 21–3
San Antonio Charro Association, 50n18
San Antonio Club, 26–7, 30
San Antonio Conservation Society, 32, 145
San Antonio de Valero, Mission, *see* Alamo
San Antonio Museum of Art,
display of royal robes and protest, 143, 149, **150**, 151
San Antonio Symphony, 5
Sanders, Heywood T., 27, 49n12
Santino, Jack, 45, 48n2
Schneider, Jane, 6, 97
Schnurnberger, Lynn, 102
Shils, Edward, 78, 160
Skramstad, Harold K., 137
Smith, John William, 21
Sobre, Judith, 113
Stewart, Logan, 46
Strong, Roy, 110

Taylor, I.T., 96
Teen Queen, 44
Tejanos, 18, 21–5, 50n10
definition of, 18
Thompson, Angela, 96
Thompson, Holland, 21
Tucker, Robert, 97
Turner, Victor, 56, 92, 156
Tyson, Farrell, 69

UTSA survey, 153–4

van Gennep, Arnold, 55
Veblen, Thorstein, 6, 52, 97, 128
Veramendi, Fernando de, 20
Veramendi, Ursula, 21

Weiner, Annette, 6

Printed in the United States
94696LV00001B/148/A